Tracks of Love
A Heartfelt Journey of Love

Tracks of Love

www.kyecrow.love

First Published October 2022

Copyright text @Kye Crow

Copyright cover image @kyecrow

"Tracks of Love" is also available as an e-book

All rights reserved. No part of this publication may be reproduced whole or in part, stored in a retrievable system, or transmitted in any form or by any means, electronic, mechanical, photocopying, recording, or otherwise, without permission of the copyright holder or publisher, other than for 'fair use' as brief quotations in articles and reviews.

To all you beautiful beings of LOVE that have come to make this world a better place, I dedicate this book to you.

Keep going & believe in yourself even if everyone else thinks you are mad!

Honouring

This book was written on the banks of a river that flows through sacred Yuwaalaraay country. A place so beautiful giant gum trees edge its banks.

While an old bougainvillea bush grows entwined with the branches of a gum tree and dangles its vivid magenta blooms over the water.

I have swum our stretch of river many times in the process of writing. For inspiration, for a recharge, for exercise, and to watch the baby spoonbills and cormorants I have come to know.

Somehow they survived strong winds and floods, even though their nests took a battering. And what a gift it was for me to watch them grow from little fluffy chicks to young fledglings that were finally big enough to leave their nests.

Thank you so much to the Yuwaalaraay people for allowing us to be here.

We also pay our most profound respect to all the different tribes whose country we have travelled through.

We honour you all, past, present and future.

One

Farewell White Feather

Our resident crow, White Feather, chortled from the tree beside our wagon. He usually settled for the night before we did, but he was restless. Crows are so intelligent. I had no doubts he knew we were leaving in the morning. He'd watched us for over a week packing up the life we'd lived among the golden blossoms. He'd also begun to disappear for hours and would return full-bellied, not wanting to eat his usual meal. The wild was reclaiming him, and I felt peace knowing that. He'd become a part of our tribe in the months we'd lived together. I was relieved to know he'd be ok without us.

Gill threw some more logs on the fire. Branches that were big enough to keep our fire burning through the night, so when we rose in the morning, I could stoke the fire up and cook breakfast on its coals. I wasn't looking forward to that early start and rising in the dark, though I was keen to go. We were two days ahead of our agreed departure date and determined not to entice another visit from the couple we'd named the prophets of doom. They had given us the strongest motivation to discard all notions of white picket fences and happily ever after and get ourselves *moving*.

I was bulging with emotions. I thought I had faced the hard reality that my goats had gone, but I felt another wave of sorrow lash me. I know it was ridiculous that I'd held on for so long, but I had. I'm an optimist. I always believed they'd turn up, but I could no longer avoid facing the hard truth. We were leaving without them.

Sitting on my swag by our roaring fire, I felt vulnerable and anxious *again*. My rawness of emotion had a lot to do with being tired. The twelve days before departure had been an epic feat of endless preparations as we mustered up the momentum to leave. It had been hard work getting our wagon packed and ready for the road, but we had done it. We were prepared to go at first light, and our camp of slumbering beasties felt peaceful. I could even hear The Colonel and his girls giving gentle clucks of contentment from their bed of dried flowers and grasses between our wagon's wheels. Everyone was happy, yet I just felt teary and tired.

I always feel like a tree. Plant me in some earth, and my roots wriggle down into the soil. The longer I stay, the deeper my roots go, and the harder it is for me to leave. I revel in familiarity with the nature I grow in. I love getting to know the birds that land in my boughs and the wild creatures that shelter in my shade. With roots, I am strong, but dig me up and get me to move, and I always feel stressed. Despite appearances, I am not a gypsy. I am a tree.

With my pulled-up roots feeling tender and raw and my grief over my goats, I also had unsettling churning in my stomach. I was on the edge of nausea. I knew it was nerves. There was no room for anything to go wrong. We had no safety net to catch us or safe haven to return to. How this next stage of our trip went was all up to us, and it felt like such a huge responsibility to hold in hands that looked so tiny.

When I asked Gill if he had any nerves, he answered casually, "No, it will be fun. I'm looking forward to being on the road again." When I told him I felt anxious, he gave me that familiar answer we'd used so many times it almost had its own set of wheels, "You know you can trust."

Trust, I'd whispered that word to myself so many times since I'd agreed to leave on this trip. In a panic, *trust*. Feeling weak at the knees, *trust*. Worried about how you're going to cope? Just *TRUST*! Laying in the dirt, badly concussed, seeing stars and aching for a fag, just *trust*! But what did it mean? I *had* trusted, and look where it had got me!

"Yeah, what in?" I exclaimed laughingly. "I've been booted in the face by a camel and had to run for my life with a wagon and a team of camels hurtling after me. I've been shoved way past every limitation, *{I think}*. What am I trusting in exactly?" I asked.

When he replied, he said something that really made me think. "You trust," he answered, "that you have everything you need to deal with anything and everything that comes up. That's all we can trust in. It all comes back to us! But we have to be alert and listen to what feels right. Then we always make the best choices."

I thought about those words for a long time as I lay on my swag, gazing up at the vast blueness of the night. Lost in its midnight mystery, breathing with the heartbeat of a trillion stars that glittered and jewelled the darkness. I stared up at the sky for so long that I lost all sense of self. I even lost my tiredness. With every breath, I felt more expansive until I became so big; I was a star, I was the night, I was the sky, and I was love. Pure love, the greatest force on the planet and the whole reason we had taken this gigantic leap of faith with all these animals. Love, I could trust in that.

I felt a weight lift from me; *stay in the moment, don't look too far ahead. Everything will unfold beautifully in the same way a rosebud becomes a bloom.* It was the voice of my wisdom speaking to me.

"But I hope," I finally replied to Gill, "this bit of our trip is easier!"

Gill laughed. "Yeah, but a comfy life won't give you this," he said as he nodded his head, beckoning me to take in the scene around our campfire. "Look at the life you are living," he urged. "Look at the person you were before you left and who you are now. It's gotta be worth the effort."

Looking around, I could only shake my head in agreement and smile. He was right. This experience was phenomenal. I would never want to be the person I'd been. I was so much stronger and clearer now. Living and travelling each day with so many animals was connecting us with them in a way I'd *never* experienced before, and I'd had animals all my life. Also, living so raw and exposed to nature with just a tiny shelter when the elements were pervasive was a holy balm for my soul.

I loved the intensity of being out in this red and rusty desert, swags rolled out in the sand around our campfire. We'd watched the last glimpse of the sun sink below the horizon, consumed in a blaze of ruby. We'd seen the dusk darken and the stars come out, with numerous shooting stars blazing across the sky. Our dogs were sprawled, sleeping in the hollows they'd dug in the still warm sand. Bella, standing so peacefully with her head hanging down over Gill, who lay in his swag on his side, facing me across the fire. Bella's body language said *all I have is yours*. She looked as if she was in a place of such surrender, and I think she was sleeping. Gill had become so used to having her right beside him that I don't think he even noticed she was there. Not this time anyway though she was often much more demanding of his attention.

I laughed as I looked around me. I'd never met anyone else who lived with a stinky billy goat as a family member in their very midst, even sharing a campfire with them. Every billy goat I'd ever known had lived on the furthest extremes of people's lives, but not our Banjo. His life had catapulted him from being so wholly misunderstood he was about to be shot to living the good life on the road with us.

Our wise sage Banjo had shown me that life's most treasured gifts are not handed out like candy. They dwell far away from false allures and propriety. They are bountiful in the acceptance of a stinky Billy goat, who guides us further beyond illusions of separation to a space that embodies more love. They are abundant in vast prickly deserts on pilgrims of trust through terrain too rugged for your slippers and almost always unreachable from the comfort of a settee. They come in wild savage places where the only footprints are our own and are the earnings of a journey that has used every muscle and is blistered from the sun. Only when we push past our limitations can we know we have an endless capacity to blitz limitations and to live life with the velocity turned right up to full. The more I trust, the more I love, and every ripe burgeoning moment is the gift.

So yup, Gill was right. There was no going back for me. I had been booted in the face by a camel, lost all semblance of a decent hairdo if I'd ever had one, and that's debatable! And had to run for my life a few times, but so what! Every moment, even the struggle, had been worth it.

After all my musings around the fire, it was late when we finally hauled ourselves into our wagon and went to bed. I'd barely slept when Gill woke me in the dark, squeezing my hand gently while whispering, "Wakey, wakey Kye, time to get up." The morning had come much too soon. Rising in the dark would always be hard for me, but we had to. With so many animals to get ready, it was the only way to be organised to leave at first light.

And then it began again, remembering a routine that was no longer honed. Making breakfast, coffee pot on, filling flasks for the day's tea. Walking dogs at rapid speed before settling them on the massive piece of canvas we'd covered our bed with just so they were safe from baits.

Feeding chickens and parrots, moving camels for an hour's extra feed. Packing camping stuff away while greeting a group of dear friends who'd come from Alice to help us on our first day. All the time listening for the sounds of goat's bells! *Just in case!* Leading camels up to be harnessed, winding up their ropes and hanging them from the railings of the back veranda. Forgetting to put on gloves, so my fingers were sore and full of prickles from all the tiny burrs clinging to the ropes. *Must remember gloves next time.* Lady Caroline's morning procession that Gill began from the wrong direction. She wouldn't budge. It had to be from the left side of the camel team, leading from the back of the wagon to the front. *How could we ever have forgotten?* When Gill remembered, with her head held high, she walked quickly into position. So much to remember, but finally, we were ready. One last listen for the goats. *There could still be time.* A flicker of hope still burned. Then Gill gave the call to "Walk em up." Our friends laughed in surprise at the noise that erupted from our wagon. Our wild ruckus parrots and our banshee dogs. I shrugged my shoulders. There was nothing we could do; we'd tried. This was us, leaving on our adventure. Nothing would contain the excitement of our cheerleading dogs and parrots.

Then we were lurching forward, leaving our haven and home behind. I looked around for White Feather and couldn't see him. I needed to before we went forever. "I love you, White Feather," I yelled as I searched for his familiar form. Then I heard him chortling from the top of a tree. Wild and regal and free. Tears rolled down my face. Yet another goodbye. *Farewell, my dear goats, and thank you, White Feather,* and then we were gone. The moment had claimed us; the past was behind us.

We had twenty kilometres to travel down the main tourist road before meeting the Old Ghan track again. However, the stretch of road before we reached our peaceful track was the hilliest we'd travelled so far. It would have been really challenging without friends to help us, and I felt so grateful for their support. They slowed traffic and kept an eye on our animals. One friend even drove behind to make sure Banjo kept up.

We had no idea where to put Banjo. His best friends Bella and Blossom walked beside the wagon, but we didn't think this ageing billy goat with his short, stocky legs would keep up. We decided to let him walk and see how he went. If he fell behind, he could ride on the back veranda of the wagon. He had come into our lives in such serendipity; we knew that even if it took a little working out, we would find a harmonious way for him to travel with us.

There was so much to renegotiate.

Jali, Jumuna's now-year-old calf, had travelled really well next to her mother previously. As the road we were on was busy with traffic, I'd tethered Jali's rope from the wagon so she could walk beside her mum, where we thought she would be happiest. Yet she kept straining to pull to the side. We kept stopping the wagon, checking her ropes, and trying to determine what was wrong but couldn't find anything. She was pulling so much that she began to rub herself raw, which was really concerning. There had to be something wrong, but what was it? It wasn't immediately apparent.

We knew our camels had often intentionally provoked us into releasing old emotions. Our wise dromedaries were not prepared to put up with the little versions of ourselves we'd been. They wanted us to be freer of our baggage and better people for them to be around. However, in normal circumstances, if they refuse to do something or act in a puzzling way, there is *always* a reason.

We had no choice but to stop the wagon and spend some time sorting out Jali. When it finally dawned on us why she was pulling like that, I almost couldn't believe we'd been so blind. We'd all been living so closely together, getting to know one another well, yet we'd overlooked the obvious. Of course, she wanted to be on the other side of the wagon. Her best friend Windy was tethered there with his mum. Jali wanted to be with her friend Windy. As soon as we put them together, all her pulling stopped, and she was happy.

There were so many camel foibles to negotiate. Yes, we could have demanded complete obedience if we'd wanted our camels to be our slaves, but we didn't. We were making this trip together, and happy animals were *the* essential ingredient. If our camels were happier walking next to their friends than *with* their friends, they would walk!

Even with several stops to reorganise animals, our camel team flowed. Several times they broke into an excited trot, and it was exhilarating to be sitting in the wagon as we breezed down that road with such ease. Even over the rough corrugations in the road, it felt like we were gliding. Our camels were as keen as we were to get back into this adventure. As the wagon rolled along, they frolicked in their harnesses, doing happy little bucks and pig rooting merrily. They were as frustrated as me at the number of times we had to stop.

It soon became evident that Banjo could not keep up the pace. I'd been riding in the wagon, focused on slowing it down with the brake as we descended small hills. When we needed to stop completely, I'd slow the wagon to a gentle walking pace before giving the command to our camels to *Whoa*. Only then could I put on our big new emergency stop dead in your tracks brake that dropped a bar across the back tire's so we couldn't budge an inch. Other than an absolute emergency, we never used this brake when moving. It bought the wagon to such an abrupt halt it would be too jarring for our camels in harness and would break their trust in moving forward.

I'd been keeping an eye behind me for our irascible billy goat, and I'd seen him falling further and further behind. I knew our friend was with him, so he was ok, but we had to stop again to get him sorted out. Our friend, Kat, told me later how she'd tried everything to get him to jump into the front seat of her 4WD. I was astounded to hear this. She had a newish car and had put so much energy into making her interior beautiful. I was relieved Banjo hadn't jumped in, he certainly had a pungent calling card, and nothing would have ever smelt the same again inside that vehicle. But I absolutely adored that woman forever for her willingness to give our smelly little love a ride. She had evaluated Banjos' need for help as more vital than her beautifully hand-stitched *by her* interior.

She reminded me of a friend I'd had many years earlier who'd come across a tiny pink mouse lost and out in the world alone and had fed this wee babe from her own breast milk. Holding this tiny pink form so tenderly, without judgement or separation, responding only as a mother, she had gently squeezed drops of her milk into its thirsty mouth. Afterwards, she searched to find where it had fallen from and found its nest built in the cracks between a pile of curing logs. She had returned that baby to its mum, fed!

Banjo was tired and was sitting under a bush in the shade after refusing to get in Kat's car. He'd had enough and just wanted a familiar face. Gill drove back in our 4WD, and our weary goat jumped enthusiastically into the back and settled for a sleep. From that day, on the back veranda of our wagon was his carriage, and each morning he would happily jump up, ready for the day.

In our dreams, we'd hoped to travel the entire twenty kilometres to the start of the Old Ghan Line while we had friends with us to help, but we didn't make it. Even so, it was verging on miraculous that on our very first day of travel, we'd progressed, with all our stops and starts, eleven kilometres.

Our friends had brought with them such strength. It was tough for me to watch them all at the end of the day as they happily got in their cars. Calling out to one another to meet for dinner the following week. Sharing how they couldn't wait to get home and have a hot bath. There was all this energy bunched up in my throat. I felt like I'd been dumped in the wilderness and left to survive. If I'd been truly honest at that moment, I would have clung to their ankles desperately and pleaded with them to stay. But I didn't do any of that. I held it all in. I tried to look happy about the choices I'd made when inside; I was feeling so lost. *What the fuck were we doing?*

I yearned to be going home to a hot bath.

Sometimes I felt it might have been easier to struggle alone than soften and relax with the support of others. When they left, I always felt the overwhelming magnitude of what we were doing *alone*, and it would flaw me. While Gill was usually jocular, this time, he felt it too. Little me and him sitting in our camp chairs by the fire with so many animals to look after, and feeling not just alone but so exposed. What we were doing was so immense that we could never hide. We were this huge in-your-face entourage that if you were coming down our road, you wouldn't miss, and I wanted to shrink down to the size of a mouse and live my big overflowing life, but unseen. *Some of the time, anyway.*

With a good night's sleep, we felt brighter in the morning. Back in our own space, filling in all the gaping holes, our friends had left. Focusing on the animals, lighting the campfire, coffee on to brew, smoke spiralling and weaving with the golden rise of the sun. Our sweet blossom breath camels contented with full bellies of acacia, the rank pong of dear Banjo as he slept snoring under the wagon with the dogs while The Colonel crowed in the day.

Yup, we'd got this. We'd be fine.

Two

Choosing Love

We travelled the nine kilometres to the start of the old Ghan line arriving in *only* a few flowing hours. The only reason we stopped was to give all our camels a drink so we could refill our water drums from the nearby bore.

We had a brick of a satellite phone that we used to call station owners along our route to let them know we were passing through. Gill had already spoken with the managers of the station we were on and asked if he could get water. They'd told him to come to the store they ran and fill up from the bore.

It was exhilarating to finally be on the old Ghan line once again. My whole body sighed with relief. No more busy roads of tourists and their traffic for weeks to come. There had been times I had doubted we would ever make it, and here we were. We had just over 400 kilometres to travel before the next tiny town, called Oodnadatta. This was the same town where our latest rescued offender Abdul had begun his life. I could certainly understand why he'd become too much for this small outback community to handle, but I hoped they remembered him. I couldn't wait to show them what a gentleman he'd become. I still couldn't believe we had Abdul! I'd never seen that one coming or imagined I would use the word adorable to describe him, but that's what he was. After all his wild rampaging years, he had mellowed into a dear sweet camel that couldn't have been more helpful.

But Oodnadatta was weeks away, and we had a lot of distance to travel before then.

Gill and I had just finished watering all our camels. A big job, siphoning water from our drums into buckets and lugging them over to our thirsty beasts. Camels can drink less water than we were giving them, but I am inclined to think that what an animal can do in tenuous and challenging circumstances to survive isn't necessarily how they should go through life. Left to their own resources in hot weather, our camels would always choose to have a daily drink. It was different when they ate lots of green feed, or the temperature was cooler. They were much less inclined to drink then. While we were on the very edge of spring and the cooler weather had yet to begin, it was still hot enough to water them frequently.

We had planned to leave the following morning, but just as Gill was getting into our 4WD to go and fill our water drums, a van pulled up at our camp. Two very flustered middle-aged women explained something was wrong with their car. It was making a terrible sound, and they were worried about driving any further. It didn't take Gill long to discover a necessary bolt had come off underneath the engine making their car dangerous to drive. Far from any mechanic and out of phone range, the only solution he could see was to get on our postie bike and go to a few car wrecks he'd spotted in the bush and see if he could scrounge a bolt that would fit.

I was not keen on being left with these women, they had a judgmental air about them, and I wasn't overjoyed to have them parked in my space, but there was nothing I could do. They needed help, they were here, and until their car got fixed, they were not going anywhere. Trying to make the best of it, I offered them a cup of tea.

"We can get our gas stove," one of them replied, "But why, the billy is already boiling?" I was confused. *What was wrong with our billy?* There was a wee kerfuffle as I plonked teabags into cups and made us all a cuppa. They were still pushing to use *their* gas stove even though the water was bubbling in the billy. I made the tea anyway and ignored their flustered appeals to bypass my hospitality and use their *own* stove.

Only later, when I sat around the campfire with Gill chatting about our day, did I see the situation a little clearer. For a moment in time, a long one for me, these two women had fallen through a crack into a world they would *never ever* usually see. One with a billy goat sleeping under the wagon with Patchi, our dog, and chickens scratching around in the *same* space we made food. Our kettle blackened from all the times it had boiled water for our tea on an open fire. To some, these aspects of our life were romantic and exciting, but for these two neatly folded women who felt so sterilised from nature, had they just experienced us and our big messy lives as unclean? I had certainly felt their disdain. Both had looked mortified as they'd sat in our camp chairs, but they'd probably have had the same distaste if they'd been sitting with their bums in the dirt like I had because I'd given them my chair!

We must have been a massive shock for them.

But there was something else I'd noticed from having them around me for the long and arduously stifling hour Gill had been gone. It was the suffocating energy of things that were hidden. I'd noticed one of them tentatively reach out for the hand of the other and be rebuffed in a sort of *not now Cynthia* type of way. I saw their yearning for each other in furtive glances that quickly looked away. These two, neat and clean and everything in its place, school teachers were lovers. It was so apparent to me, and I felt deep sorrow for them when I realised that.

In the same way, they'd try to shun my offering of tea, focusing only on dog hairs and charred kettles; instead of the love we all shared, they were doing precisely the same with their relationship. Hiding in their perceived shame instead of basking in their love is easy to do. Our world can be so judgmental.

Gill hadn't found a bolt, but he'd managed to temporarily fix their car, so they were safe to drive home. *Thank goodness!* I'd thought. I was relieved to see them go, though aware I needed to reclaim our camp from their scorn and scrutiny. It still lingered in the air. We gathered up some green gum leaves and threw them on the fire, and let the smoke cleanse all their judgement away.

It had been a strange visit with these women, and it had also delayed our departure in the morning because Gill hadn't had time to fill up our water, but that was OK. He may not have found a bolt, but I hoped witnessing us living our big messy life, overflowing beyond the bounds of sane, normal or even accepted, may have given them the courage to live *their* love out in the open.

We had spoken several times to the managers of the station we were now travelling through. They had even stopped to show their children our animals when we were travelling before. Our interactions had always been friendly, and we had made the courtesy call to let them know we were coming through. So, the following day when Gill got back from filling our water tanks and told me how he'd been treated, I was deeply surprised. I knew something was wrong the minute he got out of the car. His face was blanched white, and he was agitated.

I tensed as he told me he'd been filling up the water tanks when the manageress had come over with a phone and given it to him. It was the actual owner of the station, who we'd been told lived a few hours away. Without any conversation, she screamed abuse at Gill, accusing him of damaging her fences and stealing her wild camels. Gill had to hold the phone at a distance as she was screeching so loudly.

As for damaging her fences, unlike most other station owners, she had removed the obligatory gate required when one put in a cattle grid. Every cameleer that travelled through her property dropped her boundary fence next to the cattle grid. We couldn't walk our camels over the grid.

If she had been in the vicinity and checked her fence herself, she would have been pleasantly surprised to discover it was in better form than before. But some people live in conflict, and if they can't see the goodness in themselves, they won't see it in anyone else. Gill was just dealing with another unhappy person. We knew that. We knew we shouldn't take it on, but it was dispiriting, especially so soon after the previous negative encounter.

Yes, we were a big travelling entourage, but in the immense scale of station life and properties you could travel through for days and days before reaching a boundary fence that grazed hundreds of thousands of cattle, we were minuscule. We had the right to travel down these roads and camp on each side of them, but we were still courteous and attentive to the fact that we were travelling through people's land. That's why we had every station owner's phone number on our route. So, we could ring them, introduce ourselves and let them know we were passing through.

Would this be our greeting from station owners as we travelled? Oh, I prayed not. We wanted to get on with the people we met, to connect and share and meet the characters that lived down this track. We certainly didn't want to feel like we were travelling through hostile territory as we felt here. Gill told me when he'd taken the phone back to the manageress, she'd been standing with her husband. Gill had reached his hand out to introduce himself, but he'd turned his back and walked away.

As Gill was getting in his car, he was told scathingly, "the next bore is dry, so don't expect any water there!"

Looking on the positive side, at least we knew we had to factor in a very long stretch between bores we hadn't anticipated. How could we have known the bore we intended to fill up at was dry? It could have been potentially disastrous if we'd used up all our water and arrived there to find it dry. All we could do was stretch out our water supply and hope we had enough. We certainly were not going to be returning to this station to ask for a refill. If we could make it for a few extra days with what we had and reach the boundary of the next station and ask them for water, hopefully, they'd be kinder.

It felt so good to be moving again. Each step, each turn of the wagon's wheels, took us further away from the archer and his poison arrows who had pierced our vulnerabilities and left us feeling fragile, defensive and alert. Even questioning what the hell we were doing once again, but that soon passed. As it always did. Our doubts about what we were doing came and went and came and went. Beneficent guardians of these vast arid acres or not, this land was phenomenal. Wide open spaces with craggy rock formations on the horizon, and yes, we did see a passing herd of camels, and as hard as it was, we did refrain from stealing them! We watched them, awed by their wild beauty. Unsure if they'd be drawn to our camels, but they had passed, not giving us more than a cursory glance before disappearing into the distance. A herd of wild camels poised little threat, it was the thwarted solitary bulls we had to be attentive for, and we always watched out for their tracks.

Since Gill and I had left Alice, our focus had been so whittled down to each moment that we'd lost all awareness of what day it was. We couldn't understand why this usually quiet track was busy with traffic and trail bikes. They were blatting along with such speed and complete disregard for anyone other than themselves.

Moving through the bush with camels is relatively silent. Their big spongy feet pad gently on the earth and make no noise. The soft clanking of the camel's muted bells and the groans of the wagon did not appear to intrude on the wildlife we passed. Even the kangaroos didn't bound away. They stood upright watching us pass, curious yet relaxed, sometimes scratching their bellies, looking a little bemused but never frightened.

Nature and its wild creatures responded differently to all the trail bikes. They made so much noise. Birds were taking to the air in fright, and kangaroos were running frantic with fear, sometimes bumping into each other they were so unsure where to bound to safety. We had no idea why there were so many bikers on the track until a passing tourist told us it was a long weekend, and everyone had come to practice on the Finke desert track. It ran alongside the old Ghan line and was the route of the yearly off-road race event from Alice to Finke. When we heard that, we decided it was wise to find a place to hide until the weekend's madness was over.

We parked our wagon behind a huge sand dune that shielded us from sight and unwanted attention. It was the biggest sand dune I'd seen and reared up on the side of the track at the exact moment we decided to hide. With yet another delay, we were unsure how to cope with our limited water supply, but once again, we were looked after. Growing in abundance was an edible plant called Broad leaf Parakeelya. This succulent had long been a source of food for aboriginal people who eat the leaves and the roots and, when they've collected enough, grind down the seeds to make a paste. This wondrous plant held so much moisture our camels would not need watering as they grazed it. They *loved* munching it too! We were fine, we could relax for a couple of days until the regular grind of work wound everyone back in, and the track would be ours to enjoy in peace again.

Even though the camels didn't need watering, we were still so frugal with our water. When you have to go to so much work to get it, you treasure every single drop. Instead of our usual tin bucket on the fire boiling our water for a wash, we just splashed our faces. Gill could have driven off to find a bore, but it would have been a reasonably big trip and left me alone in camp. I wasn't keen on that. I was sure I could cope. It was more to do with the hostility Gill had met on this station. Mean-spiritedness was a space of mind that I couldn't comprehend. While I didn't want to create imaginary scenarios, I felt uneasy. I knew I would feel happier when we were off this property completely. What we hadn't anticipated was that just to be provocative, the managers of this station had lied.

We reached the dried-up water tanks a few days later, and our mouths hung open in disbelief. It would appear that the water was never turned off here, and it had overflowed from the tanks creating huge ponds verdant with life. Grass was growing everywhere, and kangaroos sheltered under the trees in the shade of their heavenly oasis. Frogs hidden amongst the water reeds croaked in unison. After enduring little water for several days and putting up with feeling grungy, there was no way I was passing this tank without stripping off and getting under that hose. Standing under an overflowing tank and being pummelled by the force of the water is an experience everyone should have. It's so revitalising. I felt charged up with life.

We filled our water tanks, but we didn't camp there. We always respected watering holes as we travelled. Our presence could easily deter stock and the wild animals from coming in for a much-needed drink. It was also the most likely place farmers lay their loathsome 1080 bait so they could cull all their victims when they came in for an innocent drink. We didn't even let our dogs out for a pee if we were at a water trough or a dam.

Feeling rejuvenated and clean, we were about to leave the water tanks when Gill noticed something sparkling in the grass. It was a massive set of keys. He thought they were for all the property's bores and had most likely been dropped by the managers. I was so tempted to throw them into their overflowing tanks. What mean-spirited little people they were. Intentionally trying to create problems for us that didn't even exist.

"We'll be just the same as them if we do that," Gill said, and he was right, and that prospect was such a terrifying thought I let it go immediately.

We gave the keys to the occupants of a passing car who were happy to deliver them to the manager's shop and say they were from the camel people. I loved this opportunity to show the miserable managers of this beautiful station what kindness and caring looked like. They may have chosen to be ignoble, but our choice was very different, even though dealing with these two had impacted us. There were days we'd really struggled with our own peace of mind. Attack energy is a pestilent seed, and we were very aware we could plant and tend it and let it fuel our own rage or choose a different harvest. We chose a more empowering harvest, and returning the keys helped us shift the flow of their negativity that had followed us for a few days down the track. And the irony was not lost on either of us that it was a rather massive bunch of keys that we were returning to them.

Ultimately, we threw ourselves into focusing on all the love we lived. Our own big beautiful lives, just like those water tanks, were overflowing. We relished every interaction with our animals and each other. Revelling in the majestic beauty of the sunrise and the pregnant and soft haven of the dawn.

We had been so nervous as we made our courtesy call to the next station to let them know we would be passing through. We had argued for a while as to who would make it. We both felt too fragile for another rebuff, and neither of us wanted to make that call. I promised I'd bake one of my cakes if Gill spoke with them. He had tried to sway me with several offerings, but none surpassed mine! It felt silly to be bartering over something as ridiculous as a phone call. I wanted to feel bolder than I was. Pick up that phone and ring unphased by whether they were friendly or not. Ultimately, Gill making the call was a forlorn win as the person ringing the next station would be me. I was so relieved to discover we had no reason to try and wheedle out of any calls.

The outback was full of generous-hearted people who were good and kind. Fortunately, the station we had just travelled through was *almost* the rare exception and known by others for its hostility.

"Thanks so much for calling," the owners of the following station said. "Make yourself at home. If you need anything, give us a call, there's water at several bores alongside the track, and you are welcome to fill up at any of them."

But the best news was that this station did not lay down 1080 baits. Our dogs could have a much-deserved break from their leads.

I felt so happy at the goodness of people I sat down and had a cry!

Three

Our Amazing Camels

While I didn't get much time for reading, I had begun to read Lord of the Rings on our days off, which didn't help my already vivid imagination. As soon as we entered the gate of the following property, my body sighed with relief. We'd made it. After dealing with orcs and travelling through their hostile terrain, we'd finally reached the elven palace and were safe. Honestly, we had to laugh! Even though we'd tried to stay focused on our own lives and not on the dismal charm of the managers, the tension we'd felt on this property left us at the gate.

There's an energy around being welcomed that encompasses you in its well-being. We all felt it. As much as Gill and I realised that our moods and emotions could determine the day regarding how our animals behaved, some feelings took longer to process. Our animals had all been so patient, though. The difference in their pace and exuberance once we were through the gate showed me they'd also felt what we were going through. They were all so excited and wanted to run. They bucked and kicked out as we trotted down the dirt track for a few kilometres. A red ribbon of a road weaving through groves of golden acacias and towering gum trees. I felt myself unravel in joy and a fragrant blossomed elation. The moment was now, and the past was already long gone. When our days were good, they were *really* good.

When the wagon finally slowed to a walk, I jumped out so I could walk beside our camels. I felt so much love for them all. These incredible beings had led me to a freedom I'd never known before. Not just the freedom of the life we were living together, but the freedom to be the real me and not the always nice one that didn't know how to set boundaries or say no.

Anyone with camels will tell you they are an endless source of fascination. Like all animals, they have such different personalities. While I loved all my animals with a passion, the camels intrigued and enchanted me the most. Mostly because they are often hidden. They won't show you who they are unless you are worthy to see them, so not many people get to see who these incredible animals *really* are. Some cameleers who work with them their entire life may never see them. However those that do get lured into their dromedary charm often find there is no getting out! Not that I wanted to escape. *Even* I thought to myself *if I have to travel red desert roads for the rest of my life, I will.*

The camels looked around, eyes bulging in anticipation at all the acacia bushes covered in their sweet-smelling vanilla and gold blossoms. It was one of their favourite foods. Kushy had a big smile on his face, but he always did. Whatever we were doing, he looked happy. We could have been entering Mordor, and he would have still been smiling. He had a purity about him that was adorable. He would cruise along nonchalantly, wearing his harness like a necklace. I think that's what he thought it was!

Chocolate brown Kunkaa, born under a tree full of crows, on the other hand, was a strong force in our camel team, and I loved singing her praises as I walked beside her. "Oh, Kunkaa," I would softly whisper, "We so appreciate you." Kunkaa would do *anything* you asked if you gave her enough praise, and as I told her how much we loved her, I could see her visibly swell with pride.

Mozzee, with his beautiful crooked nose, whilst a colossal strength most of the time, was a prankster and loved to play games. He got extreme pleasure from nipping gentle Nev in front of him, on the bum. This would have all the camels upping the pace as Nev, always a conscientious worker lurched forward in surprise. Mozzee's behaviour was a complete contrast to Lady Caroline's. She pulled our wagon with honour and pride and was appalled at Mozzees irreverence for the job. She'd look so perturbed whenever our prankster disturbed the team's flow.

Always the noble matriarch, Lady Caroline felt dignified and important walking behind her lord, Zu. He was the only camel in front of her and the *only* one she would have tolerated in that superior position. She revered him, and we shared her sentiments for this otherworldly beast. Gill and I still shook our heads in awe at how this camel had inveigled his way into our thoughts and dreams for three days and nights until we'd relented and gone and bought him. He was so phenomenal we bowed down in honour and awe of him. Zu had never pulled a wagon before we'd left on this trip. He'd never been trained to do *anything*, and yet he'd settled into leading our team like a pro. He automatically knew what to do in *every* situation. My only rational conclusion was that he'd descended like an angel from the heavens just to help us.

Pulling right in front of the wagon, we had Andaria and Jianti, and these two were hilarious. They were always the first to be harnessed, which meant they had to wait for the rest of the team. They did this with a nonchalant disinterest in anything going on, chewing their cud as if it was gum, looking around as if they were bored. If harnessing the others took too long, they'd start bickering, groaning as they half-heartedly mouthed each other. When that got boring, our beloved little Jianti would play her favourite trick.

She'd wait until all our camels were harnessed and ready and our wagon was just about to roll. Then, in a very melodramatic way, she would start bawling. And a camel bawling is *really* loud! It took us a while to realise that this clever girl was lifting her leg up high and purposely putting her foot down on the wrong side of the chains. When we finally woke up to her little game, one word from Gill was enough to have her lifting that foot up superfast and returning it to its proper position. She did this so regularly, and it always made us laugh.

Unlike many other wagon-pulling teams, we had cut the harnessing apparatus down to the bare minimum to save time. Our camels pulled two abreast, and we were aiming to work up to having four rows of them. Eight camels pulling our wagon! On each side of each camel ran a chain. From the front of the wagon, they ran the entire length of the team to Zu in the front. In total, four rows of chains. Their harnesses clipped onto the chain at each side of them. We could have chosen to use a strap called a spider that would keep the chains *off* the ground and prevent our camels from getting a foot on the wrong side or even getting tangled. Of course, if a spider had proven necessary, we would have changed tactics, but it didn't. Without this additional harnessing equipment, we were doing fine, but we did need to focus a little more at certain times. If the camels pulling the wagon in the front slowed down unexpectedly, the chains would slacken around our camels' legs. This was when they could get tangled if we didn't put on the wagon brake and slow everything down.

One of us often walked beside the camels, and we were always watching them from the wagon. Occasionally we'd notice one had stepped over the chain, and we'd have to stop. Gill often had to slide between the front of one camel and the back legs of another just to reach the camel who'd stepped out of the chains. Using a long metal rod, Gill would gently tap that camel on its foot. Our camels soon learnt to lift their legs and put them back within the chains. I felt so proud of them. They learnt everything quickly and were always so still and respectful when Gill moved in between them. He was really vulnerably. If they'd played up, he could have been really badly hurt. Sometimes our camels could be little rotters, but when we needed them to behave, they did.

The biggest challenge we faced daily was in dealing with the camels that walked behind the wagon. They were usually easy to handle in the mornings, but at the end of the day, they didn't like waiting while we unharnessed our other camels. They were impatient for a feed. As the other camels began to walk away from our wagon and feed, they would be bucking with excitement to go with them. If we were not really focused, we could get hurt. Gill was keen to get more of them in harness and rotate the camels in our team, so they all got to have a rest, and all of them got a chance to learn.

I knew we would work out all the clunky parts of handling our animals as we went along. We were undoubtedly a work in progress, and I was grateful we had the time to get it all together.

The old Ghan line was so peaceful. We'd walk for days without seeing anyone. Few vehicles used it, and those who did shared our sense of adventure. Gill and I were incredulous when we saw a tiny 2WD Barina car approaching us. It was making such a din. It was such a small car its wheels didn't fit in the well-worn ruts of the track, and its underbelly was scraping on the ground. This didn't appear to stop or even concern the elderly couple inside, who shone with health and happiness and were loving each moment of their wild outback adventure. Their vehicle was totally unsuited to the terrain, yet they were boldly and fearlessly having an adventure. They'd driven through sand and over endless corrugations in country that was so remote if they had broken down or got stuck, help may not have come for days. Whatever fuel was driving them, we shared in its trust.

As we were chatting to them, cheeky Blossom had put her head in the driver's window to say hello. They were in fits of laughter at this totally in-their-face encounter with a camel. They were so focused on her that they were shocked when Bella's big head came in the open passenger window. Our cheeky duo had discovered earlier in our trip that some car occupants gave you apples!

We were even more awed by this elderly couple when the track we followed turned to deep sand with no hard surface. We had no idea how these intrepid travellers had got through in such a tiny little car. Our only conclusion was they'd got up to a terrific speed and flown! We did not have the gift of speed, and after only a few turns of the wagon wheels, we were bogged. All we could do was get out the spades and start digging. I felt so frustrated. I was hot and sweaty, and it didn't help when some cars began to back up in front of us. We were completely blocking the track, and they were unable to pass.

A few occupants got out and came over to see if they could help. They were from the nearby Aboriginal community of Finke, or Apatula as it is now known. They were driving cross country to another community for a football game. We assured them we were fine, we'd had plenty of practice digging, and we would be out eventually. While they were reluctant to leave us bogged, they didn't want to be late for their game, so they began to look at the off-road options for getting around us. By this time, all the women and children had gotten out of the cars and had calmly walked over to the only little bush and sat down to wait in its shade. It appeared that disembarking for off-road forays and adventures was an unspoken routine for this lot. We had no idea how they would drive through the sand. To most sane people, even the idea looked crazy. They had little battered town cars that bore the signs of a tough life. Windows were missing, lights had long gone, doors didn't appear to open, and passengers embarked through the space where the window *should* have been. They slid out onto the ground, landing in a heap. We had watched with incredulity the women and children disembark this way.

I felt this nervous anticipation as they worked out the best route. A posse of four cars had turned around and driven back up the track the way they'd just come, and it wasn't long before we heard the first revving engine heading our way at *tremendous* speed. Then much to our astonishment, the first battered old sedan appeared airborne from the top of a small sand dune. It flew through the air before crashing down to earth, bouncing several times and almost losing control. With their foot fully down on the gas pedal and the back end of their sedan slithering from side to side in deep sand while their back tyres churned up a spew of sand, they slowly inched forward.

While I have no doubt most people around me watched this feat of paranormal driving with admiration and respect, I watched it in nail-biting, shit-loosening horror, but when that car finally hit the hard sand and careered back onto the track, I was jumping up and down with everyone else, screaming and cheering with excitement. What a hero. The driver alighted from that car ten feet tall, everyone slapping him on the back and high-fiving him. He was undoubtedly a man who lived life to the full *and*, as the forerunner, had mapped out the route for those to come. They came screeching over the dunes after him. Passenger free, light as a bird, flying through the air before landing with a crash and then the crazy madness as their battered bush cars slithered and screeched from side to side to get back on the road. But they all made it. This mob would not be late for their footy game, and they sped away on their adventure in a shower of laughter and love.

These sand dune driving heroes were a complete contrast to the occupant of a really expensive and new-looking 4WD who was irritably parked behind our bogged wagon. He appeared to have every accessory for off-road driving, yet he offered us no assistance. He kept complaining that we were holding him up and refused to even consider driving around us. In the hours he sat moaning from his car, he failed to find any curiosity or interest in the marvellous spectacle of our lives other than an inconvenience!

We continued to dig and rest, dig and rest. We were in no rush. It would take as long as it did, and there was nothing we could do to speed it up. Hours later, at the very moment the camels lunged forward, freeing the wagon from its entrenchment, we noticed the man with all the 4WD accessories but not an ounce of joy finally driving the off-road route around us, and we happily waved him goodbye!

Most days, we were travelling further than we had ever done before. Gill estimated we were easily managing twenty kilometres. Yet, even though we were in a much better flow, it was still hard work. Every moment pushed me, though both of us noticed the clarity we'd gained from living outside in nature, unplugged from screens for over a year. Every cell in our body felt revitalised, and I felt connected with nature in a way I'd never been before. While Gill had lived many years living simply, unplugged from the grid, I never had, and I had never felt so clear. Often our days were feats of physical endurance. We had so much to do. Travelling with so many animals and keeping them well and happy pushed me well past any prior physical limit, but I loved the challenge. I loved striding out with the camels. Even in the heat of the day, I felt so fit and strong.

Averaging one hundred kilometres every four days, we were moving! I realise it may not sound like much to many who drive cars, but to us, it was akin to the speed of light and record-breaking.

We soon reached the threshold of our next milestone, the small aboriginal community of Apatula, when just on our approach, it began to rain. For three days, we sheltered under tarps with all the dogs, chickens and Banjo and our big red rooster, 'The Colonel, who had a noble dignity just like Banjo. I absolutely adored him. We had opened our arms to all these different species, never realising for one moment that the reward would be ours.

Even days camped waiting for the rain to pass were productive. On our smoky fire with a pile of damp logs, we cooked cakes and dampers, so we were stocked up when we began to travel and even though after three days the rain stopped and the sun came out, we waited two more days for the track to dry out.

Every day we faced numerous challenges. When we saw the long crossing over the very wide dry river and how precariously sandy it was, we knew we faced another. While it looked well used, some sections were soft sand and the one car we did see cross it had almost got bogged. We negotiated this crossing for a long time before deciding our only hope was to aim for speed. Keep the wagon rolling and floor it if that was possible at five kilometres an hour!

In our new-found harmony, we always explained to our camels what we needed from them *before* we did anything. We still had days when we were all slow to move and didn't progress far from the night before but we also had many times when we needed everyone to pull together as a team. We may have faced a steep hill, or a dangerous pot holed stretch of road, but we were doing it. Some days I couldn't believe it myself. All these animals and just me and Gill. After all these years and our mammoth preparation, we were finally travelling together through the desert. While we may have blitzed many challenges, this dry river was a big one.

We had to all be in the zone before we even attempted it. As I sat in the wagon waiting, I could hear Gill's voice, "Zu, I'm gonna need you to floor it, just keep going mate, don't stop. Kushy, you're actually going to have to pull this time. Good one, Mozzee; stay focused; we need your strength. Lady Caroline, you've got this." Lady Caroline would raise her noble head high, assuming the pulling position, ready and keen to go, waiting only for the roar of loudhailer lungs Gill "*WALK EM UUUU-UPPPPP.*" Jianti was so eager to go she was throwing herself into her harness, and all the camels were bucking with excitement. "You can do this," yelled Gill, and off we went with the wind behind us. Gill yelling encouragement over the ruckus of cockies swinging merrily screeching in their cages and the dogs all barking. I was holding my breath with excitement and dread as I banged my little metal rod on the tin side of the wagon. We were all cheerleading our camels to go, go, go!

Prepping up our already frisking camels who cavorted across that dry creek bed, letting nothing, no poxy sand, hold them back. We went so fast we were almost flying, and we made it. We reached the other side. I jumped out of the wagon and hugged Gill, and then we ran around our camels, thanking and patting them and singing their praises. I loved them all so utterly much. They were all puffing up with pride, happy after their exertions.

Every day we faced so many challenges and got stretched way beyond what we believed we were able to do. We had learnt from all these experiences that whatever came up, we would find the resources necessary to transform each challenge into pure un-distilled empowerment. But we had to enter everything we did with an openness to learn and grow, and our connection with our animals was vital. When we faced challenges together and came out on the other side, I was so aware of this dynamic flow of energy between us and our animals.

Gill and I had both witnessed the negative side of our unconscious flow in our early days of travelling. On several occasions when we'd been pushed to our limits, and I felt like I'd landed in the life from hell, we'd had some crazy arguments. Often me screaming in the dirt with sticks and leaves in my hair. So pissed off, I wanted to kill my beloved, and even though we had made up, healed the rift and thought everything was good again, each time, within an hour, our dogs would fight. This was not a usual occurrence for them. Still, it showed us so clearly how vital the energy we held was in bringing every animal together in a harmonious flow. On this trip, we had to get it together and grow up. We did not have the liberty of spewing emotions. Too many animals depended on us, who were sensitive to all our currents.

But that didn't mean we ever suppressed what we felt. We just had to find a way of dealing and releasing what came up without spewing it out in camp. We'd had the odd bicker where I'd stomped off into the bush, trampling over little blue bushes in a rage, straight out into the desert, with no hope of survival. Walking, walking, walking, that would teach him if I died of thirst. Swearing blindly, I was never *ever* coming back to that arsehole and his wagon, marching away in such a livid fury; every thought was a curse until I got thirsty and thought I was about to die of heat stroke. Then I would turn around and meekly creep back into camp, staggering a little in the hope that someone would feel sorry for me because I felt so sorry for myself!

But thankfully, our trip had transformed since our earlier tumultuous time. Our own errant behaviours had become a source of such hilarity we often laughed until our bellies hurt at the mad creatures we'd been. What a welcome space harmony was, and I loved the flow we experienced from finding this place of peace.

As soon as we'd crossed the dry Finke river, Gill pulled up the camels and the wagon in the shade of some giant eucalypt trees. We all needed a moment to breathe and to celebrate. It doesn't sound like much of an achievement to anyone else to have crossed a long sandy track in a camel wagon across a wide dry river, but we were jubilant. Jumping up and down and praising our camels. Cuddling Nev, scratching Zu's otherworldly head, congratulating Kushy, who'd finally realised the fluffy thing around his neck called a harness had a use *and* used it. Singing out to Kunkaa and our dear Jianti, the pocket rocket. What a force she was! And dear Andaria, who'd pulled with such fierce determination. We were so proud of them all. As we all stood revelling in the glow of a job well done, we noticed Lady Caroline. Much too euphoric to lower her head, she stood so dam proudly she could have been receiving the order of Australia or being knighted by the queen.

Four

Watery Blessings

Our wagon creaked and groaned like an old lady as we rambled along the pot-holed track into the aboriginal community of Aputula, formerly known as Finke. We had travelled over three hundred kilometres since leaving Alice!

Sunlight danced in puddles, and the day felt bright and fresh after the rain, yet Finke was like a ghost town. Every house we passed was silent. Not a single dog barked and no childish laughter leaked from any of the houses. We couldn't understand where everyone was. *Had the entire town departed for the footy game?* Even though the soft, muted tones of our camel bells clearly announced our arrival, not a living soul came out to greet us.

I didn't mind if we slunk through town unnoticed. When you spend each day in the company of animals, you become more familiar with grunts and barks and pongs and farts. Fronting up for approaching people often took more energy than it was worth. I preferred to travel through the landscape unnoticed and unseen but happily, that was not to be the case.

We had just reached the local school when we heard the first sound of life. An excited child burst from a doorway, and behind him surged his classmates. They all came running towards us, screaming, shrieking and jumping for joy. I was concerned our camels would freak out. None of them had ever seen this much excitement before, but I should have known them better. Our amazing mob of dromedaries had already proven trustworthy in every situation where one wrong move could lead us all to plummet to our deaths. They also loved to be the centre of attention, and they were ready to lap it all up. Despite all the shrieks of disbelief at the sight of our fairy tale entourage, our beloved camels stood perfectly still, and a few even lowered their heads for a stroke. They didn't do that for everyone.

These bush kids were feral in the noblest way. Connected to the earth, barefoot and bright, with a vitality and alertness that hadn't been dulled from overuse of computer screens. They were a swarm of curiosity and wanted to know *everything*. Why, where, what, who, and when.

We showed them around our wagon and, unbeknown to us, gave them our first run of what was to become a familiar routine as we met more and more people along the way.

"How many animals can you see?" we asked. They began with the obvious, camels, a donkey, and dogs. "More," we coaxed. Then with a loud exclamation, one of the boys spotted the chickens. A wave of awe rippled through the kids as they all ran to have a look at them, clucking away happily in their home between the wheels. "More." we said, not giving them *any* clues. Some of the kids were on their hands and knees, peering under the wagon. While others were walking around it, searching every nut and bolt, checking behind the tyres as if we'd somehow secreted animals into the very framework of our wagon.

There was a loud cheer when they spotted the parrots and more cries of wonder when they saw the dove's romantic haven under the eaves. Then we told them to follow their noses. Sniffing the air and walking as if our noises were in complete control, we went around to the back veranda so they could meet Banjo. They cuddled our stinky billy goat as if he was a sweet little lamb. Even though this badly abused billy goat had had a very volatile relationship with kids in the past, he never held that against them. This loveable boy would have been the greatest friend to the kids that had stoned him, but he'd never been given that chance. I felt such joy seeing him plumped up and happy in the midst of so much loving attention. It was all he deserved and more.

Undoubtedly we worked hard every day, even on good days when everything flowed. What made the hard work worth it, though, was all the moments of genuine interactions and heartfelt connections between our animals and us and the people we met along the way. Meeting the kids from this aboriginal community was a sheer joy.

They were all cheering as we gave the camels the command to "Pull em up." The ultimate green light for our wagon launching ruckus of barking dogs and squawking parrots to begin. One of the local men had kindly offered to run ahead and drop the fence for us next to the grid so we could easily continue on our way. By this time the noise erupting from our wagon had woken the whole town up, and people stood in their doorway or sat on their verandas shaking their heads in astonishment. As our entourage passed through town, we had to call for help to catch one little errant scruff of a doggy boldly snapping at the camel's feet. His owner came and scooped him up, and we all got safely on our way.

We'd been slowly getting the camels used to having reins so Gill and I could sit in the wagon and didn't always have to lead the team. The road surface was so good when we left Aputula, and our camels were raring to go. For the next few kilometres, they trotted. We felt like a king and queen sitting up high in our carriage. We didn't even need to encourage them. We had The Waifs playing on our stereo, cups of tea from our flask and slabs of fruit and nut damper, which we always shared with the parrots. They would screech with excitement when they saw it and didn't give us any peace until they'd had their bit. What a rowdy gang of parrots we had. What a rowdy gang we all were!

Yumyum, our man attacking galah, had settled well into his new life, and he *loved* the wagon. We'd been told he couldn't fly, so we always let him out whenever we stopped and camped, but we had to set clear boundaries for him. He became so possessive when he hung out inside our wagon. If Gill or I tried to get in, he would fly at us in full attack mode. It was funny and terrifying at the same time because his bite *really* hurt. Once there had been so much noise coming from inside our wagon I had stood on our huge front wheel to look inside. I was trying to be as quiet as I could. The prospect of him seeing me was chilling. While surreptitiously peeping, I watched him frog marching across our bed like a mini dictator tossing anything he didn't want on the bed onto the floor. When he saw me watching him, he gave me such an evil look. In my absolute haste to get away, I stepped backward off the wheel and landed on the earth in a laughing, shaking heap.

He was so ferocious he left us no choice but to *ban* him from our home unless he was safely in his cage. As we travelled, he saw more action from his cage in a day than most caged birds experience in a lifetime, and he loved it. He'd screech with excitement, share our food, try and grab leaves from the trees when they brushed his cage, and he was always a very vocal member of the pre-wagon rolling chorus.

As the wagon rattled down the red dirt track with all its feathery and furred passengers on board, we could hear wild donkeys braying in the distance. In the soft sand of the road were many animal prints, including fresh camel tracks. Whether from a lone camel or a mob, they were probably attracted to the acacias bushes that grew thickly on each side of the road and were our camel's favourite food. We were constantly on the alert for our wild friends, but it appeared they had long gone, and if they were still nearby, they were obviously content enough to not bother us.

Frequently the sky would fill with the flapping wings of flocks of noisy parrots coming in for water, and as they flew, twisting and turning, their white wings looked luminous in the sunlight. I was awed by all the wild beauty. The property we were on had a wildness few stations were able to maintain or chose to in the quest for profit. I loved the way, so many wild animals co-existed. When we camped at night, dingos howled all through the night, and it felt eerie and yet exciting. One even came in really close and sat on the edge of our camp, watching us as we sat around our fire. It was bright enough to see it in the moonlight, and I was surprised at our dog's response. We'd been so relieved and happy to hear that this station did *not* lay 1080 bait. We could finally relax with our dogs, who lay sleeping in the sand around our fire, enjoying some freedom from their chains. I'd been concerned when I first spotted the dingo that our dogs would bark or even try and chase it, but they behaved as if nothing was there and did not respond in any way to the moonlit wailing of these wild animals. I felt so grateful these dingos had found some haven where they could still live wild and free. We need so many more places like this.

It looked as if the lush wilderness we travelled through would last forever when unexpectedly, the road dipped into a dried creek bed. At every creek crossing, I had to slow the wagon with the brake just enough to prevent us from hurtling down the hill too fast, but not slow it too much. The camels used the downhill momentum to cruise up each rise at a trot, and as they did, we entered a landscape devoid of comfort or feed. We had not foreseen this. There were days when if we were a little tired or wanted to get on the road extra early, we would tow our land cruiser behind the wagon instead of driving further down the track to our next camp. If we knew we had some really steep hills, we kept it with us for the day and used it as an extra brake on our descents, so we didn't always know what lay ahead.

As far as the eye could see, and flat to the horizon were gibber plains, it was like a moonscape. The entire surface of the earth was covered in sharp little rocks. Any bush that *had* miraculously managed to survive this wind-blasting terrain grew wizened and clung to the ground.

After trotting up that hill so enthusiastically, our camels came to a complete standstill. They were not prepared to take another step. All their eyes were bulging with shock as they looked around them, horrified. Surely something edible must be growing somewhere? They were looking in every direction. There was *nothing*! Lady Caroline appeared to be the most devastated by this change and was physically shaking. Her bottom lip was quivering, and it took Gill a fair time to reassure them that we were only passing through. We had not moved here to live, and the sooner we got moving, the less time we would have to spend in this camel's gourmet hell.

We had finally soothed them all enough to get them moving again when Gill and I noticed a tiny wee dot, way off near the horizon, that was heading our way. We had no idea what it was. It didn't look like a car, wasn't big enough for a bus and it wasn't travelling *that* fast. Our camels had picked up the pace again, keen to get this part of the journey over. Gill and I surmised the blob getting closer could possibly be a bicycle.

By the time the camels noticed it, it was close enough to see that it was a young male cyclist, and he had a big smile on his face. I felt really relaxed with the camels as he approached us. They had faced with calmness all sorts of vehicles and trail bikes. We had no doubt they would be okay with a bicycle, but to our surprise, they stopped abruptly. They stood in the road staring at the bike with the same horror they'd viewed the gibber plains. Then in a blind panic, our team of camels began spinning our wagon around as they all tried to run, in harness, in the opposite direction. They jack-knifed our wagon in the middle of the road, where Lady Caroline fell to her knees, shaking with fear. While she had always been a profoundly feeling and expressive camel, I'd never seen her respond in such a panicked way to anything before. Gill and I were really concerned. We didn't want any of our animals to experience such panic. *Should we take her out of the team?* But when we talked it through later, Gill and I agreed that this would mortify her. She took tremendous pride in her place at the front of our wagon-pulling crew, and if we took Lady Caroline out, we would have to take Zu out too because these two were a team, a couple even. At night they always sat together with the regal air of the king and the queen.

Her majestic morning promenade alongside the wagon and all the already harnessed camels was part of the fabric of her day. She swelled with pride every time she did it. Every single wagon launch, she was always so eager to move she would lurch forward before we were totally ready, and the rest of the team was pulling with her.

It hadn't taken her long to recover from the shock of this new experience. In retrospect, we both felt if Gill had been leading the camels, her reaction would *not* have been so panicked. We had simply underestimated her response. While we were clear we would not take her out of the team, we would undoubtedly have to be extra vigilant in future for any approaching bikes.

We camped that night in a dry old creek bed in the gibber flats whilst a storm rumbled in around us and arcs of lightning struck the earth. We'd been too exhausted and fraught to travel much further, and once again, our camels were not happy. They moaned and groaned, and it didn't help that somewhere in the vicinity of our camels, an animal had died, and we only noticed it when we were all settled for the night. We couldn't see it, but the wind must have changed direction because the smell of death and decay wafted into our camp and gave our night a spooky edge.

In the morning, as we walked around our camels, we reassured them that as soon as we reached some abundant feed, we'd stay for a few days, and they could eat to their heart's content.

It took us over a week before we pulled up at a welcome oasis, an unexpected waterhole about a kilometre long. Giant old gum trees lined the creek, their branches full of noisy galahs. Wild ducks were bobbing and diving in the water, making it look so enticing and brightly coloured parrots I'd not seen before flitted from tree to tree. Even though the summery heat had begun to wane and the days were edged with cold, after travelling for weeks through heat and dust, I felt like I'd arrived in heaven. I couldn't wait to get into the water and bob around with the ducks, but first, we took all the camels down to the water's edge for a drink. Many of our camels thought water came in buckets and were experiencing a waterhole for the first time.

I sat on the giant roots of an ancient gum tree that grew on the sandy banks of the river's shore and watched our beautiful herd of camels approach the water in an excited huddle. Inching their way nervously down to the water's edge until they got too scared. Then with a big kick and a buck, they'd all cavort back across the sandy beach to the safety of the river's bank. Then, gaining more courage and becoming more intrepid, they cautiously walked down to the water's edge again. Testing out the soft sand that made them nervous when they sunk almost to their ankles. They had many practices before they were brave enough to drink from the water. Finally satiated, they began to kick and jump playfully in the shallows, showering sprays of sunlight sparkling water everywhere. Big red Alice boldly walked deeper than the rest, sat down and began to roll, which encouraged a few more of them to sit down and roll. Soon the water was a writhing mass of camels rolling and splashing. Their wet bodies looked golden in the sunlight. I watched, intoxicated by the life I was living. So raw and free that every breath I took felt lurid and ripe with life. I felt this massive release for us all as I watched them having so much fun. We'd all been working hard, and we deserved this break.

This waterhole was ancient. Every animal in this area since the beginning of time had watered here. While it had an otherworldly beauty, there was a grief about the place that was palpable. As we travelled, we heard many stories of massacres and killings of aboriginal and Afghani people. Many lost their lives at the watering holes where they were most vulnerable. They had to drink water and couldn't avoid going to them.

When I sat in silence much later that night, after all the jobs had been done and I could finally claim some time for myself, I felt a scream in my belly, the howl of tears, and old grief lay heavy on my heart. More women and children had been slaughtered here for no other reason than their colour. It was so sickening. I began to speak softly to them, unsure if their spirits were still around. I couldn't feel them. Perhaps some sensitive souls had already passed through this popular camping place and assisted these women and children in passing over. I was pretty sure what we were here for was to release the lingering grief. It hung over everything like a cloud and had me wiping away my own tears.

Even with its ghosts, we were in no rush to leave this watery haven. Over the next few days, everywhere I went, I silently honoured the ancestors, and the innocent victims killed on this land. I didn't even feel it was necessary to do anything. Being in places that have experienced tragedy in a space of love, kindness and honouring is enough. It's our presence that radiates from us that transmutes and heals. However, a few days later, I did create a little bush ceremony with Gill.

We rose early in the morning and sat on the sandy shore under the shady bower of a gnarly big burled tree. I lit a small smoky fire of dried gum leaves topped with a few baubles of freshly gathered tree resin, my liquid gold. As the smoke wafted around us, we began to tone. A deep sound that came from my core like a long guttural moan, and I could hear Gill's voice toning beside me. There were times we sounded raspy, times our breath faltered, times we sounded so discordant. Still, we kept going, clearing all the blockages that arose until the tones we made wove together. We sat on that shore like monks in our temple. Cross-legged, eyes closed, our voices harmonising in our cerebral chant. As the smoke from our gum leaves slowly diminished, leaving only a pile of ash, the past became the present, and everything merged as one. When we finally opened our eyes, all we could see was light.

The day was still early, and it sparkled.

I felt really peaceful as I walked back to our camp and was utterly unprepared for Yumyum's death-defying heroics. We had left our flightless cocky sitting happily on the back of a chair, but he was nowhere to be seen.

We checked everywhere in camp and were just extending our worried search to the surrounding bushes when we heard him screeching excitedly from *above* us. He was flying! Flying like he'd *never* done before. He was doing big raucous show-off laps of our wagon, apparently just as surprised as we were that he could fly. As he flew through the air, he was making so much noise every hungry hawk could hear him, and it didn't take long before I noticed a falcon take off from the highest branches of a nearby tree. This was a bird that was so fast and so deadly that Yumyum didn't stand a chance.

The falcon sliced through the air straight towards our little galah on his maiden flight. Yet Yumyum put on the performance of his life. He was dipping, diving and swerving so fast as he tried to outfly his predator. The whole time the falcon was an inch away from his tail. Yet, miraculously he made it to safety within the leafy foliage of an old gum tree.

Anxious that my little bird would take off again and put himself back in danger, I ran to the tree. I saw Yumyum high up on a branch, almost hidden amongst the leaves. His heart must have been beating so fast I could see from the ground; his body was shaking. I knew he'd be safe in the tree, but I wanted him home. My legs were still shaking, and I felt weak from the shock of watching our cheeky little mutt of a bird in such danger. I couldn't even think about relaxing until he was safely *in* his cage, yet each time I called him, he ignored me.

Confident that if I gave him some time to calm down, he'd come, and not wanting to leave him unattended, I sat at the bottom of the tree and waited. Gill even bought me a cup of tea. I kept talking to Yumyum, telling him we just wanted to take him home, but an hour passed, and he was still sitting there, ignoring every attempt I made to entice him down.

For the rest of the day, I sat under the tree and by the time the sun began to set, he was still high up in the branches and out of reach from us. I had no choice but to leave him for the night. My only consolation was he wouldn't try and fly in the dark. Well, I didn't think he would, anyway.

I got up early with high expectations of being reunited with my little mate, but the day continued in the same way. I stood at the bottom of the tree with food and water for him, trying to lure my usually adoring little chum down, but still, he acted as if I wasn't even there. He didn't even look down. I was calling him, I even sang to him, but I didn't even get a curious glance. He was way up high. So high Gill couldn't even climb the tree to get him down. My only choice was to wait until he chose to come down himself and pray he didn't fly off somewhere else and put himself in danger again. He looked fine. I even watched him stripping some leaves from the branches with his beak. He was in his own little world, and we didn't exist!

It wasn't until day three of his vigil in the tree that Gill came up with an idea. By this time, I had my own little settlement under the tree, complete with books and drinks and a fire pit for brewing tea, so I didn't have to leave the Yumyum tree. Gill flopped down beside me laughingly and told me to follow his lead. Wrapping his arms around me, he began kissing me passionately on the lips.

It took all of ten seconds. Yumyum flew down from that tree like a kamikaze pilot ready to tear into Gill and would have clawed and bitten him if Gill hadn't swiftly gotten out of the way. I was astounded we hadn't thought of this before. Yumyum always bristled when Gill got close to me.

I wrapped my little parrot safely in a towel with his head sticking out, something he *loved* and nestled him like a baby. He chuckled happily as I carried him back to the safety of his cage. I could finally relax.

We spent ten days at this watering hole before we woke up one morning, knowing it was our last day. The open road was calling us once again. While I was excited at the prospect of getting moving again after such a prolonged break, it also felt daunting. Getting the momentum up again to get our massive show on the road required a huge effort I wasn't sure I had. It was always when we stopped that my fears would creep in, never when we were actually moving.

We'd travelled over 400 kilometres since leaving Alice. The dirt road we followed would now take us towards the Oodnadatta track and its throng of tourists. Our time walking through the bush, mostly in our own little world, was almost over, and I felt desperately sad about that.

Five

Tracks of Love

There were so many little details of our day-to-day lives that I had not even considered before we left on the trip. Safely ensconced in comfort zones, I had *not* contemplated how we would go about having a shit when it was pouring with rain. Or even how we would hide from passing yet often curious traffic while squatting in country as flat as a pancake with barely a tree.

It was Gill who always gave the wisest advice. He appeared to have an innate knowing about how to not only survive living out in the elements but to do so comfortably. When he settled to relax by the fire, he would mound up the earth for a pillow and dig a little hip hole before arranging his blanket. When he laid down, he was so perfectly slotted into the earth he looked like a little piece of her jigsaw.

It was Gill that wrapped my big Driza-Bone coat around my shoulders like a cape. Then he'd stand up my coat collar, tucking it under his Akubra hat that he'd plonked on my head, so I didn't get wet. Finally satisfied, I was ready for my first daunting encounter with pooing in torrential rain. I never did like hats. I always struggled to wear one, but I was grateful to be under its temporary shelter. With my spade under one arm, toilet paper safely tucked away under my coat, matches in my pocket and with warnings from Gill not to get either of the latter wet, he sent me off into the downpour. You basically make a tent of your coat, and it wasn't easy, but I did it, one *had* to, but the job wasn't finished until we'd burnt our toilet paper and filled in our poo hole. The only thing we *ever* left behind was some compost for the earth.

When there were no trees and everyone driving along the road could see us from ten miles away, Gill's advice was to use the camels as my screen. Early mornings, just when our need to grab a shovel and head bush was the most pressing, the camels were often sitting happily chewing their cud. If I dug my poo hole just a little way away from them and positioned it so perfectly that by the time I squatted down, I was completely hidden from the road, it took the paranoia out of the experience and actually made it quite pleasant. Squatting out in the early morning light, hidden amongst the humps. Listening to the birds pierce the frosty air with their melody felt so utterly organic I have struggled ever since to be able to use an indoor loo.

Apart from being spotted by tourists in our morning ritual, there were other hazards we had to face. It probably would not occur to many people that the very act of us getting through gates was a manoeuvre that required complete on the edge of your-seat life or death focus.

I dreaded them. We had so many animals to get through, and many were tethered to our wagon. Some on the sides and a few strings of camels on the back. One of us was always in the wagon riding the brake, ready to slap it on at the first shout to STOP. At the same time, the other had to ensure that every animal got through that gate, and none got wrapped around the gate post and strangled. While I always found it fraught, we got through each gate without incident, and all our camels quickly learnt not to walk out too wide of the wagon as we went through. It would seem silly to most that each successful gate experience had us jumping for joy, but they did.

The life Gill and I were living pushed us to every extreme of emotion, and endurance and both of us had continuously stepped up and faced each challenge. Oh, in my case, often unwillingly, Gill was far more stoic and uncomplaining. Of course, he'd begun this trip way fitter than me, and it was, after all, his idea. There were times I felt I was being dragged behind the wagon by my hair. Other times I would have enthusiastically traded Gill in for a different model, perhaps a more domesticated hubby who *would* like to curl up on the settee and watch TV. There were many moments in many days when the lure of comfort zones and an easier life was tantalisingly enticing, but these moments always quickly wore away.

It was my gentle bushman that would come over to me on a freezing cold morning when he noticed me shivering, with an extra scarf and wrap it tenderly around my neck or cradle my frozen fingers in his hands and rub and breathe life back into them with his warm breath. He would doctor my wounds, pick splinters out of my feet and regularly had me sleeping in a swag out under the stars. He taught me how to light a fire with damp wood and how to bake a cake in a camp oven, but the candlelit dinners and romantic nights that we had *once* had, had been overtaken by something very new. We were always so busy just doing what needed to be done that we didn't have time for *us* yet. And even though we fell into bed each night exhausted, there was an electricity between us that was ramped up. It came from the shared experience of a trillion little moments in our day that celebrated success.

We got through a gate, whoopee! We saw the most amazing-shaped sandalwood tree or ate a freshly picked wild quondong from the bush. The camels trotted up a good-sized hill without needing any commands, or we found the most magical place to camp. Success that we were actually doing it, travelling with all these animals. Success that none of our camels had a single rub mark from their halters and harnesses and had not lost any condition. In fact, they'd put weight on. Success, the chickens were so happy travelling they kept us in prolific eggs. Success that every night we climbed wearily into bed, we had a toasty warm wagon. I was so grateful for our pot belly fire and our blissfully comfortable bed.

Success for us was so many little moments that would go unnoticed by others. We celebrated them all in gasps of astonishment and cheeky little winks when we'd catch each other's eye or a quick high five as we passed each other. In the dirt and the dust, our love was blooming. Romance could wait. The coffers of our relationship were being filled to overflowing by the tough life we were living on the open road with our motley and much-loved crew of animals.

We had come a long way in miles and harmony since the station where we'd been accused of potential camel thievery and had obstacles placed on our path like a land mine. *Every* station owner since had been lovely, and we no longer braced ourselves to make that courtesy call. Some of these stations you could drive through for days, so we were deeply relieved that the custodians of these vast stretches of land welcomed us and our adventure. Our trip was so much easier when the owners were happy for us to fill up with water or call upon them if we needed help.

During our stay at the waterhole, we'd met one of the jackaroos from the station we were on. He dropped by to say hello and give us an invite from the owners to call in at the homestead for a meal and a hot shower. He was on his regular 300-kilometre round trip down rough station tracks to check all the bores were working and that all the animals had water. I couldn't even comprehend driving that distance down bumpy bush roads. Let alone driving that far and not even leaving your property. It was such a huge station, and we were only expected at the homestead *when* we arrived. At the speed we were travelling, that looked almost a week away.

Some days we struggled to travel two kilometres, and other days we felt like we were surfing a vast wave. We easily made twenty or more. It was a constant lesson to let go of striving and believing we should be making better progress than we were. We continuously thought we'd got this lesson, only to find ourselves frustrated at our slow pace later on. Our days were an ongoing process of surrender and a lesson in being present and allowing our day to flow in its *own* way. Only then could we enjoy even what appeared to be the most uninviting landscapes where there was always something magnificent to witness. The sunset, the vast starry sky at night, and the lightning on the horizon, but I especially loved the stones and the rocks. Often on those harsh arid plains, they changed colour, from hues of blues and green to streaked with purple.

We spent so much of our time walking beside the wagon or sitting looking out as we all rolled along in silent reverie. There was little to distract us from the awed wonder of living so keenly in the heat and dust, the wind and the rain and the further south we travelled, days that were curled and crisped with cold. I found living outside so utterly soothing. I had realigned with the person I'd been before computers and mobile phones and all the electrical currents that drain our life force and dull our wits. I had not noticed how slumped my life force had become until I'd left it all behind. There is a purity in nature that restores you.

We met *many* folks who were unappreciative of the endless flat vistas and couldn't see anything worth looking at, not even all the beautiful stones. I was fascinated by them. I'd had a long-time affinity with stones and rocks, and a decade before, when I'd first met Gill, I remember him pulling one from his pocket and giving it to me. He couldn't have given me a better gift, and my heart did a flip. I'd never met anyone who loved stones as much as I did. It was small and purplish, and in its very centre, it looked as if it had a keyhole. As I held it in my hand, Gill told me about the power of the ghouma rocks who like to travel to different places and how they whisper to people passing by to pick them up.

"Some come as healers," he'd told me, holding up a little stone with a crystalline centre that sparkled in the sunlight. "Others are doorways into hidden realms, and some ghoumas are so powerful even the darkest magician will not attack anyone under their protection."

One ghouma I gravitated towards was smooth, round and jet black. She looked like a little pearl who'd fallen into the underworld. As I held this ghouma, just for a moment, I was an eagle soaring in the sky above. From my great height, I could look down on our travelling cavalcade of love and see that everywhere we went, we left a blaze of light behind us.

Until then, I had thought we were clearing energy and anchoring love and compassion in the old earth grid, but I was wrong.

South American cultures refer to this energetic network of veins that circumvent the earth as spirit lines. The Chinese call them dragon lines and the Celt's ley lines. I had always known them as the earth's grid. While I was aware the earth's grid had been used to control the population through fear and separation, I had not realised it had been created for this purpose. Or that it was now in the process of disintegration.

Many years previously, Gill was fortunate to be present, with my brother, at one of my favourite stone circles in Derbyshire. A tiny little fairy circle hidden amongst the gritstone boulders in a shadowy little beech wood where the bluebells bloomed when a Druid and his students turned up. They had set up an experiment with another group of students in a stone circle a few kilometres away across the moors. They would send energy from that circle through the grid at a pre-arranged time. The Druid was watching the time on his watch and telling the group the energy should be arriving at any moment. Suddenly, my brother flipped in the air and landed flat on his back. It was a massive shock for him. The focused intention of only a small group of people sending energy had created such a jolt that it had sent him in the air.

The Druid had explained to my astonished brother that he was obviously very sensitive to energy currents. He also shared that while these energy points can be used beneficially, people needed to be aware they had been taken over by dark beings who use sacrificial energy and other abominations to permeate the grid and amplify fear and suffering. This is a potent way of keeping the population disconnected from their ultimate power, their divinity. Only fearful people can be controlled, and people have been manipulated like this for thousands of years.

However, I was shown a new earth grid, whose currents oscillated with frequencies that had never been experienced before on this planet. *You may think you have experienced love, Kye, but wait until every lower vibrational influence has been removed from this planet. Then you will experience what love really is and how it lights up and activates every cell in your body. The love you have experienced so far is a much more muted version of the love that is becoming available as the frequency on earth lifts.*

I felt so excited knowing this. *The new grid is like a tuning fork Kye; it will help people align with the new frequencies.* As I sat contemplating this new grid, I wondered if others were helping to create it. It was the unmistakable voice of wise Kye that spoke once again. *You and the animals are helping build that grid. You are creating new templates of respect and co-creation with our animal friends. It is no mistake that a smelly billy goat joined you. Together you transcended the superficial judgments that could have kept you separated and chose love instead. This is the way of the future. It is no mistake either that you have been led to animals that forced you to trust only in your own knowing and to let your heart guide you no matter what. The influences of the old grid are often fear-based. Every time you turn away from fearful choices in your own lives, the more vibrantly alive the new grid becomes.*

I had always known that the animals played a part in creating the new earth grid, and each one had come for a specific reason. They had certainly been guided into our lives in momentously unavoidable ways, especially the camels who, like all the large mammals of land and sea, balanced the electromagnetic frequencies. I'd once heard camels described by someone as 'desert dolphins', and I understood why, though I would have been more likely to name them desert whales. They did on land what the dolphins and especially the whales do in the oceans.

I hadn't fully understood the repercussions of our journey though I sensed it was way bigger than how it appeared on the surface. The currents and ripples emanating from the love and trust we shared not only reached back into the past, further disintegrating the old grid, but changed the direction of the future. Not just for people but for all the animals that had shed their blood and cried their tears too. We were overriding thought patterns lodged in the old grid from the actions of the heartless and unaware. Replacing it with a new grid of compassion and kindness, acceptance and trust as we built a bridge into a new reality. A reality we were already living! The blaze of light I had seen behind us was the tracks of love we left. I saw this clearly as I held my little black ghouma in my hand. Every person living in a sacred way, honouring our earth and all its life, does this. What beautiful tracks to leave!

In the four hundred kilometres we'd travelled so far, there had been little to distract us as we walked along. What a gift it was to walk so centred in the unfolding moment. Acutely aware of the heat of the sun on my face. A slight blister on my heel, hearing the crunch of each step. The loping shadows of the camels on the verge of the track that always made them look like some masked pagan stilt walkers, stiff-legged in their hips, off to burn the Wicca man. I loved being so present, yet each moment often appeared stretched and bulging with things we are often told should not be there. Ghosts from the past, the sounds of tears, a searing grief that comes from nowhere. They all mingled and jostled up with the joyful weavings of our day.

The further south we travelled, the more people we saw. Our days became rudimentary and physical. All other plains of existence, be they past or present, fell away. They slithered off into the bushes like startled snakes keen to avoid all the traffic, and we were left with endless questions from endless passers-by. There is a time for everything, though. I was okay with this. I loved the buoyancy I felt at people's astonishment and excitement. It was easy to become nonchalant about our life on the road and to stop seeing its enchantment. After all, this was our new normal. Still, when you stand on the side of the track with someone you've only just met as they gasp in awe at the life we were living, well that usually left me feeling pretty recharged. Yes, what we were doing *was* epic!

There was no doubt we were a sight never seen anywhere before and probably would never be seen again. One has to have a slightly aberrated mindset or a direct line to the holy spirit to travel with such a caboodle.

Many of the people we met were grey nomads, retirees who'd bought themselves the latest gleaming state-of-the-art caravan with a flashy 4WD.

One woman we pulled up alongside as she and her hubby were parked in a layby boasted of a generator large enough to power a small town. I didn't doubt it. We'd heard its throb for miles and wondered what it could be. It seemed an odd thing to be proud of, as did her lack of interest in our colourful wagon or our entourage of animals that waited restlessly outside her noisy mobile monster of a home. But we accepted her invitation to look within because we were curious.

We'd freed ourselves of almost all our possessions and experienced a lightness of being that came from that. Letting go of the attachment to 'things' had been so liberating, and I felt stifled as she showed us all her modern gadgets. She had *everything*. Washing machine, blender, bread maker, TV, hairdryer. The list went on and on. Yet, in all that stuff, there was nothing that made us want to linger. They were like a stewed pot of tea; one sip and you got a bitter taste in your mouth. Gill gave me a discreet nod which completely conveyed the message, *let's get the hell out of here* and yet leaving these two was like trying to escape a Venus fly trap.

Whenever we got close to the door, she bought something else out to distract us. She wanted to show us everything! After so long in the bush, I was utterly unprepared to deal with such predatory energy. If it hadn't been for our increasingly restless animals outside, we might never have escaped. Our animals had come to the rescue. Many times we'd stopped to chat with people, and they had all stood perfectly still until we were ready to go. I know the generator was unsettling them. I also have no doubt they were completely in tune with the knowing that if we loitered any longer with this couple and their huge carbon footprint, we'd all be sucked dry.

Outside, the air had never felt so fresh. I felt so content with my mad life as we told our beloved camels to "Walk it up." Never ones to let us down, the dogs and parrots began barking and screeching to the jangly clank of the camel's bells while our little dog Chia who *always* sat in the front of the wagon, howled like a wild hyena. Our camel team were straining in their harnesses. They were so keen to go, and we launched at a trot.

I knew what we had was good, but this couple had shown me how fantastically good it was and how blessed I was travelling with all these animals. No doubt they had peered out their window as we left horrified at all our noise and disarray, not to mention our lack of mod cons.

Unfortunately, these two were not the only odd people we met along the way. As more and more vehicles passed us, we came across a phenomenon we had not anticipated.

Many tourists cheered us on with such enthusiasm we could have been superstars coming down the red carpet. They'd obviously spotted us from a distance and parked their 4WD on the side of the road to get the best vantage point to film us as we approached. Sometimes there would be a couple of dozen cars with people sitting on their bonnets, even brewing tea on their gas stoves, parked up, waiting for us to arrive. I mostly enjoyed these people. It was those that drove past looking straight ahead, often not even slowing their pace courteously to avoid startling our animals as most good and kind people did, that flawed me most.

In the act of pretending we didn't exist, it was often the children that gave their parents away because they *did* see us. We would see their faces pressed against the windows in the back of the cars, lit up with delight. Little gasps of wonder and awe speeding by. I always felt a wave of sadness for those kids.

I had been so aware of my own fears on this journey that it had not even occurred to me that we would provoke fear in others. Even the many people we met who expressed admiration and enthusiasm, often telling us they wished they were brave enough to not only go on an adventurous holiday but walk away from their own lives *completely*, gasped for air when we explained we had no destination.

You reach a different space within yourself when you launch on an adventure that's so outside the realms of societal norms. We'd become another element of nature, raw and honest, with a slap like a brisk wind. It had not even occurred to us to tone ourselves down, but it didn't take us long to realise for our own sanity, we *had* to. When people asked us where we were going, answering *that we didn't know we were being guided* was blowing fuses in people's ability to comprehend.

"What do you mean you don't know? You must have somewhere to go." People would frown and repeat, almost with horror, "You don't know where you're going?"

They'd look at all the animals and then back at us, completely unable to grasp the trust we lived in or that there could be some higher force guiding our journey. We spent hours on the side of the road trying to explain this, and, in the end, we decided to answer vaguely, *heading south to some friends.* It was easier for us and less confronting for them. We were no longer held up explaining something that made absolutely no sense to those stuck in jobs they loathed who were too afraid to take even one tiny step towards a happier life. This incredulity was how many people that loved what we were doing responded, so I could understand why some people found even looking at us confronting. If you liked neat little picket fences and everything under control, we were rather messy. But how could anyone drive down an outback road that is straight for hundreds of kilometres through country that to the uninitiated is bleak, and then see us appearing out of the landscape like a glistening mirage and not even slow down a tad to take a better look?

This had me laughing and crying all at the same time. I had no doubt that as they whizzed past, a little bit of our love did indeed rub off. They may have found themselves at the next servo initiating a group hug with complete strangers or stopping to help a little lizard in the centre of the road. Perhaps they even broke out entirely with an eBay bid on rainbow leggings and a scruffy rescue dog from the nearest pound. I don't know, and honestly, it didn't matter. Gill and I often laughed so much at imagining the different scenarios, and I think this was our way of coping with it.

There *were times* we were out on the road knackered and over it. We got tired. There were days the wind had such a bite in it that I felt chilled to my bones, and times I dreamt of movies and hot baths. To see a car travelling towards us from a very long way away, down a long empty road and then experience them speeding past without even a friendly wave sometimes felt devastatingly lonely. Our humour often kept us going in these times. Without our humour, I would have been in tears a lot more.

Staying in each moment was always a lesson, especially when an enticing hot shower was only days away. I couldn't wait to arrive at the station. With our diluted down and much more palatable version of our destination, we did hope to make better progress. We estimated we were one sleep and a moderate day or two of brief-ish conversations away from being *really* clean.

But, of course, nothing went to plan, and two days at the very most stretched into a week.

Six

Our Beeby Gang

After letting go of so much unnecessary stuff in my life, some of my most prized possessions had become two big tin buckets we'd found on the edge of the track. Every time I looked at them, I felt grateful. I experienced their arrival in our lives as part of the miraculous flow that bought everything we needed and allowed us to live in such trust. They had no value to anyone but to us and even though they were rusty and battered, they were *exactly* what we needed. We called them our planetary alignment buckets. While they endowed us with the gift of being able to boil water for a wash, they could only be used in the precisely right conditions.

There were so *many* aspects to consider before stripping off for a wash. Feeling private and screened from the road by trees was essential as tourists had been known to waltz into our camp at all times of the day. Every animal also had to have been well watered. I had already experienced an incident when I'd had to fight to protect my bucket of water from a thirsty Banjo.

Wrestling a billy goat while naked, with shampoo dripping in my eyes, was not an experience I wanted to repeat. In the kerfuffle, the bucket got tipped over. I lost all my hot water and had to rinse my hair in water that was icy cold.

When it wasn't the animals, it was the elements. If there was the slightest breeze, our hot water would cool too fast, and we'd freeze. If we heard amidst the snorting, farting, chortling contentment of our camp, even a single irritating drone of a mosquito, *that was it*. Being bitten alive while standing naked for a hot wash was no fun, either.

Only on those nights when everything lined up would the ritual of the buckets begin. Firewood would be gathered for a raging fire and a fast boil. A few little bits of broken pallets we kept stashed in our trailer would come out for our mosaic of a bathroom floor. We'd discovered that without it, we got muddy feet from standing in a puddle.

I washed my hair and body in only one bucket of water. I had a small bowl for tipping the hot water over my head, but before I even began, on my hands and knees, I'd dunk my hair into the bucket, squeezing out all the excess water so I didn't waste *any*, and then I would shampoo. After a good scalp massage, that's when the tipping began.

Our elemental bathroom may have scaled down from the rock pool nurturance of our old home where we could both soak in a hot bath up to our necks, but we'd bought a little luxury with us. Our soaps were natural and made with essential oils. The inside of our wagon always smelt of ylang-ylang and sandalwood with wafts of lavender and patchouli. I loved our soaps so much that every time I saw them on the shelf, I *had* to pick them up and smell them.

We managed just fine with our buckets of hot water, but it was only a maintenance wash. I'd forgotten what it was like to stand under a stream of hot water and have a shower. It seemed like such a simple indulgence, yet for me, it had been elevated to the realms of the heavenly. Oh, I couldn't wait. It was the little carrot being dangled in front of me each day, and that bought its own lessons.

As we headed towards the station, the landscape became flat and bare and covered in shale. We did our usual optimistic *we will find a great place to camp around the next bend*, but it didn't improve. Finally, we pulled off the road as it swerved down into a dip, just before it crossed a dry creek bed.

Not a flat surface anywhere. I felt so grumpy. Every time I had to walk to get something or tend to an animal, I felt like I'd get a hip displacement. The surface was so stony and uneven. Our chairs and table looked wonky and precariously perched amongst all the stones.

Some days the challenges were just never-ending. All I could think to do was bake a fruit cake in the camp oven and when it was cooked sit down by the fire with a cup of earl grey tea. Just the thought had me sighing with relief. We'd come a long way since self-medicating on fags or the days when I still had a home, and I'd comfort eat blocks of chocolate or get drunk on red wine. My hard-old life had obviously given me some harmony.

I was just mixing up all the ingredients for my cake when a couple of corellas flew screeching above us before circling our wagon. This was odd behaviour for wild parrots, and Gill and I surmised they'd come to say hello to Beautiful and Charlie. When I went to see how they were responding, I was shocked to see their cage door was wide open. These two birds *were* Beautiful, and Charlie and that worried me. In the two years since we'd had them, we'd never handled them. I had no idea how we would catch them again. Since we'd left on the trip, they'd become much more communicative and connected to us. They were our constant companions in the front of the wagon, and we regularly played with them. Their favourite game was a tug of war with a stick, and they would tussle and tug at it like excited little puppies. But neither of them had any experience in the wild. While Charlie was confident taking new steps, Beautiful was timid and would often hide behind him. She'd lived for so long in a tiny cage that her confidence had been stripped.

I put my unbaked cake aside.

There wasn't much light left in the quickly darkening cerise-streaked sky and Charlie, eager to explore, took off flying along the dry creek bed with Lovely following him. Cake long forgotten, we traipsed after them as they flew from one big old gum tree to the next. It was almost dark when we saw Beautiful land on a really low branch. Between us, we managed to catch her in a towel. She looked pleased to be wrapped up safely as we carried home.

Charlie flew back with us, and while we couldn't catch him, he did at least sleep on the wagon's roof, which gave me some peace. At least I knew where he was.

My mantra for the next two days, in-between mouthfuls of the cake I'd finally managed to bake, was *Let go, Kye and enjoy*. Who was I to rush the experience of a little parrot who'd finally flown free for the first time in several decades? Once again, it was a lesson in letting go to each moment and not racing ahead, even if it was for a hot shower. Something extraordinary was unfolding in our lopsided camp in amongst the shale, and Charlie's first flight was important. Momentous even. He had lived constricted for so long, and he was birthing a new reality for himself that was so liberating I had tears in my eyes as he soared through the air screeching with joy. And just like Yumyum, he *really* strutted his stuff when he landed on the wagon. He was fluffed up with pride and so happy at his new-found capabilities that despite the discomfort of our camp, I had the biggest smile.

With all his new-found joy, I did worry a little we wouldn't be able to catch him. He showed no interest in his cage or Beautiful, but on the third day, he landed beside her and wanted to get back in. His little mate was delighted. She'd paced anxiously without him, and the two cuddled up, preening each other. I breathed a *huge* sigh of relief we'd got him, and one more sleep and we could finally leave our stony and inhospitable haven.

Our wagon-pulling team were becoming so familiar with our morning routine that after I'd undone their ropes, they'd happily saunter, nibbling as they went to the wagon and stand in their exact position. All they needed were their harnesses on, and they'd be off.

Of course, our noble Lady Caroline was an exception. Never one to mingle with the minions, she still waited, off to one side, ready for her big theatrical moment. When Gill would lead her to her place at the front of the wagon team behind the only camel, she considered a superior, Zu. She did that walk like a proud bride on her father's arm, being led up the aisle. This was her moment, and she milked it.

I'd got a fair way into my morning pack-up routine when Gill arrived back at camp with the car. I was expecting him on the postie bike and the car to be parked at our next campsite. I was mortified when he told me he'd only got a kilometre or two down the track before the trailer's wheel began to make a terrible grinding noise. He'd driven back *really* slowly and didn't think we would be going anywhere soon.

Fucking hell. I'd literally prized myself out of bed to get an early start. I was so keen to move I'd thrust myself out into the bitterly cold pitch-black morning. Getting up before the sun was *always* brutal and the first thing I did was rekindle the fire. I'd gathered twigs and leaves by torchlight and struggled to light matches with fingers so numb with cold, I'd cried. *I could have stayed in bed*, and if that wasn't enough reason to weep, I had all this work before me to undo everything I'd previously done.

I began by leading mellow Mozzee back out to eat. He'd come to us a walking skeleton covered in hide. His condition had been his fortune, though, because even the dog meat buyers didn't want him. He had a crooked jaw that looked as if it had been broken and possibly explained his dilapidated state. Yet with all the love, our little waif, with his adoring eyes, had grown as big as a mountain.

He looked a little confused as I led him away from the wagon. Even though I felt mad with frustration that we were doomed to yet more days camping in our rocky hell, I couldn't help myself swell with pride when I looked at Mozzee. He was in such good condition it was hard to remember the poor camel he'd once been. Mozzee soon found something to nibble, but he was disgruntled and grumbling. I was just reassuring him that this was only a temporary glitch when Gill turned up to give me the verdict.

There was no way to soften the news, and it hit me in the gut. The bearing on the trailer was caput, and we were not going anywhere until we had a new one. We were miles from anywhere. It had been so long since we'd been to a town; shops existed on another dimension. We had no idea how to even reach one from our dusty dirt track way out in the bush.

I was trying to suppress the grimace on my face when a white ute pulled up in front of us. A middle-aged guy got out wearing a battered Akubra hat, a work shirt and some faded old work jeans. It was obvious he wasn't a tourist, and for a lengthy moment, he stood, taking us all in before his face cracked open with the biggest grin. Until that moment, his face had been so unreadable I hadn't known if he was friend or foe. When he introduced himself, we discovered it was Jim, the station owner, our outback knight in his white ute. His arrival gave me a rude awakening back into the realms of living in trust and knowing that everything flows from this space.

Jim took the model number of our broken bearing and told us he would phone an order through when he got home, and all going well, it would be delivered by the postman in the morning.

As I was learning, postmen out in the outback don't just deliver post. They pick up parcels from the shops, collect people's prescriptions from the chemist, drop off things that need to go to town, and stop and have a chat. I had even heard of one that would empty an elderly man's chamber pot. They provide an essential lifeline for remote dwellers and are often versatile in their delivery service, as we would discover further down the track.

At approximately 11am the following day, after a much-needed sleep-in, a land cruiser pulled up beside our camp. Some tourists had been visiting the station when the postman arrived with our package. The postman had a few more deliveries before he could get to us, and it was decided the tourists would bring it to us quicker. I don't think we had *ever* had an ordered car part arrive with such speed, and we were both somewhat awed by the phenomenal grace and ease of this bush network.

I was so relieved to be moving again. We were only a few kilometres away from a 1080 bait-free zone. One of the hardest, most gruelling day-to-day challenges was keeping our dogs safe and happy. It was like living on the edge of a sharp knife. We could never let our guard down and have them wander free, and even on a lead, I watched them like a hawk. They liked to sniff at parched old bones from some long-ago dead sheep, but *nothing* went into their mouths. Nothing *ever*. I couldn't wait to relax with them, let them run free on walks and sit unchained by the fire.

Now nothing will ever convince me of the benefits of 1080, but I did respect the cautious and diligent way Jim used it. He obviously loved his dogs. He had a twenty-kilometre bait-free radius around his station and knew where every single bait he'd laid was, and regularly checked them. Some station owners threw 1080 everywhere and barely gave themselves a safe zone around their own homes.

Jim and his wife Ruby were the epitome of the spirit of the outback you hear so much about. They made us so welcome we unexpectedly stayed at this station for almost three weeks. Gill had tried to pay Jim for the bearing, but Jim had asked Gill if he wanted to do some work instead. He had a few jobs around the house, including fixing a garden gate. Gill was more than happy to give a helping hand anyway. He didn't want any pay.

From the moment we arrived, we had endless hot showers. Our camels roamed freely, having a break from their tethers. We used the washing machine and were nightly invited to eat at their huge dinner table with all the jackaroos and their one new jillaroo who were all in their late teens or early twenties and working in their first job since leaving home. As I sat listening to their happy banter, it was easy to see the allure of their chosen job and its lifestyle. This was such a huge station; some parts were days away. If the fences needed fixing in the more remote places, they'd pile up the ute with the tools they needed, their swags and eskys full of meat and, of course, beer, and camp out under the stars until they'd finished the job. They had a vitality about them that town kids rarely do that came from working hard in the fresh air. There is no room for slacking on a station. You must be a working cog, so everyone ultimately becomes fit and strong. They revered Jim and Ruby, and I understood why. While Ruby was soft and kind and the heart of the home, Jim bought out the best in his young team. He had a wild and cheeky glint in his eyes that challenged you to step up and meet him, and if you resisted, he'd poke you out of your shell. He was also hysterically funny and didn't mind telling us wild tales of his adventures. Even if they made him look like a fool and had us all holding our bellies with laughter.

I was so appreciative of them, yet I found aspects of station life hard. I would feel myself constrict when certain subjects arose around animals. I felt physically sick when I overheard a conversation on CB radio between neighbouring station owners discussing the aerial camel hunt they were going on at the weekend. To even think of an animal being shot from a helicopter had me holding back my tears. I found this such a dilemma. I liked and respected so many people I met but killing animals was normal for them. They didn't experience them in the same way I did. They didn't even know they were conscious beings who felt pain and trauma the same way we all do. To them, animals were only a commodity, a product to buy and sell or exterminate if they were considered vermin.

But I had to find a way of shielding myself. We were travelling through station country, and I wanted to do so honouring the people I met because that's who I am. I didn't want to alienate myself from them. If we turned up spouting our views and evangelising about a kinder way of living, every single door for thousands of kilometres would have closed to us.

In truth, even though I detest the animal industry, I have never made people wrong for having different views than mine. Some of the kindest people I had ever met, including Ruby and Jim, made their living from farming. Yet I also knew people who were militant campaigners for animals' rights who were so angry I found them toxic to be around.

With Jim and Ruby, I only ever experienced an open-armed welcome. They gave us a much-needed respite from the hard gruel of our days, and for that, I was forever grateful. Our generous hosts allowed us space and time to restore our strength and rekindle our passion, not to mention get really clean. I'd finally got that grungy look out of all our freshly washed clothes. I'd also had so many hot showers that the idea of a rusty tin bucket boiling water on a fire and a wash under the stars was looking romantic and appealing again. All rested and scrubbed clean, we were eager to get back on the road, and it was calling us.

It was late afternoon, and as we pottered around our camp, getting everything ready for our departure, we heard some unfamiliar dogs barking. Our camels had been roaming freely for the last few weeks, and we'd only just bought them into camp and tethered them. That way, they'd be close when we were ready to harness them up the following day at first light.

For a moment, we stood uncertain. Listening to hear where the dogs were and trying to ascertain if they were causing trouble. When the barks became more excited, and one of our camels began bellowing in distress, we dropped everything. We ran as fast as we could towards our grazing camels. Two of the station dogs had travelled five kilometres to our camp and were attacking the feet of Jumuna. She was swinging from side to side, trying to avoid their bites and at the same time kicking out at them to defend herself. We were about to race in and help her, but an unexpected cavalry charged past.

The Beebs, Bella, Banjo and Blossom had galloped over to the dogs and, working as a team, hunted them out. Gill and I watched with our mouths hanging open in awe, wishing we'd had a video camera rolling. Banjo, who most of the time behaved like a sweet and amiable pup, charged in horns to the ready and flipped one of the dogs out from Jumuna's feet up into the air. Bella, who can be a cantankerous creature if you're *not* Gill, went for the other dog and booted it in the air with her back legs. Two dogs were flying through the air howling in shock and distress, before landing in a crumpled heap. They had no time to lick their wounds. It was run for your life or be trampled. Blossom was right on their tail, cavorting and kicking and stomping her feet. The dogs bolted, and we could hear them screeching and yelping as the Beebs chased them back toward their home. I was a little anxious. I really didn't want the dogs to get hurt, though I was impressed with our camp guardians. *No one* would take advantage of us as we travelled.

Jumuna had managed to avoid being bitten, but she was sitting staring straight ahead, looking a little dazed. While Gill went back to the wagon, I sat down beside her. I felt a crazy inordinate amount of love for her that overflowed from me. We'd been through so much together, and I was as bonded with her as she was with me. My wild bush camel had come a long way since she'd had me on my knees, wanting to spew from the bloody brutality of her self-harming.

As I whispered sweet nothings to my love, she soon settled and began to rhythmically chomp on her cud.

Jali, her fast-growing calf who'd taken off in the melee and joined the other camels came running back to her mum, bellowing loudly. She had her head down, and her bottom lip was protruding as she kicked and bucked and ran circles around the tree and her mum and me. She wasn't happy. The dogs had upset her too, but after a couple more distressed laps, she came and settled down beside Jumuna and snuggled up close to her. It had taken less than ten minutes for the friction from the dogs to dissipate, and I was incredulous at this. I had been so frightened of Jumuna having another episode and done everything I could *every* single day to help her avoid *any* stress. The dogs had shown me how much I'd held on to the old Jumuna, and she was long gone. Just like us all, she, too, had grown and bloomed and now stood in her own power. I felt lighter as I got up to leave her and Jali. I didn't have to worry about my girl anymore. She could cope with the challenges of life without hurting herself or leaving her physical body and that massive miraculous moment was so dam huge I had tears of joy rolling down my cheeks as I walked back to camp.

Halfway home, the Beebs joined me, and I stopped to give them all a congratulatory pat, but I got the distinct feeling it wasn't quite enough. After all, heroes usually get some reward, don't they? Banjo was sniffing at my pockets in the hope of finding his. Perhaps a medal, ceremoniously pinned to his puffed out with pride chest.

We could all stand around the campfire saluting the little rotters, or maybe he'd prefer some culinary perks. They certainly deserved it. They'd done such a great job of protecting our camp and surprised themselves at what a cohesive and heroic little team they'd finally and begrudgingly become.

It had taken time for Banjo to become a fully initiated member of this extraordinary threesome. Bella and Blossom had not initially welcomed him, and I'd often felt heartbroken listening to him crying out for them. His yearned for mates that didn't want him, who'd sneakily taken off and left him behind. I don't know what changed. Why they began answering his cries and waiting for him when he got left behind but it made me so happy.

Our misunderstood and much-maligned billy goat had been through so much, and finally, he had his *own* little Beeby gang.

Seven

Our Culinary Postman

After all our station adventures and days of slumber and feast, we were so excited to be on the road again. I loved hearing that familiar sound of wagon wheels bumping over the ruts in the road. The camels surged ahead, renewed and invigorated after their rest. Chooks settled happily in their theatre seats, ready for the spectacle of our day. Banjo riding the back veranda looking like a dignitary expectant of accolade. While the dogs poked their big panting happy faces out the sides of the wagon from their positions on our bed.

Our next small town was Oodnadatta, a hundred kilometres away. It was the town that our notorious Abdul had come from. We'd been told he'd been reared in the local pub and taught to drink beer as a party trick. We were curious if anyone would remember him. I still shook my head in astonishment that he had finally become part of our huge family. For years, just mentioning his name would bring me out in a cold, clammy sweat and yet here he was, and I absolutely adored him. He gave me such sweet little tender kisses, and he *still* behaved like a little angel and had shown no sign of the rogue camel I and many others had been terrorised by. Although a little lazy, he was often part of our wagon-pulling team.

Now I have to confess that I was not looking forward to the challenges we faced in the next part of the track. We'd driven the route the week before after hearing we had twenty kilometres of sand dunes to travel through, and nothing I'd seen had set my mind at ease. The road didn't weave between the sand dunes. It went over them. Not only did we face the challenge of innumerable rises and their inevitable descents, but there was also limited visibility and nowhere to pull off the road. We couldn't avoid it. We couldn't change it. We just had to put our fear aside and face it. I prayed there wouldn't be much traffic on the road.

The first car we saw was a kilometre down the road when the postman tootled his horn and pulled over as if he wanted to speak with us. We slowed the camels to a halt, and Gill, who'd decided to lead the camels through the dunes, went over to see him. From the front seat of his car, the postman pulled out the most enormous, covered in icing and rainbow sprinkles, dream of a chocolate cake. Ruby's hospitality was following us down the road. With a plan to pick up the glass dish the cake was in on his way back to the station in the morning, the postman jumped in his 4WD and waved us goodbye. It looked so delicious I scoffed a massive piece of cake immediately.

We hadn't got much further when Jim drove up, and when he got out of his ute, he looked *really* annoyed. I was worried; perhaps his dogs *had* been hurt. It was the only thing I could think of. When he began to speak, it was accusatory. As if we'd nicked all his silver and were making a quick getaway.

"What are you doing leaving without your pay Gill? I thought you would come and see me before you left." He was *really* distressed. While Jim had mentioned paying Gill for the work he'd done, Jim and Ruby had done so much for us; if anything, we felt we *owed* them. Gill was happy he got an opportunity to help out, but Jim didn't see it like that. He was really insistent. "That was the deal. You shouldn't be leaving without taking your money."

We'd never been in a situation before of having to defend ourselves for *not* taking money or that act being treated as a crime. Whatever we said to soothe Jim, he wasn't happy. As far as he was concerned, there was *only* one outcome that would nullify him, take the cash. We didn't want the money. We had our savings and were using a portion of that to fund our trip. This was our only way of showing our gratitude, but there was no way he was going to let us off.

The only solution I could think of was to meet in the middle and accept half the payment. That was it. Jim had to allow us to give something back. He wasn't delighted with this, but he was soothed, and after sharing a slice of our chocolate cake with us while we told him the story of his dogs, he left with a smile on his face. His dogs were fine. He'd wondered why they'd arrived home with their tails between their legs, but he was glad they'd got their arses kicked. He didn't want them roaming and hunting.

With cash in our pockets and bloated on chocolate cake, we once again gave the command to "Walk em up," and hoped we'd get further this time.

There were many days when I just had to swallow my fears and get on with the job at hand. This bit of the track had the potential to be catastrophic. Our wagon and all our animals took up a lot of space, and there was little room for us to pull over. It was hard and slow going, and I always got tense managing the brake on hills. You have to be so focused and get it just right. Slow the wagon just enough to cull any danger of speeding downhill out of control, yet not enough to prevent the camels from gaining speed that would get them up the rise. We also had to be constantly alert to traffic, trying to pass and listening for any vehicles heading our way. We'd prepared as best we could and even made a flag on a pole above the wagon. Hopefully, traffic approaching would see it, even if they couldn't see us and get some warning we were there.

Whenever I worried about anything, I always realised later what an absolute waste of time it had been. We should have known we'd be looked after. We always were. On a busy tourist track at the start of the season, we were given the grace to negotiate these sand dunes without any other passing cars until much later on in the day.

Even so, I was wrung out and exhausted by the middle of the afternoon and called out to Gill to ask him how much further we were going. I was keen to stop. We only had another kilometre of sand dunes before us, and he wanted to get past them before we camped. I liked the idea of waking up to a new day on a flat road, so I agreed to push on. Still, only five minutes later, with no prior warning, the camels pulling the wagon determinedly swerved across the road and into a small layby. In the *very* next breath, a car came flying at such speed it was airborne, over the rise. If we had been on that track, we would have met a head-on disaster.

Gill told me later that Zu, with the rest of the camels united behind him, had adamantly refused to stay on the track and ignored all his commands to walk up. It would appear that our camels had anticipated what was about to occur and made a swift decision themselves. The day had picked up a wind, and neither Gill nor I had heard the rumble of the approaching car, but they must have.

I felt so blessed as I sat around the campfire that night. There really was some unseen force looking after us. However, I'd felt shaken by the precision in which we'd avoided calamity. Our camels were our heroes, and they were always surprising us. Just when I thought I was getting to know them, they'd show us another side. Deeper and deeper down the rabbit hole, we all went.

I hark on about how much hard work our trip was, but fucking hell, it was worth it. *This* was living, *not* the drunken couch potato I'd once been who thought she was happy and comfortable. Day by day, mile by mile, the bonds between us all were weaving inextricably together. We were this phenomenal team. We had our own herd of wise dromedaries who could anticipate and act to avoid disaster. A gang of thugs called the Beebs, we had a pack of dogs, including my wild scruffy Wunjo that had claws like talons and looked like she'd risen from the underworld. She could see right through you, and just looking at her freaked out those with deeds to hide. I had no doubt that wherever we went, whoever we met, we'd be safe, and I haven't even mentioned the chickens, our deadly insect patrol.

When 'The Colonel', our awesome rooster, had told us he wanted to come on our trip ages before we'd even sold our home, we hadn't thought of the practicalities like being woken up at all hours by him crowing. He was *only* one layer of sheet metal away just below our bed, but even if we had realised, he and his nine girls would still have been welcomed.

At first, he woke us often. We'd bolt upright from the deepest sleep freaking out at what the fuck we'd just heard until we remembered that The Colonel was in his bedroom below. He didn't just crow at dawn. He had a little banter in the middle of each night, but we got used to it. He'd be cock-a-doodle-doing at all hours, and we'd be sleeping, snoring and farting away and wouldn't even wake.

Not only did our little clan under the floor boards keep us in eggs, we saw them catch scorpions and giant centipedes around our camp. I was so relieved about this.

One night I'd awoken screaming in terror. I'd been in the deepest sleep when I was hit with a pain that was searing and terrible. I honestly thought someone had axed off my toes. Gill jumped up urgently beside me and pulled back all the covers. I was so afraid I didn't want to look. I was certain I was about to face a bloody awful, amputated mess. It was Gill that reassured me of the absence of an axeman and that all my little tootsies were still there, which had us both scrambling around in the bed to find out *what* had bitten me. The culprit was a tiny little centipede. It was so small I couldn't believe it had inflicted so much pain. The agony of that bite lasted for days. I checked our bed every night after that. Shaking out every sheet, every blanket several times or more. I couldn't imagine the pain that would be inflicted by a *giant* centipede, and I was determined not to find out.

Once, the chickens had even caught a little snake. I didn't like that. I love snakes. I ran after them as they fought over it and tried to tug it from each other. I spent a good ten minutes trying to rescue it from chickens that were much too fast for me before I realised it was futile. The damage had been done, and the snake was probably dead or would be very soon. I wasn't happy the snake died, but I was grateful to our little herd of chooks and the part they played in keeping our camp predator free. They were all blooming, they looked so healthy, and we'd even shared a couple of pieces of chocolate cake with them. Truly I'd had to. My waistline was bulging so much I could barely get my jeans on. I had pigged myself on chocolate cake, thinking it was the last of Ruby's cooking, so enjoy it while I can. I was totally unaware that our culinary postal service was not over yet.

The postman caught up with us again the following day as we ambled along the flat. Not only did he come to pick up the now sparkling clean dish that our chocolate cake had been delivered in, but he also dropped us off a fresh from the oven, wrapped in tin foil and tea towels to keep it warm, a huge dish of tuna and vegetable bake. Beautiful Ruby, with her heart of gold and more than enough cooking to do to keep up with the ravenous appetites of her own work crew, wanted to make sure we had something to eat as we travelled.

Just before we arrived at this station, I made a choice. I'd had decades in my life when I'd not eaten meat or fish. The first time I'd consciously stopped eating it was at nineteen when I'd seen a cow loaded to go to the abattoirs. When she turned around and looked at me, her eyes were so full of fear that I burst into tears. Even though I didn't eat meat for many years, I had times when I craved it. I would have preferred to have just been repulsed by it; it would have made my life much more straightforward because I love animals. I could never bare to think of them suffering and being killed. But there were times I'd succumb, and the last time I'd eaten meat was when I lived in Alice, and I'd experienced something really unpleasant. At first, I hadn't joined the dots. It was Gill who made the connection. Every time I ate meat, I had anxiety attacks. My heart would palpitate, my hands would feel clammy, I would tremble with fear, and my knees would go weak. I finally realised I was feeling the fear the animal experienced before it was killed.

And, of course, I gave up meat.

When we'd been invited to call in at Jim and Ruby's for dinner, I'd struggled for days as I contemplated this situation. The choice I came to was not made lightly. Our journey wove through the heart of so many stations and people that lived on this land. I decided to embrace and be grateful for the hospitality we were given without any judgement or separation. It felt like a much more peaceful and aligned way than asking if the eggs in the cake were free range or if they could cook something vegan.

There was a secondary reason I decided to *occasionally* eat meat while on the trip. Not to buy it or even have it as part of my daily meals, only to accept it gratefully when it was given, and that was because I was feeling depleted. After months of living on canned food or dried with a daily serving of pumpkin or potato, my body cried out for more nutrition. We had left with the best intentions of keeping ourselves supplied with fresh sprouts but had not anticipated that the salty content of bore water would kill them. We dare not use our limited and precious rainwater for rinsing sprouts. If we ran out of that, we'd die.

This choice of mine bought lessons in itself. Of course, the meals were focused around meat. Meat is a huge part of station life, but when I ate it, I didn't break out in a sweat, or have any palpitations, or experience any fear. I was curious about this and spoke with Ruby and Jim. They told me the cow was shot in the paddock while eating grass. She didn't go through the hell of being trucked before facing the nightmare of the abattoirs. How animals are killed does make a difference, and perhaps that's why farming in the old days was not such a brutal business as it is today.

I had certainly gone through an initial inner struggle, shall I, shan't I, how will I feel? But it's a choice I made at that time I have never regretted. Standing on a sandy track under a bright blue sky while galahs sheltered in the nearby gum tree, in a vast flat land the colour of leached ochre, while a bush postman handed us a still steaming casserole dish was an experience that moved me deeply. It filled me with so much gratitude I could have fallen to my knees in prayer. To accept without judgement opened me up to the graciousness and beauty of these people and their loving care. Even after we'd left their station, the hospitality of the outback continued to hold us. We went from one loving homestead to another.

We were a day away from the neighbouring station, relatives of Ruby and Jim's who'd also invited us to stop and camp and have a meal. Our tuna bake lasted until we arrived at our next culinary destination and discovered a phenomenal new addiction.

Wendy and John and their grown son Simon ran the much smaller station alone. The parts of the station we saw looked really harsh, almost desolate. Vast areas of gibber flats that didn't even have the solace of a dried creek bed weaving through. We'd found nothing for our camels to eat, not even consolatory frugal nibbles. We knew our passing through would be swift. Before we went to the homestead, we spent some time reassuring our grumbling camels that we had not moved in to live. As soon as the sun rose in the morning, we'd all be making a swift retreat.

Nothing stopped in this household for an episode of Home and Away, a soap opera I had been addicted to before I'd left. It was strange sitting at the table as we ate, watching familiar characters embroiled in their latest dramas once again beyond the realms of belief, but from my new perspective. I watched it intrigued and incredulous by the person I'd been who'd found the ridiculous plots and constant dramas in this series enthralling. I remember the day we'd moved from our sold home, and I'd watched my very last episode, almost in grief at the thought of no longer seeing the familiar faces I'd come to know and love. How ridiculous is that? I couldn't comprehend that person now.

Give me a blackened billy, a stinky billy goat and a campfire any day. I didn't need any ridiculous TV dramas to flounce out my days. As I ate my dinner glued like everyone else around me to the TV screen, I secretly revelled in my shift, but I was unaware that while one addiction had departed, another was about to begin, and one that was much more aligned with where I was now.

We enjoyed our meal with our hosts, who were such a close-knit family you could feel the love between them.

I can't even remember what led Simon to disappear out into a back room and return with one of his most prized possessions. A jam jar full of tektites. I had no idea what a tektite even was. It was Simon who explained that while they are somewhat mysterious, it is thought they're the result of earth matter that's been shot up into space from the force of a meteorite landing, which glassifies on the fall back to earth. They look black until you hold them up to the light, and then they look green and glassy.

Simon had hundreds of them, and I was so fascinated by them that Wendy and John rushed off and came back with jars of their own. These three were having a competition to see who could find the most. It was evident Simon spent more time out on the land. He had the best collection and the fullest jar. One was a perfect alien's face. It was so clear and, because of its originality, probably worth a lot of money. He told us there are many avid tektite collectors around the world.

I was so excited by the time we left. I couldn't wait to get up in the morning and begin looking. We walked miles every day and crossed many clay pans and had been advised this was the best place to find them. They really stand out on the bare earth. "You're going to pick up an awful lot of poo looking for these," Simon told us laughingly as we said goodbye. "Roo poos are the worst. They've fooled me so many times."

We were so keen to find our first tektite. When I went to gather the camels up and bring them to the wagon in the morning, I was head down looking at the ground. When I gathered firewood, I scanned the earth as I picked up my branches. As I walked beside the wagon during the day, I was looking. Scanning every bit of ground for that little black shape. Simon was right. We picked up a tremendous amount of roo poo but on the third day, bingo.

She had been sitting on the track, and I'd picked up so much roo poo thinking I'd found one, I was reluctant to bend down again. I even walked a few steps passed it, but something called me back. I was elated to have found my very first tektite. The competition was on. Kye one, Gill none. Now we just needed jam jars, and as we were getting closer to Oodnadatta, I had no doubt we'd soon find one.

It appeared that word had already reached this small bush town that we were approaching, and we had an old friend with us if that's the right word! We'd laughingly shared the tale of the infamous Abdul with a few people we'd met along the way not anticipating the bush telegraph and the speed at which news travelled.

Cars full of *mostly* local aboriginal people began to drive out to meet us, and they all had one question. They asked it apprehensively, ready to flee at the slightest provocation. "Have you got *Abdul*?" Even the police drove out to meet us and asked us the same question in the same pensive tones. So many people drove out I could imagine sirens would be ringing in the town as people spread the news of the impending horror that was heading their way. *Watch out, everyone. Lock yourself into your homes, stay safe and don't take any chances whatever you do. Abdul is getting closer, and he is only a day away.*

I couldn't wait to hear what our reformed sinner of a camel had been up to!

Eight
Crows Call My Name

Arriving in Oodnadatta was an event as miraculous as the parting of the Red sea. Against all odds, we had travelled five hundred and eight kilometres since leaving Alice, *and* we were both still alive. We'd survived the dangers of handling thirteen wild camels with no nose pegs on a daily basis. The hazards of the road, the searing sun and blistered feet. Wild bull camels, being dragged behind numerous animals, not to mention being almost trampled several times by an out-of-control wagon on a downhill sprint with all its accompanying camels. In fact, the parting of the Red sea was a mere mini miracle compared to our epic feat.

Oodnadatta had always been the midway point of our journey down the red dirt track from Alice, right down to Maree, where the dirt finally turned to tar and who knows where we'd head after.

Through every struggle and every wave of doubt that we would ever get anywhere, we had consoled ourselves with the goal *we will all be flowing together by the time we get to Oodnadatta,* and we were!

We had perfected every aspect of life on the road. From the time it took to wind up all the camel's leg ropes to the speed at which we could unharness our team. We could get the fire lit and the billy boiling while chopping spuds to throw in the pot for our evening meal. Then fit in a dog walking session while dinner cooked, timed precisely to allow for a brief relaxation and a cup of tea before our meal. Most of the time, Gill and I worked together in such a cohesive flow we had the precision of a fancy swiss watch. On the days we *did* want to kill each other, we'd stride out manically into the bush. Far away from all our sensitive animals who were barometers of our every mood. Have a yell and a shout, get everything out of our system, cuddle and make up and return all peace and love as if nothing had ever happened. We were mastering even our foulest moods. The days of spewing it all out in camp and travelling under a cloud of our gloom were long gone. Nothing had ever flowed when we'd done that. Every animal went in a different direction, and everything that could go wrong *did*.

Those days I'd felt like throwing myself from the nearest lover's leap. They were so fucking hard. When you feel like you have nothing left to give and all you can see in front of you are never-ending demands, you have to dig really deep to find some energy. Exhaustion by itself was usually relatively easy to move through. When exhaustion was laden with Gill and I arguing, life was much more challenging. It was so true that everything flowed from us. When we were disjointed with each other, everything became overwhelming, even little things we would have normally faced with ease. You can hit some deep dark lows if you don't get your head into a better space. I know I did, and it was in these moments I realised how our challenges were also our saving grace. In the busy pace of our day, something inevitably happened to catapult us into a completely new experience that would instantly help us shift our mood. The key was often being willing to let go. Every past experience was already water that had flowed downstream. Gone!

It could be the enthusiasm of a tourist who was deeply moved by the bravery and trust we lived in that helped us realise, once again, how extraordinary our lives were. It could be sitting around the campfire in a landscape of black and white stones, wondering where the heavenly smell of sandalwood was coming from. Then realising our fire was lit from its dead branches gathered unwittingly from a nearby tree. It could be our powerful little pocket rocket of a camel, Jianti, coming over to Gill as he sat by the fire and sitting with him. Wrapping her long neck and head around him and giving him a cuddle. Or the time we went to a well for water. As we approached, millions of swallows spiralled out of the well's dank and mossy depths and took off in a flurry of chatter and feathers across the landscape. They looked like a spiralling willy-willy.

There was nothing mediocre about our path, and both its gifts and plunders were immense.

Arriving in this tiny outback town was a huge moment for us. It had been the focus of all our achievements and the holy grail of our success for hundreds of kilometres. I knew, without any doubt, chocolate called, but I'd known that for over a hundred kilometres.

As soon as the animals were all happily settled, we got in our 4WD and headed for the roadhouse. We'd passed endless handmade roadside signs advertising their wares on the long dry road that led to town. Keeping us informed of the distance we had yet to travel to reach them. Only eighty kilometres to go for fuel and takeaway. Only seventy, only twenty! Every day we got closer, and after endless miles travelling at the pace of a walk through a landscape that on my less-connected days begged fantasy, I was consumed with a craving for chocolate by the time we arrived.

We arrived back at our camp laden with treats, but our first brief little visit to this town was the last visit we made into town together. We'd set up a few kilometres away on the outskirts of the town common. As we drove back in, we saw Munki in the headlights being attacked by several dogs who were all lunging for his feet. Our gang of thugs, The Beebs, were all tethered near the wagon because they often ran behind us if we drove out in the car. We hadn't wanted them following us into town, so they'd been no help for Munki. Gill picked up a big stick and, yelling like a madman, charged at the dogs, who soon bolted yelping in fright. We settled Munki down and checked his legs and feet, and we were relieved to see he hadn't been bitten. We'd got back just in time. Even so, I felt terrible for leaving our animals vulnerable like that. Neither of us had anticipated hungry camp dogs coming so far out from town to predate. That was it. If we needed anything else, one of us would have to stay home and guard our animals.

It didn't take long for news to spread that we had arrived, and the sun had barely risen when we were woken by the first of many cars full of people. It soon became very apparent that *everyone* remembered Abdul. They came twitching nervously, almost too afraid to get out of their vehicles. They would speak to us with one foot on their accelerators pumping the gas, ready to flee back to safety if the King Kong they remembered Abdul to be, escaped.

Our sweet little adoring love had terrorised the residents of this town. We heard tales of him entering people's homes in the middle of the night like an oversized cat burglar. He was so smart he not only worked out how to open doors, he even opened up their fridges. One woman told us she'd arrived home late one night, a little merry after a late-night drinking session at the pub, to find that Abdul had pulled all her food out of the fridge. What he hadn't been able to extract from its package was strewn around her kitchen in a slobbery sucked mess amidst camel poos and a giant puddle of piss. While he was long gone, he'd left enough evidence to prove beyond doubt who the culprit was.

Another local, an older bloke, told us he'd woken in the middle of the night sick with fear to find Abdul standing over his bed. Fortunately, Abdul didn't put up much of a fight and left when the man began to shout for help. Others had barricaded themselves in their homes as he rampaged around them, trying to get in. Breaking into people's homes certainly added another element of terror to Abdul's escapades. No wonder the townsfolk had driven him out of town.

It was funny yet tragic listening to so many stories of yet another orphan camel who'd grown up without any boundaries. The centre of attention and the source of much amusement until he grew beyond his endearing calf-like frolics. I understood, but it must have been so confusing for little Abdul to be driven out of town and left to survive on the local rubbish dump for doing the very things he'd been encouraged to do.

Even though we led the reformed villain up to their cars and showed people how he had changed, few were willing to risk getting out. There was an affability about their memories, though. People's faces would crease with big smiles when they recalled his antics. They'd nudge each other laughingly as they recalled how they'd climbed the tree to escape from him or the day they'd locked themselves in their car out in the hot sun.

A few people gave him a nervous pat. It was three young aboriginal girls who slipped barefoot and fearless from the back seat of their car who embraced Abdul. Giving him so much love, his big head sunk in contentment towards the ground, where they cradled it in their arms. Even Banjo was lured into their circle for some love, and they cuddled our stinky pissy love without even noticing his pong.

I couldn't have adored these girls more.

We were told laughingly by an older woman who visited with her grown-up son that the only time this town had known crime was when Abdul lived there. They both recalled the 'terror of Oodnadatta' It was such a close-knit community, and while they did have a somewhat redundant cop, the law was kept by families. Everyone knew each other, and no one could get away with anything. If any youngsters played up, they'd have a whole town of aunties and uncles berating them.

There was a lot I enjoyed about this quirky outback town.

But the hungry camp dogs did not make it easy for us to stay. We had to be constantly on our guard, and it was stressful being unable to relax. We stayed because we needed a new gasket for our 4WD, and it took us four days to replace it. On the fifth day, feeling sick and swearing we'd never eat chocolate or ice cream *ever* again, we gathered up our big family, our newly acquired jam jar for our burgeoning collection of three tektites, and left.

We had four hundred and twenty kilometres ahead of us before the Oodnadatta track hit the tarmac at the small town of Marree. Our destination after that was *completely* unknown. I always felt a pang of anxiety when I thought of what we would do when our red ribbon of a dirt track came to its inevitable end. Still, I couldn't look too far ahead. I had to stay focused in the moment. It was pretty momentous for us to be finally on the other side of the town we'd been walking towards for *months*. Our goal of all flowing together had been surpassed long before we reached Oodnadatta. I was overjoyed that so many hard-gut-busting experiences were now a thing of the past. I was also secretly celebrating the demise of a character I had suffered under called Goblin Gilly. I hadn't mentioned him before, partly because so much was happening every single day. Some parts of the adventure inevitably get left out in the telling. It's hard to cram it all in, and other things you don't notice so clearly until they are gone.

In all my imaginings before we'd left Alice, I'd never considered the camel training boot camp I was about to enter. Or how my handsome, gentle bushman would become the biggest, fiercest, frothiest bull camel I'd ever seen. In those early days when we were all over the place, and almost all our camels were dangerous and wild, there were days Gill roared around making so much noise, I felt really stressed. I dreaded those times when Goblin Gilly appeared. The tension catapulted me straight back to school days and memories of being caned with a ruler for not spelling correctly. The bright, inquisitive student I'd been at my previous happy school diminished in fear of being wrong. I'd never been able to learn in tension. Even doing the most straightforward job, my mind would go blank. I couldn't even remember how to safely tie a bowline knot in a camel's rope. I'd be fumbling, struggling to do something my hands had done automatically hundreds of times before.

We'd quietened our earlier camels with zero stress, never rushing any step, and I'd wanted to do that with all of them. *Couldn't we at least talk about it?* I felt really pissed off with Gill. He wouldn't listen to me. If I tried to broach the subject, a steel door would slam shut between us. I had never known him to be so sharp with me before.

One night in a flood of tears, I berated him. We were sitting around the fire. The jobs were all done. Bedtime beckoned luringly, but I couldn't sleep. I needed to talk with Gill. He made some flustered gesture of couldn't it wait until morning, which made me even madder. I had no idea how anyone slept in the midst of emotional turbulence. I also didn't want to wake up to a fresh new day and face the military drill our journey was becoming for us *all*.

In all my fury, I had failed to even contemplate that I may end up feeling remorseful at the lack of support I'd given Gill. I'd never even considered what he was going through or the burden of responsibility he carried for keeping us all safe. I'd even interpreted his raging around as anger when it was bluff. We had invited a lot of danger into our lives by taking untrained camels without nose pegs with us. I understood that. I saw Gill dealing with them daily, which often freaked me out. One kick and everything could be over, and with nowhere to return to, that was not an option. For us to be safe, Gill had to make our boundaries *really* clear.

"It's all taking so much effort at the moment, Kye. It's not that I don't want to talk. I just don't have the energy. Most of the time, I'm running on momentum. I'm exhausted. If I stop, I'm gonna fall apart. I know it will get better, but I've just gotta let them know that being dangerous is not on!"

I understood. When you have a one-tonne creature rearing in the air above you, threatening to stomp you into oblivion, and your *only* control is a rope, you have to find a way to be blatantly clear. That's *not* fucking on! Dangerous behaviour we could not tolerate. Our lives and well-being were much too important for that.

Yup handling our untamed beasts would have been much easier if they all had nose pegs, but they didn't. We'd made that choice a long time ago. All that Gill had was a rope. If they were dangerous, he used his rope to pull them down into a sitting position and tie them so they could not get up. They were often mad. They'd writhe around, struggle and bellow and spit if we went too close. Still, something significant always shifted in them during this time of struggle and surrender. Gill was on their side, and neither of us wanted to hurt them. We'd saved most of them from being killed for dog meat, and we wanted them all to have the best life they could, even if that life was different from what they'd known. They had all come with such synchronicity. Refusing them would have felt like wading upstream in a fast-flowing river, but I'd always felt they'd chosen us, not the other way around.

Once they'd stopped struggling, Gill would return to them. He'd talk to them so soothingly, reassuring them in a soft voice that everything would be ok. They often looked so nervous when he reached out to touch them, but weaving his spell around them, Gill would begin to gently stroke them, often for the first time. If they went to bite or spit, he'd walk away again, staying in sight of them the entire time, knowing they needed a little longer.

With almost all the dangerous camels, being roped down once was usually enough to create a massive shift in their behaviour, and unexpectedly, it built trust. Many of our camels had already experienced the worst of people. Yet, when they were at their most vulnerable, Gill hadn't hurt them. That shifted how they viewed him. They realised they didn't need to be defensive, and more often than not, they gave him their trust.

But we had come a long way since our early days of dangerous camels. Thankfully Goblin Gilly had only been with us in the first few weeks of our trip, and I was glad he hadn't come any further. Still, there was an aspect of this experience that made me curious. I was the soft one who believed in the power of love, who would prefer to sit all day in a yard talking with an animal rather than tie them down. Yet from the moment camels had come into our lives, it had been Gill they favoured. The general mood amongst our camels was almost a unanimous adoration of even Goblin Gilly. They loved my usually gentle bushman in all his phases. They would nuzzle him with their big soft lips, look at him dotingly, and their long eyelashes would flutter whenever he spoke with them. They treated him like he was their little guru, while I was barely tolerated if not treated like shit. Camels without nose pegs, free to make up their own minds, have little time for you if you're not fully embodying who you are. Gill was Gill, and Kye wasn't yet sure who she was.

I was glad Goblin Gilly had been buried a long way back up the track, in some unmarked grave. Never to be recalled or dug up again. His widow had even refused to buy a tombstone, but I must admit those camel boot camp days had taught me a thing or two. All love and light didn't cut it with these dromedaries. They wanted the authentic version of me, and between Goblin Gilly and our pack of press every trigger until she combusts, camels, I had gotten real. Finally, stuff love and light, I had collapsed on my knees, a sobbing, broken mess of a woman, and screamed.

I got little nuzzles of approval after that. Our humped lords and ladies seemed to approve, but it made me ask. Had Gill and I *needed* to be pushed to our furthest extremes for us all to finally meet in the middle? It certainly appeared that way. As the wagon creaked its way south and an endless trail of cinders and ash from old campfires marked our progress, Goblin Gilly had softened, while all love and light me had become more real. The endurance of our trip had broken us into perfect pieces to fit more harmoniously together. We were a much better team, and I even had a few camels that adored *only* me.

One of these was a fine-boned red-haired camel we called Rockhole. He was different in looks and temperament from all our other camels and had this adorable afro mop of curls on top of his head. He was also very skittish, making me wonder if he'd been castrated much too young, never developing his masculinity. He'd arrived in our lives *with* a nose peg we'd never used. I loathed the sight of it. We'd tried to get it out a few times, but Rockhole had freaked out. It had taken a lot of gaining his trust before he finally let Gill cut it out of his nose with some pliers. I couldn't believe how huge the plastic circle was that sat inside his nostril. It must have felt really good to get it out. Once again, it would have made life so much easier if I'd been willing to use it, but this gentle, sweet camel was already sensitive about his head and nose being touched and bawled in fright if we got too close. With me beside him soothing his alarm at life, he wasn't necessarily dangerous, but I had to be totally aware. He could panic. I didn't want to add to the fears he already had and willingly took the hard path if it meant gaining this sensitive camel's trust.

My love for Rockhole engulfed me. From the moment he arrived, tied down in a sitting position and delivered to us on the back of a car trailer, it was love. The woman who'd had him could no longer keep him, and she'd wept tears of relief he was coming to us. He was basically untrained, would bolt at the flutter of a falling leaf or the flap of a tiny wren's wings, and I had to reassure him about *everything*. He, too, would shut down and get confused when Goblin Gilly prowled around, as would my beloved Jumuna, who always preferred me. After all her trauma and self-abuse, gentleness with this girl was the only way. After everything we'd experienced together, we had become really close. She was always so maternal to me and nuzzled me like I was a little child.

One of the other camels was Kunkaa, my little chocolate brown first love. While she was now fully grown, she was the little calf who'd arrived all those years ago, opening the camel floodgates and changing our lives forever. She was also the camel who'd booted me in the face. I'd known that was my fault. I hadn't been paying attention, so I could hardly hold it against her. However, I needed time to rebuild my confidence with her. Gill had handled Kunkaa for a while, but on such a labour-intensive adventure, I couldn't avoid her for long. She was a feisty girl rather than an aggressive one, and she'd taught me a genuinely epic lesson. I had to be totally focused when handling *all* of the camels. In fact, this epic lesson was a significant component of living an empowered life. Focus is essential; whatever I do *if* I want the best results. It may seem crazy to say that Kunkaa's kick had been a profound gift, but it had.

As I walked beside the wagon, watching the rain clouds and their crystalline chariots of ice building up in the south, I was mulling over who we'd become and the parts of ourselves we'd left behind. I remembered the time Nev had communicated with me. Not in words but in a wave of knowing that was palpable and clear. It expressed that when Gill and I let go of our resistance, our camels would stop resisting us. We must have been making good progress. Handling our camels was undoubtedly easier.

I had spent many years learning healing techniques and doing courses aimed at helping people live more fully. While some had undoubtedly been worthwhile, nothing in my life had broken me open before like this trip with all these animals. When I looked back at my life before we'd left, I lived in a straight jacket. I had never really expressed myself because I'd had such a distorted belief about love that came from all love and light new age-ism. It was the camels who helped me trample that veneer. They led me to a powerful truth. Love is not a space of always being 'nice'. It's being honest and authentic. I'd walked some hard miles with our animals of wake-up calls. Each one had shown me when I am who I am without judgement, the more vibrant and alive I become. There are no love and light rules to being ourselves except do no harm. When we live on the pulse of each moment, we feel everything. Love is the freedom of being able to howl like a dingo or scream because we are mad. That's love for me, being here on this planet in my wild untethered fullness, the way I was when I was a child.

And I was unfurling from such constriction. Living amid so many animals who naturally do what they need to do, was liberating and often very funny.

When I'd first met Gill, I'd had many hang-ups, and a major one was that I'd been inhibited about farting. An old partner with his own issues felt sick if a woman farted! So, I suppressed mine for years. Bent myself to his misshapen shape, not realising how weak I became every time I hid a part of me. I can't even believe I did this now! When I'd finally told Gill what I'd done, he'd looked at me utterly aghast before bursting into laughter. He couldn't stop. "Well, we're going to sort that out," he'd said. "Come on, I know you've got one in you. I want to hear a fart."

At that moment, I would have found it easier to attempt to walk over a tightrope at Niagara Falls. I felt so bunged up from my inhibition and totally embarrassed, but Gill is the man for getting you back to nature. After much coaxing and encouragement, I finally managed the sweetest, most polite little fluff of fart, only to have Gill roar, "You call that a fart!" That statement had become a standing joke that never lost its gleam. As the years passed and I became relaxed with a bodily function that should have always been considered normal, we laughed so many times over farting. One night around the campfire, as Gill sat with his back up against Munki, Gill had farted. It was loud enough to notice but not comment-worthy. The next moment Munki let out a huge fart that was mega loud and lengthy. Gill and I had cracked up laughing and, simultaneously, uttered, "Now THAT'S a fart!"

So yeah, while I'd let go of my inhibitions around farting before we left, the five hundred kilometres we'd travelled since had seen us bury and discard so much more. And in the letting go had come the freedom.

I had never felt so present to life as I strode out beside the camels. I was aware of everything. The footprints I left in the ochre-coloured sand of the track. The slight sting of my cheeks from the cold. The way my body felt muscled and taut. The sound of a loose end of rope flapping against the tin of the wagon in such a rhythmic way it sounded like a wonky heartbeat. Then, the sudden movement of two crows startled from their grizzly roadside meal, taking off in a flap of ebony wings. They landed in a roadside tree so caked in dust that it looked ghostly. Their Cackles and caws were so velvety as we passed. Kyiiiiiii, kyiiiiiii, kyiiiiii. They sounded as if they were calling my name. Even Gill called over to me, "Kye; the crows are calling your name."

I heard them call me too, and I wasn't surprised. At that moment, I felt so one with life; of course, the crows were calling my name. I was the road kill rabbit they had been eating and the wind that ruffled and skewed their feathers. I was the wintry sunshine that held little heat and the ghostly branch of the tree they perched in. I was the pause they waited in, keen to return to their feast.

Nine

My Beautiful Mob

Despite being a tyrant of a camel for many years, Abdul had previously been in the guardianship of a belly dancer who'd taken him out in public as part of her exotic performance. I'd seen this naughty camel covered in excited little children who were scrambling all over him. Abdul had been so well behaved and stood perfectly still. He loved to be the centre of attention every chance he got. Whether he was terrifying others or centre stage and being adored, he had such a Jekyll and Hyde personality. For many years he brought up such contrasting feelings in me. I could break into a cold sweat at the thought of meeting him, yet when I imagined his big eager, friendly face, I smiled.

I wondered if memories had surfaced for him since returning to his hometown. He'd shown such eagerness to greet the folk he'd once terrorised but had been rarely met. I'd felt protective of him as almost everyone shied away from his enthusiastic in yer face greetings. I couldn't blame them; I had done the same, but Abdul was a misguided innocent, and after each rejection, he'd looked so confused.

Now, with every turn of the wagon's wheels, just like us, he was leaving his past behind. Everyone he faced now would be new, and people could meet him for who he'd become and not who he'd been.

It felt so appropriate that the road ahead was lined with tourists waiting for us to arrive. Even a big bus full of passengers was embarking so they could stand on the side of the road to get the best view as we passed. There was a jauntiness in Abdul's step. His head was held high as he looked straight ahead, and he was *actually* pulling the wagon and no longer wearing his harness like a mayor's chain of office.

We always stopped for groups of tourists. We should have had a donation tin, but we hadn't been pecuniary and thought about that. So many people stopped for us. We could have sold postcards and reaped our fortune running wagon tours. Instead, we stood out in the cold for free, often sharing the same story over and over because everyone asked the same questions. However, with these tourists, I made a point of introducing Abdul. He looked so regal when he heard me mention his name, but that didn't last long. As people approached him, happy to be the centre of attention again, he broke into a goofy smile. This adorable camel loved people. I told the crowd gathered around our wagon that Abdul was a legend who had begun life as an orphan camel, growing up without any mother to look out for him. "It's a miracle he survived," I said. "Many orphan camels get shot because the behaviour that's encouraged and laughed at when they are little becomes dangerous as they grow."

I had no intention of dragging Abdul's story with us; I just wanted to celebrate and honour him. We had just stepped out of his past, and that past had pretty much rejected him. Even refusing to entertain the idea that he had changed or be open to meeting the loving being he'd become. Whether a person or an animal, I love hearing stories of personal transformations. I find it empowering to know that the past does not equal the future, and regardless of struggle and strife, anything is possible. That was what I wanted to share with people. Not the struggle, though that was relevant. It was Abdul's transformation despite every adversity that was important.

"This camel Abdul has faced massive rejection," I shared with the crowd that had gathered around us. "He has been hugely misunderstood, and narrowly avoided being killed. Yet in that eleventh hour when everything had looked so bleak, a miracle had occurred. This crusher of cars had unexpectedly found himself being welcomed into our haven of love. After all the ups and downs of his life, he finally found his home and at the same time, found love."

I bow in honour of all our beloved animals, especially the camels. So many, just like Abdul, had faced insurmountable challenges. But this was his moment, and I could see the emotion in people's faces as everyone gave him a pat and congratulated him.

On a dusty outback track, under a weak and wintry sun, with a whole group of strangers, Abdul had finally birthed as the beautiful camel he'd always been. He was no longer a victim of his past. We all laughed when a middle-aged man with piercing blue eyes and a mop of sandy brown hair piped up. "He sounds just like me. I spent years trying to please my wife; whatever I did was never enough. Then one day, I came home from work, and she was gone. She'd bloody well run off with a lover. I was devastated, but six years later, I have never been happier. I'm finally living the life I wanted, and look," he said as he put his arm around a woman with long chestnut curly hair who was smiling adoringly up at him. His words sounded like a purr when he pulled her close and told us, "this gorgeous woman loves me for who I am." It was a priceless treasured moment in the hard miles of our trip. All around me, people were smiling and *really* smiling as they held their hearts in acknowledgement of the tenderness of this man's love for his partner.

I felt like I was farewelling old friends as I climbed back into the wagon. People reached up to give Abdul a farewell pat before waving us off. I undid the brake and gave the camels the command to "Walk em up." Our wagon lurched forward to a chorus of cheers, screeching parrots and howling dogs. I could see people laughing. No one had anticipated the noise our cheerleaders made. Connecting with people in such a heartfelt way was manna from heaven for me, and there could not have been a more synchronistic meeting to honour Abdul's release from his past. It was equally wonderful that he shared this moment with a passing stranger with a similar tale of love. Our impromptu roadside meeting was an experience that filled our chalice, and we both needed that. The stretch of road we travelled was pretty desolate. Little grew on its wide-open plains. I could hear the earth saying *I'm sorry; I have nothing left to give.* I was so grateful our animals were all fatties, and we had always prioritised travelling at a pace that maintained their well-being. We didn't want them to lose *any* condition *ever*.

The next ten days of travel were so hilly, and progress was inevitably slow. We had put eight camels in harnesses so we could train more of them as we travelled, and so they each had less work to do. Together they were very strong. Eight camels are an absolute powerhouse and could easily get us up hills, but they were just like us with their moods. Some days they'd plod along so slowly. On other days, they'd trot for miles and Gill and I would sit in the wagon feeling like we were Gods riding our chariot through the heavens. We never ever pushed them to trot, they did it *only* when they felt like it, but I loved it when they did. It was so much fun and felt exhilarating.

We had faced all sorts of different vehicles coming down this track, and the camels had become very relaxed with motorhomes and big 4WDs pulling plush caravans behind them. They didn't even mind the big tourist buses. They trusted Gill so much that if he was beside them, reassuring them, they were OK. While they may hesitate for a moment, they usually put a brave step forward. Of course, we hadn't even considered they'd panic at a bicycle. We were super alert to tiny black dots on the horizon that could possibly be cyclists.

The second time we heard a bike was heading our way, we asked a passing tourist to tell the cyclist to make some noise as he approached and let him know our camels were nervous about bikes. Gill and I had pondered if it was the silence that could have alarmed them. While their reaction to the second cyclist was definitely muted, they stopped for a moment, looking ahead with *what the fuck* expressions on their faces. This cyclist was making so much noise. He came towards us, yahooing and yelling, "halloo everyone, just passing by, whoopee doobie doo. I am here." I had never heard anyone make so much noise. He was like a boom box on wheels, but it worked. Beyond a momentary alarm and an expression of shock on Lady Caroline's face at his utter lack of decorum, the camels came to a gentle halt beside a tiny little lycra-clad Japanese man. He had a huge smile, and he popped his bike on its stand and, in a gasp of awed astonishment, came over almost in a bow, hand outstretched to say hello. This madman was cycling to Darwin, over 2000 kilometres away. He appeared to be having a jolly good time riding slowly over corrugated ruts and through arduous and hilly terrain.

We took photos for him with *his* camera, by the camels, in the wagon, standing by the wagon and finally, with big smiles for the camera, a photo with Gill and then me. After giving him a cold orange from a bag a tourist had gifted us, we waved farewell to this lovely adventurer who exuded passion and love for life. We both felt a little flat that his beaming presence had gone.

Life on the road was like that. We fell in love and said goodbye in the same conversation and did it many times along the way. Of course, there were endless people that just waltzed into our lives to bludge some energy and not give anything in return. I tried not to focus on them, but sometimes that was really hard. Some people were just so rude. We were over having video cameras pressed into our faces by complete strangers who hadn't even said hello. There were times we did fume for a while, but we always came back to the truth. These takers were not worth our energy; only the kind people deserved that, and we met so many of them. Many days felt like a chain of love, from one heartfelt embrace to another. We were valued, we were honoured, and told we inspired. I had never anticipated that. When we'd first set off, if I'd had an invisibility potion, I'd have taken it and travelled unseen. I am glad I didn't have that potion. So many people clutched our hands gratefully or reached out to hug us with tears in their eyes, telling us we gave them the courage to live their dreams. If we inspired people to do that, I was humbled and happy we'd been seen.

Many faces we met merged as one, not because they were not special or had failed to touch us profoundly but because their underlying stories were the same. The desire to break free of their chains and walk away from all their obligations. Whereas the people that stuck with me were those that already had broken free. A German Vet, tall and lean with sun-bleached hair and a berry brown beaming face and eyes that shone with joy. He told us he was living on a huge wooden boat and sailing around the world. He had moored his boat in South Australia to make a quick road trip to Uluru to see Ayers Rock. Our brief meeting was a communion of souls. We chattered excitedly with him, overjoyed to meet a kindred spirit, even if it was for ten minutes. When we went to part, we all hugged each other in tears, knowing we may never see each other again yet so aware our hearts connected us. I was grieving for a few miles after saying goodbye to that man. Moments like this were the blessings of travelling down a busy outback track in tourist season, but there was one thing that *really* peed me off.

We wanted to pass through without leaving a trail. We put out and covered up all our fire pits, cleaned up our camps and were fastidious with our poops, even though no one else that travelled this route appeared to be. If there was one big moan I had, it was that every bush near the side of the road had toilet paper tangled in the shrubs behind it. There wasn't a roadside bush that hadn't been pooped behind. If there was a big stand of bushes, one could expect masses of poops and toilet paper littering the countryside like streamers. It made us both mad. *Don't these people know how to use a spade and bury it? For fucks sake*, I felt like asking people we met if they knew how to have a bush poop, even checking their vehicles to find the necessary spade. I could see myself roaring. "*You haven't got a spade!*" Even giving lessons on how to dig a hole and bury it. I was told by one bushman who brought up the subject of the toilet paper streamers fluttering in the breeze that he thought dingos might have dug their poops up. I know toilet paper, and that paper had definitely never been below ground.

We were getting close to our next blink, and you'll miss it town of William Creek, and the track was getting really busy. Loads of people were heading north to Alice to find an early camping spot for the Finke desert race the following week. I felt so grateful we had travelled this part of the Old Ghan line when it was quiet, or every bush along its red dirt banks would have had the toilet paper streamers too. All sorts of vehicles passed us, with dirt bikes on trailers or wild-looking hoon cars. My favourite cavalcade was the gang of about thirty people travelling around Australia on postie bikes. Having our own postie bike that we considered one of the best buys we'd ever made, we could appreciate the adventure these people were on. However, another aspect of this group showed me they were kindred souls.

As they all whizzed by, their bikes laden with camping gear, waving and tooting their meek little postie bike horns, I was thrilled to see small shovels roped onto the sides of their panniers. A definite sign that this was a gang of conscientious poopers, and even though I totally *got* their postie bike enthusiasm and could feel their excitement at the adventure they were on, I felt so uplifted to see those little shovels and know that others out there in the wild unknown were also burying their own poop!

I totally understood this gang of travelling postie bikers. We loved our little postie bike. It was an absolute hero and had become an indispensable aid on our trip. It had never let us down and easily dealt with rough roads and wild bush tracks. While we were clocking up the kilometres in the distance we had travelled, that distance was almost tripled for Gill. My beloved travelled our route once on the postie bike, once in the 4WD and once in the wagon or walking.

Most mornings, he drove our 4WD with the trailer attached and the postie bike on its ramp to the next location we would camp. After unloading the postie bike, he would ride back to the wagon. Our much-loved postie bike would then be loaded onto the ramp at the back of our wagon and remain there for the rest of the day as we all travelled to the 4WD. It may sound like a complicated process, but having our postie bike and 4WD created so much ease in other aspects of our life on the road that we always felt grateful for them. I must confess though gratitude seems such a pallid word to describe my feelings. I *loved* them both so much and often sang their praises with Gill. "Isn't this just the best bike you have ever bought?" I'd say proudly to Gill as I stroked our postie bike affectionately.

The 4WD and the postie bike had taken so much stress from our trip. They enabled us to choose a nightly camp with the best feed available for our animals, and with their help, we could easily keep up with the needs of all our thirsty animals. Being able to drive out to a bore or a water tank and fill up all our drums with water was one of my favourite jobs. While we waited for the water to siphon into our drums, we would usually swim in the tanks.

Unless we were falling into bed exhausted at night, we had few occasions in our day where we could *really* let go. Our water-filling trips gave us a fantastic opportunity to relax, even if it was only for half an hour. I loved floating in a concrete water tank way out in the desert, staring at the brilliant blue sky. I often felt so present to the luminosity of the moment that I could feel myself soaring with the eagles in the thermals above. These were moments that felt so wild and beautiful and free. We may not have had a fancy swimming pool, and honestly, I wouldn't have wanted one. Give me wild places over tamed every day. From our watery oasis, we could lazily watch the giant red kangaroo drinking from a nearby trough or the little swallows that would swoop down over the tank and drink in mid-flight. It wasn't just the drums of water that got filled from our trips to the tanks. We were as well. I always returned to our camp revitalised.

And it wasn't just the physical ease of our vehicles that I appreciated. Both our 4WD and our postie bike reminded me to stay in trust. Every time I looked at them, I remembered a potent truth. When I am living in flow, everything I need comes. There are no obstacles or limitations to this. This holy space of living has no impediments. It doesn't matter if I am in a very remote location and barely meet a soul. What I need will always come. Life will find a way to deliver. Really knowing this gave me the courage to step forward boldly. To live my life without needing a safety net. When I forgot this truth and let my fears momentarily blind me, I only had to look at our postie bike or our 4WD and remember the miraculous way they had come into our lives to realign.

The postie bike will always represent freedom and trust for me, and I felt so much excitement watching this huge gang of conscientious pooping postie bike fans toot and rev past.

For a beautiful moment, I daydreamed. I imagined racing over to our postie bike and unloading it from its ramp. I'd need to grab my swag, a few clothes and our rather large spade, but I could strap it lengthwise along the bike. Yup, I even thought of that *and* the possibility that Gill would have the same idea, and I may even have to rugby tackle him for the bike. But the lure of a flirtier adventure soon paled.

Who else in history had travelled with such a massive menagerie of animals and on a journey that didn't even have a destination *and* had done so for no other reason than *love*?

Oh, it may have been a fleeting lure to be so free. To feel my hair blowing in the wind as I revved my postie bike. I had even seen me giving Gill the finger as I sped away from responsibility and hard gruels of days and roosters that crowed all through the night. As I watched these bikers toot and rev past, it was abundantly clear to me. The lure for me was always love and I could never have left without leaving *everything* that mattered to me behind.

For better or worse, I was with my mob, and I loved them all so much.

Ten

Every Life Mattered

As we pulled into the tiny outback town of William Creek, there was no avoiding the crowds. They came from everywhere, spilling from the pub, bursting from cars parked in the street. We were soon surrounded by a throng of people taking photos and recording our every move. I was not in the mood and felt grateful Gill stepped up. I watched him from the wagon standing in a huge group of people taking his photo, wanting him to poise with the camels, pointing video recorders at him as they asked the same questions we'd answered a million times already. He could have been a movie star.

Our camels stood so perfectly still that they looked like statues. Often, and only in public, they were so buttoned up and stately that they had the demeanour of Buckingham palace guards. Looking straight ahead unwaveringly, unwilling to even lower their haughty heads for a pat. I heard a guy in the crowd exclaim, "My God aren't they regal," and then he saw Abdul, who, while the only one, just couldn't help breaking rank. Our loveable pup of a camel with his big goofy smile just loved people, and there was no way he could restrain himself. He reached out excitedly to slurp the face and drool over anyone who gave him attention. For that salivary pleasure, there was a queue! I could not see Lady Caroline's face from my seat in the front of the wagon. Yet, I had no doubt that her bottom lip would be quivering in indignation at Abdul's complete lack of poise. Abdul just wasn't made for being buttoned up.

We had no reason to stop. It was still early enough in the day for us to be hopeful we'd make it further down the track before making camp, but the sky was becoming so dark and stormy, and the air stank of rain. We knew it wouldn't be wise to travel on. Camels, though perfectly designed desert creatures have no grip on their huge padded feet and don't like walking on any surface they could slip. The last thing we wanted was for us all to be stuck on a wet, muddy track out in the rain.

As we resigned ourselves to pulling up early, we had no idea it would be ten days before the weather cleared and the road dried out enough for us to travel, but we were not the only ones stranded. This tiny little town temporarily cut off from the rest of the world, became an island oasis for numerous caravaners and tourists and a few mud-splattered dirt bike riders. They had been on their way to Alice for the Finke desert race. It was those bikers that left me with a memory I shall never forget.

After a week of sheltering under a leaking tarp trying to avoid the drips, the sun finally came out. We had been unable to walk anywhere because of all the mud. Lured by the tantalising possibility of chocolate or even some hot chips from the local pub, we decided to brave the boggy path to town.

I've had so many moments in time that are so vivid I have thought as they happened; I *will remember every little detail of this in twenty years.* Walking along the street in William creek after a week of heavy rain was one of them. Everything looked so bright and crisp. Light shimmered from all the puddles, and raindrops glistened from the leaves of all the trees. So many others, just like us, had been marooned in this tiny town with its one pub and its café, and for the first time since we'd left Alice, we were incognito and able to enjoy others taking centre stage.

On the *only* strip of tarmac for hundreds of kilometres, down the main street of town, several dirt bike riders performed epic and lawless stunts. I normally loathed the sound of dirt bikes, but I clapped and cheered with everyone else as some leather-clad riders roared up and down the entire street doing wheelies at 120 kilometres an hour. Sometimes coming from different ends of the road and passing each other in the middle, and other times surging down the street in tandem.

This was the highlight of our stay. While much of the time was spent sitting under a dripping tarp reading books, we did make a significant change in how we managed our camel's grazing that would transform the rest of our trip.

We'd begun tethering the camels from a long leg rope to a tree, but this was not ideal. We were sensitive about travelling through *other* people's land and respectful not to let our animals wander all over the place. However, when the camels were tethered to a central point, they caused damage. Little shrubs and bushes within their reach would get tangled in their ropes and uprooted. We didn't like this *at all*. We'd intended to travel through the landscape and leave no trail.

Several times Gill had suggested hobbling the camels, but I always resisted. I felt like I was treating them as prisoners by shackling them. I know; it didn't make any sense. We had to tether them anyway. I just didn't like the idea of them shuffling around with their front legs almost strapped together. Gill felt if he hobbled a few and let the others wander freely, they would all stay together and not go very far. We could also rotate the hobbled camels so they all had time unrestrained.

I finally relented, and what a relief because Gills's idea worked. Not just for the landscape. Our camels could eat a much more varied diet and fill up their bellies much faster. After a few hours of grazing, they would contentedly settle down around the wagon to chew their cud. There was no more getting tangled. I was overjoyed. Untangling their ropes from bushes was the worst job of all.

When a camel has walked around a spiky bush twenty times, and the rope is coiled around its trunk and knotted up with tufts of grass, the choice is to crawl into the bush and untangle it or chop the bush down. Of course, we never chose the latter, even though it would have *always* been the easiest option. I often came out from under those bushes, scratched and bloody, feeling entirely over the whole dam adventure.

Why the hell didn't our animal communication work all the time? Why didn't our camels simply respond when we asked them to graze close to camp? It was apparent there were glaring chasms in our communication skills, but why? Why did it flow sometimes and feel non-existent at others? I often thought about this in the hours I spent walking beside the camels. After our communications with our animals *before* we'd left, I'd expected to experience this with them immediately, all of the time, forever. Not the shenanigans we'd gone through. Of course, it makes sense that communicating with an animal or anyone for that matter, is much easier in a calm and relaxed space. Certainly not flying through the air after them hanging on for dear life to the end of their rope.

When I asked our lord of the harem, Zu, for some clarity on this subject, he looked at me so gormlessly that I questioned my sanity for even thinking we'd shared intelligent communication. He always did have this slightly dopey look. His bottom lip hung down, so his mouth was always slightly open and yet I was not fooled by his veneer. I'd seen him lead his herd several kilometres back to our camp after blocking their return for weeks. He had done so immediately after we'd politely asked him to bring all the camels home. I'd also seen him veer the wagon across the road, saving us all from a potentially catastrophic oncoming collision with a speeding car. I had also seen how he had responded to being put in a harness, pulling our wagon like he'd pulled it hundreds of times before when he never ever had.

I knew he was much more astute than he liked to appear, and yet why did he often act so dopey?

The stream of communion we dipped and dived into was never there around chores and routines. Understandable, that's when we were super busy, but I honestly felt it was much more than that. When it really mattered, the camels showed up and responded from a place of awareness. Even in the early days of our trip, when they kept getting the wagon bogged in deep sand, I knew they were doing it intentionally. They all had such wry expressions, and I am sure they were passing winks. Their faces communicated the unanimous agreement between them that they had two very dysfunctional and unaligned humans to whip into shape and train for this trip. That meant relieving us of all our baggage. The times we'd yelled and screamed red-faced with blood vessels bursting, or I'd sobbed hysterically, a broken mess in a snotty gush of self-pity, was us being broken and mangled and rearranged. We were in the best personal growth boot camp and had put ourselves into it willingly. And camels are so clever. They knew exactly how far to push us, when to let off, and precisely how to inveigle their way back into our good books. I wanted to blame them for putting us through hell, but I couldn't. I wouldn't have wanted to travel with me either!

But Gill and I had gone through our rites of passage, hadn't we? Their wry looks, with time, had become smug. As if they were preening themselves when they looked at us that they'd *done good*. We were their little project, and I was in no doubt they were satisfied with our progress, so why didn't we communicate all the time? Why was it so hit and miss? I really wanted to understand.

There was certainly so much more trust between us. Trust had been a huge thing for us all to earn with each other. *Any* good relationship can never be one-sided. They had to trust us, as we trusted in them. We'd chosen the hard way to handle camels. The easy way would have been to break their spirits or beat them or control them with a nose peg, and many chose that route, but not us. We had chosen to grow, connect and find the way forward, travelling together in mutual respect and harmony.

While I have already mentioned our camels were the best catalyst of personal growth I'd ever encountered in my entire life, I could only recommend them with a hazard warning. They'd obliterated my life as it had been and had a devastating effect on my comfort zones. Some days I couldn't make up my mind if they had bound me up like a fly in a spider's web or woven their enchantment around me, but good or bad, laughter or shit storms, all I wanted was more. Wherever these quirky, loveable, yet totally exasperating humped beasts were taking me, I was following, and I didn't even need to be roped!

So many aspects of our trip transformed as we all began to trust each other. I no longer held my breath, knotted up with anxiety when Gill slid in between our harnessed camels. Four rows of two standing quietly while Gill slid behind the back legs of one and the front legs of another. He might need to tie a rope, tighten a buckle, untangle a chain. He would talk to them, letting them know what he was doing, "don't move guys, I am coming in-between you," and they always stood perfectly still. They'd even lift their legs up when he asked them. "Come on, Kunkaa, lift up that foot," and up it would rise while Gill fixed the chain.

I might not have understood all their mysterious ways or why our communion with them was so haphazard, but I was never surprised by all the people we met who told us the love we shared with our animals was palpable. Many were moved to tears by it. I understood. I often felt moved to tears by the love and camaraderie we all shared. We had developed such a strong bond, and our union with them *all* was for *better or worse*. There had been no thoughts of abandoning Jumuna because she was beside herself in grief and prone to self-harm and would likely never pull the wagon. Even giving Rockhole the boot because he was flighty and nervous and if we weren't *always* on the ball, likely to run us over or Banjo because he had ungodly habits and pissed all over his face. Even 'The Colonel', who crowed regularly throughout the nights, was a much-loved member of our family. Even if someone had offered us a pot of gold, we'd have turned it down. Our family was *not* for sale, ever.

We had committed to each and everyone, and that's why more often than not, they gave us their best.

I'd felt so proud of our camels when a very experienced cameleer joined us around the campfire one night. He'd been astounded that our camels stayed so close even when they were unhobbled. Yup, we'd all come a long way together, and while it hadn't always been like that, I knew it was the bond we all shared. It was as simple as that.

Several years previously, as novice cameleers, Gill and I had gone on our first-ever weekend trekking trip. We took Lady Caroline and Gidgee, her three-month-old calf, with Nev and our two young camels, Kunkaa and Jianti. We were camped in a very treed area, and the camels had been grazing nearby. As we were still getting to know Nev and Caroline, we had hobbled them. As the billy boiled on our campfire, we'd periodically checked them. They were grazing nearby, and everything felt relaxed, yet ten minutes later, they were gone. At first, we were casually walking around calling them, confident they would appear at any moment, but they didn't. My calls became more frantic. Gill and I split up and walked around calling them, but neither of us saw any sign of our camels. Not a single track. We couldn't even hear their bells. At one point, I could see Gill searching in another area. He wasn't far away, and I began calling him. Louder and louder, but it was evident he couldn't hear me. The wind was muffling my cries. Was this why the camels were not responding to our calls and why we couldn't hear them? We spent hours searching. I was freaking out inside. I couldn't bear to think of them being lost and hobbled, and I was sick with worry.

Eventually, we trudged the five kilometres home to get our 4WD. We could cover more distance and check to see if their tracks crossed any dirt roads. We just needed to pick up their trail. We spent the next two days searching and searching. We were up at first light, searching until dusk. I couldn't sleep, I didn't eat, and I was inconsolable.

On the third day, another cameleer offered to come out and see if he could track them. Fortunately and very fortuitously, we found their tracks crossing the dirt road. We followed them for a while. I remember this cameleer squatting down in the sand, assessing the direction they were travelling and saying to me, "They are not messing around. They are getting as far away as they can. They're going straight back out to the desert and are not even stopping to eat."

I had been sick with relief when we found their tracks, but I was gut-wrenchingly devastated to hear his words. I was in a huge dilemma. If our camels were racing away from us at the first opportunity without even pausing to eat, then all I could morally do when I found them was take off their hobbles and let them go. I felt ripped apart at the thought of this, but I couldn't see any other choice. I loved them so much I could not keep them as my captives. I had tears streaming down my grubby face. I was trying to hold myself together long enough to find them and free them up. I was exhausted. I'd been running on coffee and had no sleep. I was so emotionally fragile I was struggling to cope. When I heard my friend's subsequent prognosis, it was a balm for my soul. "Hang on, they've turned around and are coming back this way."

As we followed their trail, it soon became evident that everywhere Gill and I had stopped our car in the previous days, pulling up and beeping our horn and calling them and calling them, the camels had hobbled towards us. You could see our footprints in the sand where we had got out, and right over the top of them were our camels. They had been responding to our calls. Hobbling madly towards us, yet in my anxiety to find them, we had never lingered long enough to give them time to reach us. I wept with unhinged joy when I realised that and lay blubbing in the dirt. I felt sick with relief.

I felt like I'd finally reached the Promised land when we found them in a sheltered valley grazing. They looked so relaxed and nonchalant as if they'd known we'd find them. I ran over to them, so happy to see my precious loves and began fussing over Lady Caroline. In my worry, I had imagined their poor legs would have been rubbed raw from several days of walking in hobbles, but there was not a rub mark anywhere. I knelt at her feet, massaging her legs where the hobbles had been, still crying with relief and joy. She gave me such an imperious look, yet the feeling I got from her was motherly. *Come on now, child, pull yourself together*, and I did.

Our camels had made a choice, and it had been us.

I *loved* sharing our connection with our animals. I yearned to see a world not only where animals are treated kinder but one in which they are recognised as the sentient, conscious beings they are. Gill and I had become a living, breathing demonstration of an ever-learning, conscious communion with animals. And we would always be learning. What is known is never all there is to know. I knew the animals would take us deeper and deeper and deeper. The more we could surrender, the more we would be shown. Our relationship with our animals was the ultimate journey, and it did not have an end.

We didn't always get everything right. Yet it was easy for people we met, who may not have ever experienced animals, to witness and feel for themselves the palpable bond that connected us with our fury and feathered tribe. Without that bond and the trust we all had in each other, Gill and I would still be kicking and screaming, scratched and blistered somewhere up the track, a lot closer to Alice. We would never ever have made it this far. What we had achieved had *only* happened because of our connection with each other and the love that we all shared. They were important to us, and they knew it. We travelled only at the pace of our animals' well-being, and our chickens were just as well regarded as our camels were.

Each and every life mattered.

Eleven

Salty Pink Bliss

After being bogged in William creek in the deluge and the mud, it was invigorating to be walking beside the wagon, breathing in the familiar scent of my camels once again. All the little shrubs and bushes had sprung to life from the rain, and water sparkled in the clay pans on the side of the track. After such a prolonged break, we knew it would take time to find our rhythm again, and we only managed five slow kilometres before deciding to pull up for the night. It was never worth pushing ourselves or the camels. We were all a little tired, but there was another distraction. The abundant feed!

As we pulled off the track, Lady Caroline's bottom lip began to wobble and quiver. Her eyes were nearly popping out of her head in anticipation of all the culinary pleasures. There were lush patches of ruby docks with their lantern-like mottled pink flowers. One of her favourite foods and not seen growing this prolifically since we'd left Alice. I certainly shared her jubilation, and it wasn't just over the feed. While most of the clay pans had water in them, there were vast areas of red sand that were vegetation free. The perfect environment for our obsession.

I haven't mentioned our tektite fervour, but since our visit to the family of avid collectors, it had not waned. Not one little bit. In fact, looking for tektites had become a normal part of the day, like putting the kettle on or feeding the chickens. Everywhere we walked, we were heads down scanning the earth for those little black glassy looking stones, and our collection had grown to about thirty.

Once Mozzee had nearly walked right over the top of me because stupidly, as I was leading him, I'd suddenly gone, head down, bum in the air and hadn't given him *any* warning. I was excited because I thought the roo poo I'd picked up was a tektite.

Sometimes we'd have big rushes of finding them, then none for a week, but we never gave up, forgot to look, or got bored looking. We loved looking for them, and as soon as all the animals were happily chomping, we headed off on a tektite gleaning adventure in the last rays of light. The fading light gave a sharp edge to our pleasure, lacing it with panic. Soon it would be too dark to see them, even if they were there. We had no time to waste, the sky was darkening fast, and we were just in the final crack of light when we unexpectedly heard shouting coming from nearby.

We thought we were far from people, and we were startled to hear a man's voice. We stood absolutely still, alert and attentive as we listened and tried to decipher what was being said. After a few moments and none the wiser, Gill decided to walk towards the voice and find out. Gill is so stealth-like and can be the creepiest thing in the bush. He can move through the night without a torch and be totally silent. It doesn't matter if it's a dark moon and everything looks totally black. He still manages to see in the dark and move seamlessly. It's like everything holds its breath, and even dead branches dare not snap, and not a crunch of a leaf can be heard. Even if someone meant menace, I have no doubt they'd shit their pants the way Gill silently appears from the bush or sits in the dark watching. I wasn't at all worried about him when he took off towards the man's voice, telling me in a whisper to wait at camp. I knew he would check out the scene before making an appearance. Still, I was keen to find out what was going on.

Twenty long estimated bush minutes passed before Gill appeared silently out of the darkness like a ghoul, but it also could have been an hour. We didn't have a watch. In fact, we didn't do time *at all*. We had no need for it. We rose with the sun, knew we had to pull up and make camp each day when the sun reached a certain lowly position in the sky, and we went to bed when it got dark. We had no appointments, nowhere to be. All that mattered was 'right now' unless one was *waiting*, and then time dragged.

I'd gone through a few different imaginary scenarios waiting for Gill to return and thought the most likely cause of the shouting was a couple arguing. Only I hadn't heard another voice. Just a man's voice, and he sounded panicked. I'd felt uneasy listening and was relieved when Gill returned and filled me in on what had occurred.

A retired couple was camping nearby, and the husband had been shouting at a dingo that was trying to take down a full-grown kangaroo. Fortunately for the kangaroo, the man's yelling had distracted the dingo's focus on its prey. The kangaroo and dingo had bolted in different directions. I was happy to hear that. I know the dingo has to eat, but a much smaller prey would mean a much quicker death than being mauled.

Slowly we wound our way south through a rocky and rugged landscape. The further south we went, the drier the landscape became. Not everywhere had received the abundant rain. Every little shrub on the edge of the track looked gasping and beaten. I felt introverted and quiet and was trying to stay focused on each step. That track, my little thread of safety, would soon peter out. But I didn't want to think of that or try and work out what we could do when it came to its inevitable end. I knew everything would work out then, and *only* then. I was learning that. Learning to live in each moment and not look too far beyond the next breath.

When I stayed in each moment, I didn't miss anything, and It didn't matter how straight or seemingly bleak and barren the track could be. There were always surprises. Something always pulled us up and had us gasping in awe. The perfectly bleached white skeleton of a lizard merging into the rusty coloured earth, the hazy heat shimmering silhouettes of a herd of wild camels far away on the horizon, the tracks of a dingo down the middle of the road, with the tiny soft print of its cub. There was always so much to see and experience. Often the road was so long and straight that it really heightened my appreciation of blind bends and unexpected vistas when we reached the rise of a hill. Especially when it unveiled a scene I'd never seen before.

Our track had just dipped into a dry creek bed. The camels were feeling exuberant, kicking and bucking excitedly as they cruised up the rise, taking us out onto the flats. My mouth fell open in astonishment. In the distance was a massive pink shimmering crystalline expanse stretching as far as the horizon. It was the first time I had ever seen a salt lake, and if Gill hadn't told me it was much further away than it appeared, I would have run over and laid down on its pink salty surface.

We camped within its sight that night, and as I sat around the campfire, I could taste its salty lick in the cold night air. While Gill had led the camels out to graze, I had begun on the jobs around camp. Feeding the birds, then letting out the Colonel and his girls for their nightly forage before walking the dogs and then settling them all down on their beds with their bowl of feed. Our nightly routine was always busy. Yet throughout every job, I'd watched the lake changing its hues with the dusk, from a soft pink fairyland to a radiant blaze of magenta. By the time we had sat down, grateful for our end-of-day moment when we both gave a huge sigh of relief as we collapsed into our camping chairs, the moon had risen. So big and bulbous but not yet full. It had bleached the lake into a wintry snow-clad wonderland.

Despite all the gifts of our journey, I had days I wanted it to be over. It was constant hard work, and even when we had a brilliant day, we *always* had a weary one. I ached for a home. I am much more a homebody than a gypsy, but as I sat around the campfire that night, I realised something profound. I never wanted the way we lived to end. Ever. I still wanted a home, but I never wanted that separation again between us and our animals. I loved living with them, bad breath, stinky farts, roosters crowing. Even Banjo's pissy-soaked beard and the way, every night, he pushed his way in front of us to get closer to the fire.

How could we ever go back to him, or any of the others living outside and us living in? Would we, with time, forget how special and extraordinary this journey had been? Would we once again be lured by the false and phoney charms of TV and stop sitting outside under the stars, around our fire? Oh, I hoped not. Would it be possible to create a bridge and share with others this phenomenal experience, and would they believe us? Would they think we were telling tales when we spoke of sitting under the moon watching the salt lake flouncing her jewels as she basked in a silvery moon? Would they believe this survived endless challenges, chocolate box scene that was our end of the day, and everyday life? Sitting around the fire with our tribe.

Munki, who'd grown as big as a mountain chomping his cud with Gill sitting up against him as a backrest. Both so relaxed and at ease. The bond between these two was palpable. Munki could not have been happier than when he was with Gill, and even though he had his faraway dreamy look, he looked as if he was smiling.

Our irrepressible, over-the-top, in-your-face, belligerent and honky donkey Bella, who always stood on the edge of the flames as she slid into her nightly reverie. Her eyes would close, her head would hang down, the smoke would waft and billow around her, so you could barely see her. She looked like some ethereal being emerging from the mist.

Invincible Yumyum, who could fly faster than the hawks, sitting with his head tucked under his wing as he snoozed on the back of the chair Gill had vacated to join

Munki. While Chia, our little hyena of a dog who lived life with the ferocity of a shooting star, lay curled up on her bed by the fire with Patchi, her giant of a brother. Our fires were always such a crazy scene, yet I had never felt more at home. The world we had left behind was the mad one, not this. Around this fire were friends. Around this fire was a holy communion of souls that went way beyond little mortal bodies and the limitations of believing ourselves as humans or of being superior to any other species! We had that so wrong! Oh, so wrong!

I had grown so much as a person since opening to learning from our animals. Our ancient and wise camels that, beyond the little glimpses they allowed us to see, were still a mystery to me, were all sitting around the outer fringes of our fire and wagon in a circle. They felt like our guardians, sitting like silhouettes under the moon. While the familiar rhythmic chomp as they all ground, their cud palpitated the air almost like the echo of an ancient drum beat. Merging with the territorial sounds of the night, a howling dingo far away, the shriek of an owl, the crack and spit of the fire as she roared, sending sparks up to dazzle the blue night sky.

It would seem unbelievable to many that there were days when our life on the road would feel so routine that it verged on being mundane. Though I'm glad to say, only ever briefly.

Gill and I knew what we shared with each other, and all our animals was much too beautiful, too precious, and too fleeting to ever take for granted or let fade or dim. This mad, crazy, yet more sane reality than anything I'd *ever* experienced before may have been our 'normal'. Still, I wanted to relish every moment and savour every step because this incredible journey *would* eventually come to an end.

And as I rose to go to bed that night, I had tears rolling down my cheeks at the thought.

Twelve
Naughty Gill

Even though it could be harsh and cruel, I loved the red desert country. The hardness that unbuckled me came not from dust storms and blistering heat or irrepressible flies but from the quest for ever-increasing profit. Greed permeated *most* of this vast land.

I'd never heard of people shooting kangaroos until we travelled in the outback. The first time I ever saw the roo shooter's lights arcing across the landscape, searching for their prey, I'd felt sick in my guts. I couldn't relax. I didn't even enjoy sitting around the fire. How could I when I knew that in the glare of those lights was a killing field? There isn't a palatable way to share this, and it would be easier to avoid it, but this happening created a seam throughout our trip that was a constant struggle for me to deal with. We didn't always see the lights. Sometimes weeks would pass in-between. I'd relax then and breathe more easily. Still, it was always a brutal shock when they appeared again, sweeping menacingly across the land.

There was a level of antipathy amongst many farmers, however friendly and warm they were, for any animal that took a blade of grass from profit-eating stock. Rarely did we meet tolerance for coexistence, and the ones that did respect the balance were spoken of badly or viewed as odd. Yet these stations were the places I loved, and I remember every one of them with delight. They had a wildness, an untouched beauty. Very often, more fodder was growing on the land and more wildflowers. Even more trees because these farmers realised how vital balance in *all* things was to harmony on their land. In harmony, *everything* thrived.

I felt a freedom on these stations that was exhilarating, and I felt much more at home. I loathed leaving these properties. I wanted to stay on them forever. The shift between realities often felt acutely dire when we passed through the gate into the neighbouring station. Back into a landscape where everything was controlled and the only animals to thrive were those that made a profit. These were the stations where the roo shooters were welcomed.

The truth is, nothing could take away from the experience we were sharing with our animals. They were always my focus, and we experienced many beautiful moments every day, *but* whenever I was aware of the roo shooters, I felt queasy and distressed. I had to *really* try and shift my focus. Being angry or upset served nothing, which didn't mean I didn't feel these things. I did. But I had to bring myself back to my centre. I had to be present for myself and our animals. Sometimes that meant sitting with my back to the lights to really anchor down into the reality I was in. I would remind myself that the love we each put out made a difference and could be felt, and in that vast hard, profit-driven land, there was one fire at least burning brightly for all things good and kind, and it was *ours*.

I knew this was one of the reasons we were all there and not just Gill and I, the animals too. Not to try and change anyone else's view or get angry. Our job was to plant seeds of kindness along the way that would when the time was right, sprout.

I got such strength, especially in these more challenging situations, from our matriarch camels. When I sat with them, they reminded me of the times I'd sat in the dirt in a circle with a group of aboriginal grandmothers. The presence of these old women had felt so deeply ancient and grounded that even though I consider myself a strong and practical woman, compared to them, I felt as inconsequential as a soap sudd. Their connection with country was so much a part of who they were. It *was* them. They *were* the ancient forest and the mountain range, the raging rivers and lakes, as they were the dirt beneath their feet.

The camels had a similar connection with the land. They *were* the deserts they roamed, the red sand dunes and the ancient gullies. As they were the rocks and the stones, and just as Gill did, they merged so completely with the landscape that they were almost impossible to see if I didn't look through different eyes. I would have to soften my gaze and gently scan. As my eyes gently roamed across the wide-open plains, I could almost see a distillation of energy where the camels were. The difference between their energy and the nearby bush was often so subtle it would have been easy to dismiss it as imagination. Only experience had shown us this was a viable way to find our camels.

While I loved the desert, I didn't have the natural affinity for it that Gill and our camels had. I knew the feelings that came from connecting with land. I felt them each time I returned to my homeland, the UK. The very minute I touched the earth, I'd feel myself lapping up familiar and ached for currents. I'd soak up the pure vitality of the trees and plants and flowers, the rocks and the streams. On that land, I did feel ancient and earthed. Yet all the holy currents of my life had led me far away to the red desert. I may not sink in and merge with it like Gill or the camels, but I was here.

If I closed my eyes, I could feel the land of my blood and bones and its ancient stone circles and holy sites following me like the resonance from a tuning fork. Even so, being in the desert was a big adjustment for me. I hoped that would change. Many times, I'd felt the boundaries between species slipping. Just for a moment,

I'd see the luminous being I was communing with, not the camel, dog, or goat. I was learning every day that we all had the potential to see and experience beyond our limited perceptions. Did land hold the same sway to bind us to our limitations? Was it possible I had not merged with this land because I'd defined my identity by location? I was not indigenous to this red desert, but I was indigenous to earth and surely, far from home, that was a more relevant beacon. I felt these truths so succinctly when I sat amid the matriarchs. They held a space like a holy chalice, and just being with them stretched me beyond all the beliefs and identities that kept me small. I was forever stretching beyond small!

Each time I saw the prowling lights of the roo shooters, I'd feel myself contract, like a spasm in a tight muscle. Yet, if I went and sat with the matriarchs, I'd feel myself shift into deep peace and only peace. They had no fear for their own lives, so why should they fear for others? Death was just a doorway and not an end. They just sat chewing their cud. Everything was perfect. Everything was at peace. Life began and ended and began and ended, again and again.

Did it matter if death was a blood bath? I wanted to know the answer to this. *Surely death has to be our choice and not taken by another?*

It was Jumuna that answered the question I posed and not with words or nonsense or stuff that could be misunderstood. With her presence. Once again, I felt the space between us disappear and the truth of who we truly were, emerge. It would appear that to emerge, one has to merge and what I saw when I did, challenged me. Everything that I'd judged and feared came from my separation. Nothing was by chance, and everything was called in. Even the rabbit plucked from the earth by an eagle had thrown himself into that moment of death as a dance into the infinite and miraculous where everything became love.

I didn't like it. On a much deeper level, I understood, but I still sat with my back to the lights. The matriarchs continued to chomp and chew. They recognised my resistance, and even that was no cause for concern. Limitations were like the leaves on the trees. When the time was right, and the wind blew, they'd fall.

I felt so grateful for these wise beings. It had taken so long to move beyond my false notions, bullshit and veneers. Especially around our mistaken notion that Gill and I were somehow guiding this trip. Only when I shifted from swaggering around as a cocky know it all little human who knew nothing at all to approaching the matriarchs with humility did our whole relationship change. They *finally* began to open up to me.

We treated all our animals with love and respect, but the matriarch's received the same obeisance we'd give a tribal elder. Now I always found this really strange, but often when I was with them, I would recognise an energy from them that felt maternal. They were mothering me, and while it wasn't fussy or clucky, it *was* caring and sweet.

I am pretty sure it would have challenged most people we met to comprehend that animals were conscious beings we could learn from and, *if* we had any common sense, *would*! People were not ready to jump that far from the limited societal view of animals. Many didn't even know if animals had personalities. This was one of the most common questions we got asked as we travelled. And quite frankly, although I always answered this politely, I was staggered by how many people asked. *Had they never had a dog? Were there so many people out there who had never interacted with an animal?* Of course, I gave them the benefit of the doubt. If these people had somehow managed to go through life without knowing the answer, well, here was a golden opportunity to help them step up a rung.

"Yes, they most certainly do!"

They all have such varied personalities. It was like travelling with fifty different people and hanging out with them all, all the time, every day. As you can imagine, they took us through a range of emotions. We had animals that loved to be the centre of attention and others that were shy. Some were bossy, some were funny, and some even annoyed me. Some even found *me* annoying!

Munki, who worshipped Gill and would let him do *anything*, treated me like I was an irritating fly. Whereas Rockhole and I adored each other, and yet Rockhole didn't like Gill *at all*. We had pushy animals, some that were more demure. We even had dopey and gullible ones like our big dog Patchi, who every night would get fooled by Chia, his little sister who, compared with him, was the size of a mouse. She was a clever trickster, always sneaking around playing games. Every mealtime, she'd toss her kibble into the air, scattering it around her bowl. She looked playful, *but* she'd cunningly laid her bait before walking away, feigning complete disinterest. To the innocent observer, it looked as if she'd finished her food, but we knew she was hiding, poised and hackled, ready to pounce. Loveable, innocent, and guileless, Patchi would *always* amble over to finish her food. He fell for her trickery every time. His little sister would leap from her hiding place like a wild banshee and defend her kibble.

I often felt like a time travelling storyteller, standing on the edge of the track, sharing our animal adventures of life on the road with a crowd of people. Looking as if we'd come from some more expansive future time where it was perfectly normal to travel in a brightly coloured wagon with fifty rescued animals and not know where the heck we were going.

The way people stared at us in awe, we could have even come from another planet! They loved our stories and wanted to meet the animal involved. We shared many of our animal adventures along the way, but there was one such tale I never told on the road. Call it decorum!

I had just built up the fire and put the kettle on when I heard Gill yelling loudly. My heart did the biggest lurch. I immediately thought something awful had happened, and I ran with a dread of arriving and a sick feeling in my gut. It was rare for Gill to yell with such urgency, so I was sure something must be *really* wrong.

At first, I couldn't make out what was happening. It all looked very confusing, and I was still taking in the scene when Gill yelled at me to grab Lady Caroline's rope and lead her away. In my instant sum up of the situation, I was relieved to see no blood, and no one looked hurt. In fact, the camels appeared to be enjoying themselves.

Lady Caroline, evidently able to maintain decorum in the midst of passion, was sitting very regally with her head held high, looking straight ahead while Zu was mounting her from behind. It was Gill who looked the most uncomfortable. He was hanging from the back of Lady Caroline's hump. Twisted at an awkward angle with his foot placed over the entrance where Zu was enthusiastically attempting to plant his seed.

Gill, as our on-the-spot family planning coordinator, was multitasking his work boot as a camel contraceptive! I had to give him full marks for ingenuity and another clap on the back for hilarity. Despite my uncontrollable laughter, I managed to grab hold of Lady Caroline's rope and lead her away. She had been pregnant many times before she'd even come to us. She didn't need to be pregnant again.

Zu always blew me away. We would never have given him a home if we'd known he was a bull, yet he had proven to be one of *the* greatest blessings of our trip. As Gill led him away from Lady Caroline, he followed like a little lamb. He didn't even put up resistance. Our big baby of a bull camel that would drop his head into our arms when we stroked and rubbed his face and yet led us *all* on our mad adventure like a heroic king was one of the most noble and wise animals I had ever met. I felt so grateful that it was our lives he had descended into, and we'd trusted enough to welcome him.

We had a different relationship with every animal, but there were two, especially, that filled me with pride. Abdul and Banjo. I still shook my head, awed by the flow of events that had led us to them. Both had shown behaviour that was so destructive or dangerous they had almost lost their lives, and yet here they were. I always laughed when I thought of our caravan of love with these two ex-villains, tucked in lovingly amongst us all, and both had proven to be little angels, *most of the time.*

Many tourist buses had regular routes up and down the Oodnadatta track taking their paid passengers from around the world on their outback adventure. Of course, we were a major attraction. A phenomenon even, and every time they passed, they'd all disembark for the, *You're never gonna believe this, Kye and Gill tour.*

On one of the visits, I was tired and had no energy to chat, so Gill went over to talk with them. I was happy to wave hello from my chair beside our campfire but completely lacking in ardour to answer the same questions *again*. Gill had his odd moments of seeking hermitage, but he generally loved chatting with people and being the host. Sharing our wild tales of bull camels or the time I'd been kicked in the face, or almost run over by an out-of-control wagon, *twice!* People would look over at me with incredulous gob-smacked looks on their faces. Shaking their heads in astonishment, totally awed that I was even *still* alive. I was indeed a little miracle!

I sat contentedly watching Gill as he stood in a circle of backpackers who were listening to him, enthralled. Periodically I heard big gusts of laughter. Everyone was relaxed and happy and enjoying themselves as Banjo walked into the circle. Gill just kept talking. He did not pause for a second to warn them about the odious beast in their midst. I watched, thinking they would smell him. They were bound to get a whiff, but they didn't. Gill kept talking as Banjo went around the circle. Everyone was loving him, stroking and patting him and giving him a rub on his head. I was sure that at *any* moment, Gill would warn them about our pungently affectionate billy goat. Nup, nothing. He didn't say a word. The wind must have been blowing Banjo's pong away because no one flinched. Not even when Banjo began to rub his face and pissy rank beard up and down on people's jeans. I looked over at Gill in astonishment. *Was he going to tell them? Not* a word from my beloved. I was up and down in my chair; *shall I warn them?* I *really* didn't feel at all sociable. I dithered in indecision long enough for me to realise I was already too late. The damage had been done.

As everyone was climbing back onto the bus, I went over to wave goodbye. I asked Gill why he hadn't said anything about Banjo. "Oh, they're on an adventure. It's all good fun. They'll remember this time," he replied as we watched the bus reversing to get back onto the track. Even over the noise of the engine, we could hear everyone exclaiming inside the bus,

"Pooh, what the fucks that smell?" Everyone was looking at each other as they searched for the culprit of the pong. "What a foul stink. What the hell is it?" They began getting up from their seats and checking their shoes to ensure they hadn't stood in dog shit. I stood watching, a little mortified. This was not a smell that would easily wash out. I couldn't believe that my gentle, loving bushman, who'd sleep all night beside our orphan camels, so they didn't miss their mum and who treated me with such tenderness, was now laughing hysterically because everyone on the bus now stank of billy goat. He was laughing so much. He was bent up on the ground holding his belly, and as much as I thought he'd been really mean and what he'd done was despicable, I just couldn't help myself from laughing too.

Thirteen

Little Willys Everywhere

I never doubted that a new home was our ultimate destination, and while I had no idea where it was, I knew we'd find it. I'd let go of the idea of it being somewhere over east. That prospect was thousands of kilometres away, and we were heading in the wrong direction, and even though we didn't know where we were going, it felt so right.

On days when it was bitterly cold, or I felt low in energy, I would imagine the home that awaited us. I could see it in every detail. The tree-lined driveway, the wooden veranda with the beautiful view where I'd sit and meditate in the morning. I had no doubt in my mind that after letting go of everything, including our home and after being so willing to walk, even if it was a little fearfully, into the unknown, a new home would be waiting. This home would suit all our needs. I could even feel the surge of excitement as I saw us all arriving there.

But there were many days when the thought of arriving at our destination filled me with panic. I knew we were living an experience that may never come again, which made me sad. But of course, it was a double-edged sword and the life we experienced each day with our animals often varied greatly from the world we travelled through. Perhaps in a softer and kinder terrain where everyone loved animals, we could have travelled forever.

My biggest challenge was the roo shooters and aspects of station life that failed to acknowledge the sentience of animals. Whereas for Gill it was rude people and we met many of them. There were days I could have happily set 'The Beebs' on them and watched them run to safety being butted and booted up the arse. It would have given us great pleasure. Having video cameras shoved in your face or people talking about you to each other as they wandered nosily through our camp as if we were not there was maddening. Especially when we were exhausted. Generally, I didn't get *as* frustrated as Gill. I understood how he felt, but we *could* tell people to leave without being rude or creating antagonism.

When you travel in the outback, everyone for hundreds of kilometres knows your coming weeks before you've even arrived. News spread in the pubs, by tourists filling up for fuel, through the network of grey nomads and often by amateur radio. I got the impression by the constant welcomes we received that good things were said, and we wanted to keep it that way. The ease of our journey depended on the people we met along the way.

I didn't want to waste time on people not worthy of it. They were rude and ignorant and didn't care. Shoo them away and get on with our lives, and while we had the odd one, we carried for longer than needed and fumed about for hours; generally, that's what we did. And if I felt Gill was getting irate, I'd just remind him they were not worth it. We were good anchors for each other and helped balance each other out. Rude people, just like my fears, challenged us momentarily. The feelings they left passed with a few deep breaths, sometimes a muffled scream into a pillow and a reminder to self to be eternally grateful we were not them.

It was easy to pick the nature of people by the way they approached us in their cars. We took up a lot of space, and more often than not, people had ample warning we were on the road. Even so, some sped by completely disregarding all the animals, not giving a fuck about anyone, leaving us in a cloud of dust, coughing and spluttering. On they went, racing through the countryside, not seeing a thing.

A common occurrence that was *maddening* was people that would drive around us and then stop their cars on the road right in front of us. They would completely block our way and force us to either stop or move our entire wagon onto the other side of the track if we wanted to keep going. *How could people be so rude?* I just couldn't fathom it. There was so much room for them to pull up off the main track without interrupting our flow. Were they really that selfish that all they thought about was themselves? It certainly appeared like that. It really made us appreciate all those that slowed their speed to a crawl *before* driving around us or stopped their cars completely at a safe distance to watch us pass. And when people approached politely and asked us if it was OK to take a photo, I felt like hugging and kissing them. To show such courtesy to others was becoming so old-fashioned!

There was one car that felt really menacing even as it approached us, and it looked out of place on a tourist track. It was a large and flashy gleaming black 4WD with black tinted windows. *Keep going*, I whispered to myself before realising it was slowing down beside us. I looked up and down the road, hoping more cars were coming, but there were none. With its motor still running, it stopped on the track alongside us. The windows were so black we couldn't see anyone inside, yet they just sat there. Was the long pause before the electric windows wound down calculated for maximum predatory effect? It felt like that, and I wasn't surprised to see five big beefy unsmiling bruisers of men inside. They looked like they'd come out of some bully mould. My inner radar was telling me to be attentive. Menace was prowling around, and I had no doubt Gill felt it. I saw it in his eyes when he gave me a discreet look.

When you live with so many animals, your senses, your ability to read body language, and vibrations become so heightened. You don't even doubt. You can't afford to. Doubt or inattention is the kick in the face. It's the moment when you have mistrusted yourself enough to disconnect with the flow of the moment and allow an accident or catastrophe in. It's as simple as that.

I've experienced a couple of times in my life when I have been hit with a wave of energy that was so strong it had me moving *immediately* in the opposite direction from where I'd been heading. Each time in *that* moment of awareness that I had to move, and *now,* just ahead, was the possibility of an event that could have ended my life violently. I didn't feel that intensity of warning with these men. I knew my life wasn't in danger. It was more a feeling that these men wanted a feed. They were energy vampires that fed on fear, but neither Gill nor I were prepared to give them that. We remained bright and friendly even though we could see their condescending sneers, and the only response we got was a grunt from the driver.

No fear, no feed. Windows were sliding back up again, and off the bully boys went. I was glad to see the back of them. I looked at Gill, relief all over my face, and we both uttered a different word in unison; *"*Crims,*"* I said, while Gill uttered, *"C*ops.*"* We cracked up laughing at that. It's definitely a fine line, and sometimes hard to tell the difference. *"Or Orcs,"* I laughed. On days off, when I managed to devour another chapter of Lord of the Rings, I often felt a kindred soul in Frodo. His was a different journey, but it was also one of trust that pushed him beyond all his limits.

Even though we were laughing as we stood with all our beautiful animals under a bright blue sky where the wintry sun was shining, I felt as if I'd been doused in dirty water from our brief engagement with these men. All I wanted was to get clean.

It was only mid-day, and I asked Gill if he felt OK about us stopping and making camp. We'd already met a few dickheads, and I'd had enough and wanted to be off the road. Gill was more than happy to retreat. Earlier, he'd been out in front leading the camels, and a car had come towards us at a frightening speed. He'd stepped out into the middle of the road and waved his arm up and down to try and get them to slow. They'd accelerated even more as they sped past, showering us all in grit. If they'd been driving in the same direction, we might have concluded they were escaping from the bully boys. Then we may have understood!

It was rare to make camp so early. Getting everyone ready each day was such a massive effort. If we were going to have a lazy day, we at least wanted to start it with a lay-in, but the feeling to stop was so strong. I knew we had to trust in that even though, at first glance, it wasn't the most appealing place to pull up.

As we followed this rough, bumpy track that snaked across the flats to a small grove of trees, I suddenly noticed the stones. They were black, just like tektites, but unlike our obsession, they were everywhere. Bending down to pick one up, I got the shock of my life to see a jet-black smooth rock in the shape of a perfect penis with testicles. My first thought was it must have been someone's long-lost and rather weird fertility pendant, but as I looked closer at the ground, I saw little willys *everywhere*. At the same time, I heard Gill yell out laughingly from the other side of the wagon, "My god, we've arrived at dickhead flats." The irony was not lost on me that after our dick head kinda day, we were in the perfect landscape.

Our response to the negativity in our day had been protective. You don't earn the relationship we had with our animals lightly. Not only had we been bashed and beaten, triggered and trampled to get where we were, but we'd also lived outside in nature *with* all our animals and *only* them for company for over a year. That changes you. It takes you back to the purity of who you are, untarnished. We had reached this *mostly* omnipresent place of peace, and it was *only* from this space everything flowed. I treasured this and was fiercely protective of it. If either of us felt we had to stop and renew, that's what we did. And yet, after the brief few hours we'd spent on the road mingling with the ignoble, neither of us had anticipated the aching belly laughter our day would also bring.

We were camped in a sea of little willys. Little willys everywhere. Some had one testicle, and others had three. Some were limp, others erect. *What an earth had caused this?* Neither of us had ever seen anything like it before. The strange thing was that every willy was circumcised even though the formations came in two very distinct stones.

One was very smooth and jet black, and this one came with testicles, while the other looked like a little canon ball that had been fired onto the site, perhaps by some Gods. It wasn't as black and had a rough surface, and though I know nothing of geology, they looked as if they could have had iron in them. They were slightly misshapen, each one the perfect circumcised bell end of a penis.

We knew no one would believe this discovery. We wouldn't even be able to tell our friends without laughing, so they were unlikely to take us seriously unless we had proof. So, in the gap between jobs all done, animals all happy, and dusk, we went out into the last glowing embers of the day to gather the evidence. We were down on our hands and knees, selecting a range of assorted members to the screeching chorus of a flock of corellas as they flew into the perishing light. We gathered bulging pocketfuls, giggling at our treasures like naughty children.

I had tears rolling down my face from laughing as Gill and I sat on a little hillock in the last gust of light and spontaneously began acting out a puppet show where we gave our rocks voices. Big Barry, a rather well-endowed chappie of a rock chatting with Triple Trev, a rock with three balls and boasting. And as the sun disappeared over the horizon and the dark settled around us, I felt like I'd had the best day. We'd been so right to trust in ourselves and stop. Not only were we guided to the ultimate cosmic joke, but I had also laughed so much that I felt cleansed from inside.

As we made our way back to camp, heading for the silhouettes of our camels and the blaze of our campfire where Banjo was already muscling in, we had our arms wrapped around each other. We both felt buoyant with love and gratitude for our life that never stopped giving. I felt so expansive I could have been twenty feet tall and irrepressible. Whatever load I'd arrived with had been alchemised into pure gold. Feeling worn out from people, I'd sensed my fragility enough to retreat and, in doing so, gone through so much laughter and release. How could I not have seen that even dickheads are heavenly messengers guiding our path? I'd had that huge lesson before with the angry land owners who'd reticently agreed to our two weeks' request to pack up and leave. How could I have forgotten that?

Without the blessings of grit in our faces and cars bulging with bully boys or orcs, we'd have carried on down the track and missed this phenomenal place.

Although it wasn't a place for the prudish or faint-hearted, I had no doubt people would have flocked to this location if they'd known the earth was strewn with little willys. But their secret was safe with us. On a long and boring stretch of road, no one was likely to stop unless the rocks lured them in as they'd done with us. This was a place shielded from the busy, fast-paced lives of those that lived disconnected. Only stalwart adventurers cycling up the track or those on crazy love pilgrimages, like ourselves, were likely to find them. The rocks at this place were holy, and nature always protects its treasures!

The following day we experienced such a shift in the people we met. They restored our faith that there were many good and kind people out there. One very brief and memorable meeting was with a luminous and beautiful young deaf and dumb woman who stood watching us from the edge of the track with her friends. Many other onlookers had also pulled up to stop and watch us pass by. There were so many faces, and yet it was her we noticed. Her face was radiant with joy, and as she held her hands together in a prayer position, she made a circle in the air before placing her hands on her heart. There were tears unashamedly streaming down her face. Her simple tribute had been offered with such raw vulnerability. It was heartfelt and had my own tears flowing.

Others gave us gifts. A bag of oranges, a couple of cold beers, a bar of chocolate, and a loaf of Italian bread. Absolute treasures when you are far from shops and living on a diet that rotates between four different meals and often had us craving treats.

One couple, on their way home from a weekend's camping, dropped off all the food they had left over. They had asked us uncertainly if we would like it. "It's not much," they said, "there is a bottle of wine, some chocolate, a bag of cherries, some pistachios, cakes and biscuits and various gourmet dips. Do you think you'd want it?"

"Holy Fuck, YES PLUEEESE" had been my rather enthusiastic response which had the couple laughing. We failed every previous lesson on binge eating and had the best feast and the worst gut ache after. Dare I say it, "we were never EVER going to do that again!"

But there was one man we met who really stood out. He had a story I will remember forever. We'd met him briefly a few times on our trek. He had his own minibus and operated small outback tours. Each time we'd met him, he'd had tourists on board, so we'd never had a chance to chat, which was always disappointing. I found him intriguing. He exuded serenity and had the most incredible crystal clear, bright sparkly blue eyes. Probably in his late sixties, and to add to his general vibe of peace and beneficence, he had a long silvery Santa beard.

Our 4WD was already parked ahead at the place we'd intended to camp, and it was late in the day when we finally reached it. This man who introduced himself as Harry was already there and asked us if he could camp with us. I was delighted by this. He was taking a break from the tourists, and finally, we had him to ourselves.

Having such a deep connection with our animals, I am always aware of how other people greet them. There's an equality often missing for our dear animal friends. People can call into a home where a dog lives and not even think about saying hello, and yet that's *his* home. For many, animals are lower-class citizens unworthy of attention, let alone honour or respect. When I saw Harry down on his knees introducing himself to our dogs, I knew precisely why I'd been drawn to him. He was one of us, and it was easy to see that the animals loved him. I could even see the camels turn their heads towards him, deeply curious about this human whose energy field felt so free and unburdened. They were unused to that. They were slowly helping liberate Gill and me, and while I felt Gill was much more masterful than I was and held in much higher esteem, Harry was off the charts.

After we'd eaten, Gill built up the fire, and we sat around it watching the flickering flames. Banjo's stanky danky pissy pong of a head was nestled in Harry's lap while

Harry stroked our loveable billy goats ears and massaged his head as he told us his story.

In another lifetime that seemed very far away, Harry had been a very successful high-flying entrepreneur living the good life. He flew around the world meeting clients and went on luxurious holidays with his wife. He lived in a beautiful mansion, had a holiday house or two and had everything that money could buy him, including several luxury cars. Then one day, something happened that turned his world upside down.

He had a passion for riding trail bikes. One sunny afternoon he was blatting along a bush track when an emu ran out unexpectedly in front of him. There was no time to swerve or try and avoid it, and he hit it at speed, throwing it into the air. He told us everything appeared to happen in slow motion. For a moment, just before they both crashed to the ground, time suspended completely as the emu and Harry looked into each other's eyes.

When Harry came too, he was lying in the dirt, the bike was on its side still running, and the emu was lying beside him, dead.

"That was the moment when my life changed." Harry told us

"When you look into an animal's eyes as it passes over, its spirit leaps into you, but of course, I didn't figure that out until much, much later."

When he'd returned home from that trip, he'd told us, nothing about his life made any sense. A switch inside had flipped. All the things that had mattered to him suddenly appeared nonsensical. He couldn't comprehend doing *anything* for money. He stopped going into his office and wasn't bothered if everything he'd built fell apart. He just didn't care. His huge house that he'd been so proud of now appeared pretentious and ugly, and he didn't even want to be in it. The only peace he felt was in his garden, so he built himself a little bush shack that he moved into. He stopped mowing the lawns and let nature reclaim his extensively manicured gardens. His wife thought he'd gone insane and left him, cleaning out all the bank accounts, selling the silver and taking the deeds to their other homes. He didn't care about any of it. For the first time in his life, he felt happy and free. His garden became such a wilderness. It was a haven for wildlife. There he was in posh suburbia, with his hair growing long, his beard even longer, his pants and clothes ripped and tatty and all the wild creatures for miles and miles flocking to his haven. It all sounded so beautiful and sane to me. Of course, it wasn't long before the 'good Samaritans' on his street began complaining to the council. His uncut lawns were letting down the neighbourhood, and heaven forbid, they thought he was pooping in the garden. They began to cause so much trouble he knew his only rational choice was to leave. He felt very sad to leave the animals. He had developed a wonderful connection with them and let them all know he had to go. He could feel the spirit of the emu inside him urging him out into the desert, telling him to let go of everything and roam free.

He packed up his 4WD with his essentials, said goodbye to his animal friends, sent his ex-wife the key and drove away to his new life, and never looked back.

After a year of following whims and currents and wandering like a wild emu across the desert, he decided to turn his Landcruiser 4WD into a tour bus. That way, he could still roam freely while sharing his love of the desert with tourists. Some paid, some didn't. Money didn't matter to Harry. He was finally doing what he loved.

We all sat in silence after Harry finished his story. Such a transcendent tale needed a big pause for breath. We'd all been so immersed in Harry's story that the fire had dwindled to a pile of red-hot coals. Gill threw a few more logs on, sending embers shooting up into the night sky. I felt so blessed sitting with this man. Finally, a person we could be ourselves with. Even when we told him we didn't have a destination, I knew it wouldn't be a big deal, and it wasn't. We all lived trusting in life, living in flow, and we had the same gentle ways of being and respecting nature and the animals. I didn't even need to explain why we were living so boldly or tell Harry that animals were conscious beings. He had the spirit of an emu and had spent months living in his garden, communing with nature and the birds. It was a relief being with a kindred spirit. That was so rare for us, and our time together was precious and holy.

I felt quite sad as we waved him off in the morning, unsure if we'd ever meet again. He was going in a different direction as the tourist season had come to an end. A flagrant reminder that our track would imminently end, and we also needed a safe haven before the temperatures began to rise.

I certainly pondered the synchronicity of meeting Harry, or Emu man, as we fondly called him, because our next destination was to the homestead of a man known as Eagle man. All I knew was that he fed the wild wedge-tailed eagles. While I couldn't wait to hear his story, I felt really unsettled because of a dream I'd had the night before.

I hadn't mentioned it to Gill in the morning. Partly because we were both revelling in the last few moments with Harry, but also because I'd dismissed it as just a dream which wasn't exactly working. In fact, I couldn't stop thinking about it, and it made me feel really anxious. I'd had similar dreams before, and they'd always happened.

This dream was about my sulphur-crested cockatoo, Jo.

Whenever we stopped for a couple of days, we'd let Jo out. He looked so majestic flying through the sky. It was hard to remember the broken-spirited bird he'd been when we offered him a home. I'd worried about how he'd cope with being more confined as we travelled, never anticipating that he'd also grow and bloom in unexpected ways. We were all expanding beyond our limitations. The love we all shared gave him a firm foundation to be himself, and the more confident he became, the cheekier and more playful he got. He loved to grab hold of my jacket and tug it or nick something I was using and fly away with it. He had such a cheeky nature.

As Jo's trust in me grew, so did our telepathic communication and sometimes disturbingly so. He could get right inside my head if there was something he wanted. He did this better than any other animal we had. One woman we'd met from a station had said, "Oh, I don't like those birds. It's like they get inside your head." While I couldn't comprehend anyone not liking a bird, I understood exactly what she meant. Jo would do it with the most piercingly intense look that bored into me. Even if I wasn't looking at him, I could feel his deeply penetrating gaze.

I loved Jo so much and felt really distressed to have a dream telling me I must let him go; he was ready to leave. I knew what this meant. I'd had a couple of these dreams before with different birds. Always birds, and each time these dreams had sent me into a protective frenzy. I'd do everything in my power to make death impossible, yet each time I'd failed. Something completely out of my control had occurred that I hadn't anticipated.

I kept trying to convince myself the dream was just a dream. Everything was fine. Jo wasn't going to die. The dream had only bought up my fears about losing Jo. It was obviously triggered by knowing we were about to visit a man who fed several wedge-tailed eagles. Well, Jo would have to stay in his cage. There was no way I was letting him out with eagles around. If I had been honest with myself, I would have seen clearly what Jo already had. I was prepared to keep him in a cage not only until the eagles had passed but until my fears had, whenever that may be. Oh, but I was good at convincing myself. *It's just to keep him safe from the eagles. Deep breath Kye, no need to worry. Just shake off all that stress. Jo will be fine in his cage.*

As we trundled down the road, getting closer to Eagle man, I could already feel the intensity of Jo's gaze boring into my back, trying to get my attention. He didn't mind a few days in his cage but an indefinite stay because I was afraid? There I was locking Jo up, and I hadn't even asked what my very bright and highly communicative feathered friend wanted. He didn't like that. Who would? But I was so afraid that I wasn't prepared to budge. I loved him, and I wanted him safe, and I kept convincing myself I was doing it for Jo. Yet, I had a sickening feeling like sand slipping through my fingers, and it wouldn't go away. If I'd been wiser at that moment, I might have recognised that the sickening feeling was because I'd dumped everything I valued. I'd replaced the love that I lived by with fear.

But growth takes time, and sometimes when we are standing in the dark, it's hard to see even when one of your dearest friends is doing everything he can to get your attention. Jo was piercing me with an intensity I could not ignore, and there would be no peace until I listened.

This was *his* life, and he mattered!

And I should never have forgotten that truth.

Fourteen

Initiation

When we finally met up with Eagle man, I had to wonder if we'd gone through some sort of vortex back at Penis Plains as it later, rather jovially, became known. It was as if we'd landed in a parallel dimension. We had gone from bullyboys and orcs to big-hearted open men in one vast willy of a night. We'd even met a tourist on the road who'd told us, kinda incredulously, about a seaside café further south. It was run by a woman that spoke with aliens and was anticipating the arrival of the inland sea!

That surely couldn't be true, not in the rugged outback!

Eagle man had given Gill directions on the phone about where we could camp and told us he would call down later. The sky was a pastel wash of lavender, and the sun was just a simmering glow on the horizon when our host appeared. Most of the chickens had already retired to their home for the night, but The Colonel was still pecking at the dirt around our feet. We must have looked funny. Us standing out there in that red dusty desert, in the cusp between day and night, with a big red friendly rooster besides us. Not to mention all the other critters!

But the moment I saw Ronnie, or Eagle man as he was known by many, I loved him. He was an Arabana aboriginal man and one of the custodians of the land we were on. He had a smile that lit him up and emanated from his whole body. Nothing about Ronnie was watered down or feeble. When he offered me his hand to shake, the strength that came from him was like plugging into a power socket. When he pulled us both close, giving us the biggest hug, it felt like being in a freshly laundered rocket launch. After travelling so long, washing the same old raggy clothes over and over again in buckets and bore water and never really getting them clean, the smell of those freshly washed clothes was intoxicating. *Almost* as delicious as chocolate.

I felt an immediate recognition. My heart, body, and spirit knew this man from some other time, and just like Gill, I felt rapt that our paths had met again. I felt so welcomed, like I was a little lost chick who'd finally been tucked safely back under her mummy hen's wing. Only I hadn't known I'd been lost.

I didn't ask Ronnie how we smelt. Wafts of 'odour du billy goat' and smoky fires laced with a salty, sweaty slap was very likely. He did, however, offer us the use of a bath house. It was in a building that stood separately from an empty house across the road from his home. There was unlimited hot water, and we were told to make ourselves at home. "Relax and enjoy," he said as he disappeared back into his house, "I'll catch you tomorrow."

It was an old bathroom that could have once been for the station workers. The water was heated by a wood fire lit under a giant donkey that Ronnie must have cranked up earlier in the day when he knew we were coming. He'd told us we could use all the hot water. It was *all* for us! The floors were concrete, and it was very utility, and I liked that. I felt relaxed and comfortable. We didn't have to worry if we splashed water on the floor or got the bath mat dripping wet as there wasn't one. This was the perfect bathroom for me, and it had an old enamel bathtub that was the most enormous bath we had *ever* seen. Gill and I sat at each end, up to our necks in hot water, and we could have easily fitted another person or two in-between. We sat in a steaming oasis of cleanliness for hours. I hadn't realised until that moment how familiar my body had become with bruises and scratches, aches and pains. There were so many marks on my body I hadn't known were there. Bruises I had no memory of, purple stains on my skin and one big, slightly livid scratch across my thigh. *When had I got that?* These were the everyday repercussions of a life that gruellingly pushed us past our limits every single day.

But all our wounds received absolution in that bath that night.

The following day when we called in to see Ronnie, he was out the back of his house. Two huge wedge-tailed eagles sat regally perched on his garden fence. They were completely at ease with him as he threw them hunks of fur and bones, which they grabbed from the air, held in their talons and ripped apart with their massive beaks. Shredding whatever animal it had been into pieces in seconds.

With two majestic eagles sitting behind him, *just a typical day for Ronnie*, he began to tell us his story.

"Until my bike accident," he told us, "I had never been close to an eagle." I certainly had a feeling of déjà vu as he began his tale, and I heard, just like Emu man, it started on a motorbike. Evidently, a key ingredient in these sacred initiations.

Ronnie told us there'd been so much rain the earth was covered in wildflowers. All the bush quandongs were full of fruit that was ripe and juicy, but the rabbits had bred up too, and they were everywhere.

It was nighttime, and he was riding his dirt bike down a bush track with the headlight on, driving slowly because rabbits were darting across in front of his bike. He was very attentive as he tried to avoid them. Suddenly he felt a massive whack on his back, and he was thrown from his bike. When we regained consciousness, he was laying on his back in the dirt with wedge tail eagle feathers scattered around him. The only logical explanation he could find was that an eagle, focused on the rabbit in the headlights, had not seen him on the bike and collided with him.

It was such a similar story to Harry though Emu man certainly appeared to have had a more total metamorphous. His encounter had led to the death of the emu, which mirrored the end of life as Harry had known it. The eagle may have survived, yet these men had both been hugely influenced by the birds they'd collided with.

Ronnie told us how he used to have a reputation as a fighter. He got into pub brawls and could take on several men at once and beat them. I must have looked aghast because Ronnie laughed at my expression. I could not imagine this peaceful, beautiful man fighting, *ever*! But then he shared that he had been a drinker and lived a very different life to the one he lived now.

Neither of these men saw these encounters as accidents. Events that catapult us so intensely into new awareness are initiations.

It was no surprise that Ronnie had been chosen by the eagles, a bird that soared above all others. He appeared to be a man of presence and power, as well as vision. A unique industrial sculpture park had been built on the land he cared for. Well known by travellers up and down this track who couldn't drive past it without seeing the small planes standing upright on their tailless ends or the huge water tank that looked like a giant dog.

I'd felt an instant rapport with Ronnie. If I had a tribe, he was in it and feeling this was extraordinary. After our night with Emu man when I'd thought I needed to wring every morsel of goodness out of the night and cherish it forever, because meeting kindred souls was so rare, here we were with another remarkable man and only a few sleeps later!

The connection between us all was palpable, and it felt so precious. To describe it or even speak of it would have sounded clunky. We could tell Ronnie felt it, too. He made it very clear we could stay for as long as we liked and even threw around possibilities of us staying there forever. It was indeed a tempting thought to entertain.

The following day he gave us directions to drive out to some abandoned buildings where the original station had been and look around. I felt excited as we drove down the roughest dirt road and across a dry creek. It was hard to even see the track. It had been a long time since it had been used. Decades even. Many times we thought we had lost our way completely because the trail was so rough. *Was it even a trail we followed?* We didn't know, and we were just about to give up and return to Ronnie's when we saw the buildings. We made it!

Once, this station had been a bustling place employing many workers. Now it was all crumbling and falling down. Old horse carts and early model cars were sitting in clumps of grass, fading into the landscape that was claiming them. I find these old places so intriguing. In the periphery of my awareness, the ghosts of the past were all still there. The air was laden with their whispers. All their voices that had faded and frayed with time.

We knew a little about the history. Since leaving Alice, we had travelled a route stained with the blood of the aboriginal people of this land, but here we found a happier story. This place had been a safe haven. It was built in 1922 by a white settler called Francis. He was the son of a prestigious politician and had married a local Arabana woman named Braida and bought up a family of seven children.

As we travelled, we'd spoken to so many different people and heard all sorts of stories of aboriginal children that had been hidden in an attempt to keep them safe from the government officials who prowled the land, stealing them. Some were put inside the tucker boxes the camels carried, or lowered down wells, or even tucked inside hollow trees. Of course, taking the children was done under the guise of 'helping them, but if you break up *any* family or separate anyone from their culture, you stand a much better chance of disempowering them.

Frances had stood firm here, and none of the children were taken. He flat-out refused. Later, a school was established and a church and children received a traditional and European education. It was a thriving mission until nineteen fifty-eight, when Frances died. Within two years, it had closed. Without the visionary, the vision had died.

I always found it galling seeing buildings fall into ruin, especially when, with a team of people, they could have been saved. I could have seen us building something so worthwhile with Ronnie, but not on this land. It was beautiful. I even loved the remoteness, but the energy felt bound up, and I didn't know why. I could only presume it was because too many people were involved in the decisions concerning this land. With too much divergence, that dynamic can stifle.

I felt sad as we drove back. I knew this wasn't our home, and that felt so clear, but it had given us a safe haven. I'd deeply relaxed and got *really* clean, but best of all, there were no 1080 baits laid. We were able to take our dogs to some natural springs for a swim and a walk. This station had many natural springs, though several had dried up since the mine had opened at Roxby Downs. The underground water was becoming more and more depleted. This was a considerable concern for Ronnie, especially as the mine was planning expansion.

Leaving wasn't black or white for me emotionally. I knew it wasn't the right place for us, but I still found myself pondering if we could make it right. Even with the natural springs drying up and family dynamics, I was still torn. Tired and torn. There was a part of me that felt such love for Ronnie. I just wanted to call it a day and settle down. I know how rare it is to meet people you really connect with. I didn't want to let that go. Was it possible that we could create an epic vision here despite the issues? I would have moments when I would sink into imagining it, but it never felt like a straightforward option. I just got a messy feeling, like the feeling inside a house where no one ever took the rubbish out. Staying with Ronnie was not an option, and we only had one choice. That was to go. If only it had been Ronnie's land, I would have stayed happily nestled under this man's wing.

Life didn't make it easy for us. The day we left, it was bitterly cold, and we were travelling into the wind. The prospect of a world outside Ronnie's vast presence had felt cold anyway. I sat hunched up in the front of the wagon, wearing so many clothes I could barely move, yet I felt chilled to my bones. There had been no words to say goodbye. Just hugs and feelings and tears.

We were now in the final leg to Maree. Only fifty kilometres to the end of the Oodnadatta track. We had found out that the dirt track continued further to the town of Lyndhurst, but it turned to tarmac after that. I had no idea what we would do then or where we would go. I could only keep myself as much as I could present to each moment and remind myself, once again, to trust.

While we never usually made deadlines, we were aware that the Maree camel races were on the following week. We didn't want to navigate a town, even a tiny one, with all our animals when it was busy. If we could get through *before*, all well and good. We had no desire to see the races. I've only been to them once in Alice, and I was appalled. When a camel is bawling, it is distressed. When it is shitting itself, it's either afraid, upset or stressed. I saw so many camels at those races that were in evident stress, and yet all around them, people were getting drunk and laughing at the noise they made. It's no wonder people think these beautiful creatures spit and kick and are so gobsmacked to find a happy camel is the complete opposite.

We'd met some lovely cameleers that we'd stayed with further up the track who really loved their camels and usually entered the races, but none of their camels had nose pegs. That would have created a very different dynamic that involved mutual cooperation. I might have formed a different view if I'd seen happy camels not being bullied or harassed to race in races they didn't want to run. Instead, I saw nose pegs used as tools of abuse by people who called themselves a cameleer. I lasted less than ten minutes at the races and left in tears. Walking past loads of people I knew, trying to hold myself together long enough to get to my car, where I broke down crying. I had no intention of going to another camel race. I wanted to get through Maree way before the races occurred.

We travelled fifteen kilometres the day we left Ronnies. Our camp for the night was in a beautiful place with huge peeling barked gum trees all along the big wide creek bed. We were no longer on his land, and prior to ringing the station we had just entered, I'd felt very nervous about phoning the land owners of the property. Apart from that one miserable woman, everyone had been welcoming and friendly. Yet we had been warned by a few people that this man loathed cameleers and was likely to be rude. I lost the toss, so the call fell on me. I didn't want to ring up with an expectation of how he would respond, so I tried to set it aside. Of course, it's never nice dealing with nasty people, but when you're out in the world with such a big tribe, there are times you can feel really vulnerable. When you're tired, or it's cold and windy, or worst of all, when you just want to go home but you don't have one. That feeling is a bummer! This time my sensitivity was still adjusting to coming out from under Ronnie's wing.

So, I rang this man, and what a surprise. He was lovely. In a sweet voice, he thanked me for phoning and letting him know we were travelling through and told me to have an enjoyable time. I had been dreading that call. It was another lesson in embracing these situations openly without prejudice. I felt that communicating with people courteously *before* we arrived at their stations paved the way for us to be received so well.

I let out a huge sigh of relief after the phone call. We could relax, all was well in our world, and we had been welcomed.... once again.

I was pretty sure we were far enough away from the danger of Ronnie's eagles to finally let Jo out. He had been caged for almost a week and was getting restless and screechy, but the prospect reawakened my fears. *But what about my dream?* I hadn't given it any thought since we'd arrived at Ronnie's, but now faced with opening his cage door, I felt anxious. Jo was staring at me with an intensity so fierce I could feel him boring through my skull like a drill. When I tried to ignore him, he began to squawk, louder and louder. It's the most deafening noise, so loud and tortuous you will do anything for it to stop. But he wasn't going to stop until I listened to him.

When I spoke with Gill, he told me I should listen to Jo, "it's his life and his choices, not yours." I knew he was right. I knew I couldn't keep limiting Jo's life because of my fear.

My hand shook a little as I undid his latch and opened his door. "You stay safe, Jo," I warned him. "Make sure you come back." I'd already told him about the dream a hundred times. He still wanted out. Death is of no consequence to animals. It is only us fearful mortals, separated from our divinity, who think the body is all there is.

The relief that came from him was palpable. Tension unwound, a sigh of relief. He left his cage with a raucous screech. Big white wings flapping as he flew up into the sky and headed for a big silvery barked ghost gum growing on the edge of the dry creek and landed on a branch. I watched him for a while, scanning the sky avidly for predators. I'm unsure what I'd have done if I'd seen one. It's not as if I had wings and could fly up and save him, all I could do was worry, and I did enough of that. I had to let go. I couldn't control everything. I felt stressed, and only when I sat down with a cup of tea did I realise it wasn't just about Jo and his safety. It was the end of the dirt road. I felt so vulnerable and completely at the mercy of people's good intentions or not.

And I know I always talk of the good people we met, but we always filtered who we were. Would people have liked us if we'd been ourselves? Because while I loved so many good and beautiful people we met, if I could have changed the way they profited from animals, I would have loved too. I would have stopped all the roos being killed and banned fucking 1080 bait, and let the dingos live wild and free.

The completely contrasting way we lived our lives regarding our animals bought up my vulnerability. This was always a very dualistic aspect of my life on the road. And it wasn't a lie to experience the good with people. I generally love people and can usually find a common thread to connect. People do what they have always done and often don't question. That's all. When animals are your income, you can't see their sentience because your focus is profit. There is no space for conscious connection and holy communion. You can only have that sacred relationship when you have let go of dollar signs and self-gain. Only then can you meet an animal in awareness and actually see who they are.

And yes, I always look for the good and try and stay focused on what matters, but I was tired. Really deeply tired and not so much from the physical challenges, but from the harshness of the outback. It can be so hard. It's not a place of soft feminine energy, which didn't help my fragility. *What on earth would we do when the dirt road ran out?* And it was me that answered myself. The wise version, not the worrying one. *Stay in trust, Kye, and keep focused on now. You know you are being guided. You will be shown a way.*

Fifteen

Holy Circle of Love

I stood under the huge gum tree, shading my eyes from the early morning sun, looking up to see if I could find Jo amidst its leafy branches. When I found him, he was nonchalantly chomping his way through some tender leafy shoots he'd stripped from the branch as if he had all the time in the world and no adventure to return to. When he saw me, he dropped his leafy shoots, and they spiralled down to the ground and landed like a half-eaten gift beside me. I watched him with amusement as he shifted his position to peer down at me. With his bum in the air and his head below the branch, staring straight at me, he gave me that look that could pierce my very being. He communicated with the precision of an arrow going straight for its target. Bullseye every time! I had zero doubt that he was not coming back…yet. He was so full of attitude. He sat himself up, threw back his head with such drama, his pale-yellow plume feathers fanned out on his head like a crown and then, with his best cocky swagger, he took off marching along his branch, screeching. What a show-off.

Our coffee percolator was just starting to bubble as I returned with the news. Jo wasn't ready to leave his tree...yet. After such an extensive time in a cage, I couldn't blame him. We had planned to drive to Marree and check out the condition of the road. It wasn't far, but I didn't really want to leave Jo out.

I loved sitting around our campfire and having our morning coffee. Before we left Alice, we'd found in an op shop the most perfect stainless-steel coffee percolator that brewed two perfect cups. While it was completely blackened from all the fires it had been on, it was one of our most treasured possessions. Gill poured the coffee, and we sat enjoying our morning ritual. It was always a time of solace before the outbreak of our day when it was usually go, go, go! We both sat contemplating what to do with our wayward bird. Gill finally said, "We won't be long. I reckon Jo will be OK."

We drove into town, did what we needed and drove home. When we arrived back at camp, I gave Jo a call, and I heard him screeching in reply from his tree. I had this little happy moment, feeling so much gratitude for the love we shared with these animals. Jo was excitedly responding to me, calling him. I couldn't help smiling as I watched this jovial clown of a parrot launch himself into the air to fly back to camp. He could have flown anywhere, yet after all his years of being shut up, he was flying back to us and his home in the wagon. I was laughing. He was making so much noise. *Look at me, look at me.* Bountiful waves of exuberance emanated from this bird who'd once been a shadow of himself. Knowing that we had helped him find his joy in life made me feel even happier.

I was just about to gather some wood for the fire when I felt a physical chill rush up through my body, and I knew it was to do with Jo. I turned and looked up at the sky, holding my breath, feeling desperately anxious yet praying it was only my imagination.

Jo was almost home when from out of nowhere, a huge wedge-tailed eagle appeared. I didn't know if it was Ronnie's, these birds live everywhere, but it was flying in pursuit of Jo. Big slow flaps of its giant wings while Jo still screeched exuberantly with all his attention on me.

I ran out into the open, yelling at the eagle, pleading, praying. "Please, please don't get my Jo." I had never felt so powerless. I wanted to faint and spew and scream. Yet, despite this, I was also aware that something beyond my current awareness was happening, and it felt colossal. As if all of life had been distilled down into this very moment. The sky had become a vivid blue, and with each laboured, heaving, teary breath of mine, I could taste the fragrant blossoms in the gum trees. I could smell the soft sweet chalky smell of Jo. I could even hear the heartbeat of the eagle. In the intensity of the moment, which felt like one long slow drip from a tap before it splattered on the ground, I knew Jo had never felt more joy, and he had never felt freer. He screeched his happiness to the heavens.

I watched it feeling sick. My precious Jo was plucked from the sky by his predator. It was all over so quick. One minute he was clowning, making such a ruckus and the next, hanging limp in the talons of this mighty bird. I ran out, yelling at the eagle. I wanted Jo back. He was so full of life that he couldn't be dead. Surely not? I screeched at the eagle, "Give me Jo back." The eagle dropped him. I ran so fast to where he'd fallen and found him, my little white love, lying on the shale-covered earth. So perfect and warm, he looked nearly alive, but his neck had been broken. I crouched over his body, sobbing. I'd known he was getting ready to leave us, but knowing, hadn't helped. My friend had gone. I wept on my hand and knees until Gill came and led me back to camp as I cradled Jo's still warm body to my heart.

Even in my raw pain, I knew that death was not the end. I sat holding Jo until my sobs subsided. I had such an empty ache inside. Then I heard some words, spoken so clearly as if a wiser part of myself had stepped in and taken over. *Jo left because he was ready. He had consciously chosen his death because his earthly cycle was complete. He left this earth soaring with the eagles, and in the moment he was plucked from the sky, he could not have been any happier.*

I sighed with relief. It didn't stop the ache of his loss, but it helped. He'd made his death such a public affair. I knew he hadn't wanted me to worry. It could have happened while we were out, and I wouldn't have known where he'd gone. I'd have spent weeks out in the bush looking for him. He'd also passed over in the most gregarious display of joy, even gathering those he loved for his parting ceremony. Yet I'd given tears and not flowers. We as little humans have so much to embrace around death and its joyful and unfolding expansion into the realms of love. I knew all this, but on the human level, I was in grief. I have all my conditioning too.

In the golden hues of last light, raw and puffy-eyed, I made a little cairn of stones over Jo's body with Gill. We had tried to dig a grave, but the ground was rock hard. It was like chipping into stone. I was still crying as we said our farewells and thanked him for coming into our lives. I kept thinking any moment he would wake up and this would have all been a dream, but he didn't, and our pile of stones just grew.

I felt lighter by the morning with an unexpected sense of release. I'd been burdened with dread for weeks. Worrying about my little mate and how I could guard against his death. It had been an enormous strain, and it had suddenly gone. The deed was done, and the weight had lifted. I still felt heartbroken, but Jo was in my heart where he would always be, and I'd tucked a few of his tail feathers under my pillow.

The following morning, as Gill said the magic words "Pull em up," and the parrots and dogs began their morning cacophony, it was much more subdued. Even so, Lady Caroline, was pushing impatiently into her harness, keen to go. When our wagon surged forward, it was with such enthusiasm the rest of the camels began to cavort excitedly. We were off in a bound of excitement. Feeling the energy, our dogs and parrots howled and screeched even louder, but Jo was still a massive loss to our cheerleading team. Without his vast presence, our wagon felt empty inside. The squawks from our other parrots were nowhere near as boisterous. It would take a while to come to terms with our Jo-less wagon, but I wanted to make up for Jo's loss of noise. To leave with his spirit of rowdiness and fun. I picked up a long metal rod and began banging it on the tin of the wagon. For the first time, I was a part of the morning ruckus. As we lurched forward, making an almighty din that Jo would have been proud of, I was clanking and clanging and yelling out, "We love you, Jo, WE LOVE YOU, thankyoooo, we love you," and in all the exuberance of the moment, I couldn't stop myself from crying.

Under an overcast and thunderous-looking sky, we travelled fifteen kilometres before it began to plop with rain. We had no choice but to pull up. We had hoped to reach Maree, only a few kilometres away, but that didn't happen. For the next four days, it poured with rain. Never-ending torrential mud splattering rain. We lived in a sea of mud, and every time we had to go out to tend our camels, who fortunately were all enjoying the lush feed, we came back with shoes the size of footballs. They were so caked in mud. My feet were so heavy I could barely move. One slow lumbering step after the other, each one heavier than before. It was a relief to get back under our tarp even though our fire was smoking from all the wet wood. We'd put our boots beside the fire to dry and then crumble off the mud in layers. When our boots were mud free, it would be time to go out again.

Our camp was a steaming, smoky muddy huddle of dogs and chickens. Right in the middle, keeping himself toasty and warm as all billy goats with high self-esteem do, was Banjo. I had no idea how he had ever survived without us. This goat loved his home comforts.

We camped in this spot for a week until the road dried out, and we began to see traffic on the track again. We knew by this time that the camel races if they'd even happened with all the rain, would be over. As long as the roads were quiet and we missed the hoo-hah of the camel races, before or after didn't matter to us.

The first car that stopped, intrigued by the spectacle of our life on the road, was a farmer and his twelve-year-old daughter. He asked if we'd been trying to get to the camel races. When I told him that camels are usually very sedentary and don't like racing, he looked relieved. With tears in his eyes, he told us he'd taken his daughter to the races, but he would never go again. "I breed cows and sell them," he said, "but I was horrified at what I saw, and my daughter shouldn't have had to see it."

I felt physically sick as he told us what had happened. I'd really stood alone with my stance on camel racing. So many people that I knew liked it. They entered their camels or rode in them. I'd had times I'd questioned if I'd been too reactive. Had I only witnessed a one-off incident, but I always kept coming back to the camels I'd seen in the yards, and so many of them were showing signs of distress. Anxious animals were enough reason to be repelled by this sport, but the abusive handling of the camel I'd seen *should* have been totally unacceptable. Many people saw that young cameleer using all his weight as he hung from his camel's nose line when he couldn't get it to sit. The race was about to start, and it was down to brute force to get that poor camel into position. Not only was the camel bawling, but it also happened right at the start line when everyone was watching the track.

Very often, camels do sit down if they're stressed. If they get pushed too far, they shut down. Evidently, this was what had happened at the Maree races. A camel wouldn't get up, and they wanted to position it to race. They tried to get it up by hitting it with black plastic poly pipes. It just sat there bawling. When it still didn't respond and had even refused to move when they pulled its nose line, they put ropes around it and dragged it behind a car as it sat on its knees.

"It was horrible," he said, and I could feel the emotion in his voice, "I felt so sick from watching them hurt that animal, and it really upset my daughter. No animal should be treated like that. I'm appalled."

I felt sober and sad hearing this man's experience of the races. He was wise enough to recognise cruelty and abuse and not just see a nasty spitting animal, as many do. I would prefer not to see any animal used for sport, but *if* it is going to happen, why not lift the standard? These events could showcase a harmonious connection between a cameleer and his camel. We have horse whisperers. Where are all the camel whisperers? And no, it's not us. If there was any whispering to be done, it would be our camels demonstrating how they'd whispered to us and *not* the other way around.

I have such a deep appreciation for these animals. My life was irrevocably woven with our camels, and gratitude comes nowhere close to describing the beautiful bonds of affection we'd developed with them all. These quirky, frustrating, hilarious, loving creatures that many misunderstand, believing they are nasty, aggressive animals that only spit and kick because they have only ever seen them poorly treated. I was happy to introduce our camels to everyone we met because I wanted people to know the truth for themselves.

I felt a grief about me as we approached Maree, missing Jo, sadness at our conversation with the farmer. Lonely. We had just reached our insurmountable destination, and there was no accolade. No one cheering us on. No friends to greet us or celebrate with us the heroic feat we'd accomplished. We'd finally made it to the outskirts of a tiny outback town that was the completion of the Oodnadatta track. Unbelievably we had travelled over one thousand kilometres! Many thought we wouldn't make it. I'd thought we wouldn't make it, and here we all were.

The town was spookily quiet, like a ghost town. The camel races had evidently been and gone, thank goodness. We could hear the rusty creaking of roadside signage flapping in the wind, really adding to the unnerving empty feeling of the town. The camels were looking around nervously though they kept going, but they were alert. The biggest scare for them was all the huge signs, one after the other, as we entered the town. Advertising the servo, the pub, the caravan park and everything and anything this tiny town had to offer. After hundreds of kilometres of bush, it was such an infringement on the usually bare sides of the roads. We kept going, reassuring the camels as we looked around nervously ourselves. Where was everyone?

Gill was out in front leading the team, reassuring Lady Caroline. She was looking around anxiously, though trusting in Gill enough to know that if he was leading, she'd be safe.

On we went, past the silent servo, on past a few houses that felt empty and bereft. What was going on? Had everyone been sucked into a black hole, never to be seen again? There was no childish laughter and not even a dog barked!

We could even see the bush opening up on the other side of town. Not far to go. The camels were picking up their stride, keen to leave the ghostliness of this town behind, when something *really* unexpectedly wonderful happened.

We were literally only a long fence and one house away from leaving the town. We were about halfway down the long fence when a man wearing a turban popped his head over the fence and exclaimed, "Oh my goodness, look, everyone, camels." Suddenly a gate creaked open, and people began to stream out into the street in vast numbers. Screeching, screaming, cheering, and laughing. All of a sudden, we were surrounded by hundreds of people. Media crews were filming us, and people were taking photos. Others stood with gob-smacked expressions as if they couldn't believe their eyes. They kinda mirrored my own expression. Where had all these people come from? Many of the men wore turbans and looked of Indian descent. The camels had stopped walking in all the commotion and were standing perfectly still, so I put the brake on and jumped down.

My only concern was my highly-strung flighty love of a camel, Rockhole, tied from the back of the wagon and surrounded by people coming in so close. I didn't want anyone to get kicked. I gave a few warnings to people to give the camels space. One kid was even firing a cap gun, yet our magnificent team stood there looking so proud and beautiful. Oh, my goodness, I adored them. They made me buckle at the knees with pride and joy.

We knew beforehand that at the same time as the camel races, there was to be an Afghani cameleer reunion, but we thought they would be long gone. We had not anticipated or expected to arrive in the midst of their party.

This reunion was for the descendants of the original Afghani cameleers. They began arriving in outback Australia to work the teams of camels bought into the country from Karachi around the 1860s. These cameleers came from numerous countries that had a tradition of camels, including Pakistan, parts of India and Kashmir. Still, they were all lumped under the term,' Afghani' The Afghanis and their camels were responsible for opening up the outback and making it possible for white settlers to live in more remote places. The camels carried in loads to places where horses could not go. Yet despite this, the Afghanis received the same persecution the aboriginals did. Many Afghani descendants are also part aboriginal because it was the aboriginals these cameleers often lived with and eventually married.

Tears had been pretty close to the surface since Jo had gone, but standing among all these excited people, my tears flowed in joy. Our friends hadn't been there, but that holy current of love that ran through everything we did, keeping us connected with a force way bigger than little us, had bestowed us with its own celebration of our achievement. It could not have been better. We found ourselves swept up in the hospitality and admiration of these generous and beautiful Afghani people.

One elderly turbaned man came over and held both my hands in his, and looked directly into my eyes. When I met his gaze, I was astounded by his beautiful clear green eyes that shone with kindness. He shared how blessed he felt that we had arrived at this time of their gathering, "please come back and eat with us tonight." I could only nod in happy agreement.

We camped on the outskirts of town, just five minutes walk away, and when everyone was settled, we returned to the reunion. The elderly man who'd taken my hands and greeted me with so much love told us they were all talking about camels when they heard camel bells. At first, they thought they had imagined it. Several times the conversation stopped and started because of the illusory sound of the bells, but they realised it was only getting louder. They couldn't believe their eyes when they looked over the fence and saw us all coming down the street. He clutched my hand in his again and gave me that beautiful piercing green gaze. With tears in his eyes, hugging my hand as he spoke, he told me something that moved me so profoundly. "When we saw you coming down the road with all the camels, we felt as if our reunion had been blessed. Thank you for coming." I had no words. I just put one hand to my heart while my tears plopped onto his beautiful brown hand.

The converging of our paths had evidently blessed us all. I should have known that the currents and flows that had guided our trip would delay us so we could arrive at this perfect moment in time. An Afghani reunion far surpassed thousands of cheerleaders, even if they had all been chanting *Kye and Gill, Kye and Gill*. They would never have recognised or acknowledged what these wise and beautiful men could clearly see. Not just the completion of a rather epic part of our journey, but an aspect we both took immense pride in, the condition of our camels. "I have never seen camels in such good condition," said the elderly green-eyed man I was falling in love with. "It's astounding that they are this way when you travel so far." His words were met with numerous nods and grunts and words of appreciation from the other cameleers who clearly agreed. Our camels were in excellent condition.

I could not have imagined being met with more honour if I'd tried. We had gone through famine and feast with our dear friends, but for every night of poor feed they experienced, when we came to abundance and all the bush tukka they loved, we gave them several nights of binge. Our animals, especially the camels who had done the work, were what I was proudest of. We had arrived here with not a *single* rub mark from a harness on any of our camels, with them all looking bright and happy. That was success for me!

To come to the end of this track and arrive in the very midst of this reunion was not just a coincidence. It was truly the most magnificent and ultimate divine timing.

Even though it had been a huge dilemma for me, I never regretted my choice to eat meat on this trip. Accepting people's hospitality in the way it was given allowed me to connect with many incredible people. This night, shared around the fire, eating spicy foods and being treated like a guest of honour, was one of the most memorable and blessed moments of my life. In all my memories, this one is stitched in pure gold and carried in my heart forever.

Later in the night, as the women cleared the food and put the leftovers into containers, we found ourselves sitting in a group of elderly men. They wore traditional dress and told us they had grown up with camels. Their fathers had been cameleers themselves. I'd often wondered how Afghani cameleers had behaved towards their camels. Their relationship with their dromedaries would have been based on survival and competition. Those who could carry the most oversized loads were most likely to get the job. I felt grateful that my own experience of life and the times I lived in had allowed me to experience my camels so differently. Even so, I was curious about the relationship between Afghani cameleer and their camel. I knew several people who'd claimed to have been taught by traditional Afghani cameleers, and their methods seemed brutal and cruel. Were these men like that? I didn't know, though I could see they held the camel in really high esteem, revered them even.

There was one very elderly slender man with stunning green eyes who had been listening and smiling and appeared very interested in what we had to say, but for a long time hadn't said anything. When he did speak, it was about the camel races. I'd purposefully not mentioned the races. I hadn't wanted to spoil the magic of the night by hearing these men had cheered them on. I was in for a surprise. As this gentleman spoke, his emotions were welling up. Unashamedly tears began streaming down his face. "They were so cruel," he said. He spoke so softly. It was easy to see he was a very gentle man. "Many of the camels were too young. They should never have been raced like that. And they beat one camel as it sat down, over and over." He looked traumatised from what he'd seen. He was shaking his head, his face streaked with grief.

I had been surprised to see him cry so openly. I realised I had my own preconceived perceptions of what I'd anticipated an Afghani culture would be. I had assumed it would be disdainful of more womanly emotions. Yet, the entire group of men were all nodding their heads in agreement and looking teary. They had all been moved by the plight of the camels they'd seen at the races. If anything, Gill and I had restored their faith that there were cameleers who deeply regarded and cared for their camels.

After so long of feeling alone in my views on camel racing, on a short stretch of dirt road, I had met one upset farmer and his traumatised daughter, and now this beloved and beautiful circle of old men. They openly wept for those camels they'd seen be abused. While I was just as disheartened that this behaviour with camels was seen as OK, I also shared the hopes of these dear men. People would eventually wake up and see these incredible animals for who they *really* were.

"They deserve to be treated with respect," one of the other cameleers said, and the group nodded in agreement.

I felt cocooned in a haven of kindness as we sat in a circle with these old cameleers. For a moment, our conversation paused. The women that looked after these men were always busy, and the sounds of plates being gathered and emptied and pans clanking, continued all around us. A muted noise in the background of our poignancy. The pause between us felt pregnant with hope as if all our desires were held in this moment. The tears passed, and the lanterns had been lit. As we sat there, in the silence of our reverie, my heart felt so full. What a precious, treasured moment in time I had been gifted.

When the silence broke, we were all smiling. We looked from one to another, our smiles turning to wide grins, and then we all began laughing. Laughing and laughing.

In this holy circle shared with the ancient and wise and all the ancestors that walked with them, there was a feeling so palpable. It was like a pure sparkling raindrop that had landed in the fragrant petals of a deep red rose and was about to plop onto the earth and water the seeds of love sewn by us this beautiful night.

Sixteen

A Lone Camel Waits

I woke early the following day. The soft caws of a crow in the tree outside our wagon merging with my dream. I smiled sleepily, thinking it was White Feather waking us for his breakfast, but the sounds of raspy caws only intensified as more crows flew down and landed in the branches around us. Then I remembered. Almost a thousand kilometres separated us from our black feathered friend. We were not at the start of the second part of our trip. We were almost at the end. The crows were not waking me for their regular feed. They had come for the bones.

Then I did laugh as I remembered the night before. We had left the celebrations laughing and giggling like a couple of kids, not only feeling we couldn't have been more blessed but also rather tipsy after only two beers. We were also piled high with leftover food. There were bones for the dogs, leftover salads for the chickens and various containers of spicy and exotic meals for us. Not wanting the dogs to miss out on the celebrations, we had given them each a bone before we went to bed, and by sunrise, the crows had seen them.

Snuggled so contentedly in bed, I was in no rush to get up, but I did. If the crows had already spotted the bones, it would be the ants next. I needed to throw them further away from camp.

The early morning sky was the colour of pale pink roses and cast a softness across the arid and bare landscape surrounding Maree. As I dealt with the bones before rekindling our campfire, I thought the colours of the sunrise magically reflected the purity and softness of the love I felt.

The smell of coffee woke Gill and had him join me around our early morning fire. It was rare for us to be up early without having much to do. Usually, we were so busy getting everyone ready for the road. When we had days off, we slept in. We had arranged to meet a few people and give a couple of media interviews. So we were in no rush to move on, but something else was tugging at the edges of my awareness that I couldn't quite explain. As if there was another reason for us being here, one we had yet to see. I couldn't work out what it was. All I could do was let go.

Gill and I sat for a long time in silence, enjoying our cuppas as we basked in the peace of sleeping animals and nothing to do but watch the day awaken. The pure dawn chorus of the magpies, the golden glow of the sunrise, the arrival of a few more crows, a beat-up sedan driving down the dirt road to who knows where.

We had both noticed we were in the perfect landscape to easily see tektites. Flat with low-growing vegetation that grew sparsely, leaving bare earth exposed. We were both really excited. In fact, I was feeling excited about *everything*, even the end of the dirt road, an hour away by car, or a day's trek with camels. Just *one* night feeling supported and loved had left me with my trust in life restored. I knew we would be fine. Life looked after us, and that had never been more apparent.

As we went about our morning jobs, I was searching the ground and was surprised when I began to find quartz crystals. They were everywhere. I wasn't even aware we were near water, but we must have camped on a floodplain. I was about to yell over at Gill to tell him of my discovery when I noticed him picking up something from the ground. He held it up in the sun as he yelled, "Kye, look what I've found."

Our first-day camping on the edge of Maree was memorable and not only because of our bulging pockets of beautiful quartz crystals. We did a media interview and met two young aboriginal girls who came down to meet the animals.

The media interview because our doves decided to fly around us while we were being filmed. We looked like a couple of St Francis of Assis's disciples on our journey of love. Sitting there, animals around us, while our holy messengers of peace and love circled us in the air.

I have no idea if the footage was used or if it's still sitting in some archives, unseen. We were so immersed in our lives we didn't even think to follow it up. We'd had a few interactions with mainstream media during our trip. While our interview with accompanying doves was sweet, I felt we were too outside the box for them. Our answers to their questions left them startled and gasping for air, *and* we'd watered ourselves down! It's hard to be who you are in a reality that's so constrained.

Earlier in our trip, one guy from a popular newspaper asked Gill to pose for photos. Instead of walking down the dirt road leading the camels in a relaxed and cruisey way, as he was doing, the reporter wanted Gill to look as if he was pulling not just all the camels but the entire wagon himself. Gill had done it for a laugh and not really given it much thought, but it had portrayed what we were doing in a completely different and utterly ridiculous way. We both realised we had to be on the ball and *not* pamper them by trying to fit into their version of what they thought we were doing.

The other memorable event was being visited by two young, vibrant and effusive aboriginal girls who came to meet our animals. Our relationships with children were always more honest. We didn't have to hide with them. They gasped in awe as we told them about our adventure. However, with their childlike innocence still intact, we were well within the realms of magic and wonder and unlimited possibilities, and they loved it.

Banjo, never one to let the wounds of the past hold him back from a good cuddle, came and plonked himself down between the girls, who, without missing a beat, continued talking while cuddling Banjo. I had no idea why the kids where Banjo had lived had been so mean, but all the ones we met loved him. They didn't even notice his smell. They embraced him so naturally and without any fear.

One of the girls had been telling us all about her pampered pooch, a scruffy little white dog. Then she told us a story that explained to me the feeling I had of being tugged around the edges of my awareness.

It was about a camel called Adjani who used to be so quiet that every Christmas, Santa would ride her into town with his sack full of presents. Often the kids would jump up and ride on Adjani, too. She'd been Santa's helper for many years. I noticed as she was speaking it was all in the past tense. "Does she still do this?" I asked. Acutely aware that the tugging I'd felt had intensified. "No," she replied. "She got really angry, and they put her in a paddock with horses. We haven't seen her for ages."

"Does she have any camel friends?" I asked. "No", she replied, "only horses." I knew by this time that the tugging I felt was Adjani. She was calling us to get her. I knew without any doubt that she was going to join us. We just had to go through the formalities first and ask for permission.

After finding out who owned her, we paid him a visit. He was a lovely man with his own history of cameleering. He explained that Adjani had been one of his best camels until he leant her to someone. She had come back really angry and a few times had tried to hurt him, either by going for him with her teeth or barging over the top of him and trying to run him over. He'd narrowly avoided being injured. After a few occasions of trying to get a rope on her, something he'd been easily able to do, he gave up and put her out in the paddock with the horses. She'd been out there for years. "But surely you don't want a dangerous camel," he asked. "I don't want you to get hurt. She's a big camel and could do some harm. Why on earth would you want her?"

Explaining why we were willing to take on a dangerous animal was a little like telling people we had no known destination. Combining these two bits of info about our life had most people gasping for air. In the realms of what we accept as everyday life, it just makes no sense. It didn't always make sense to me, and I was living it, but I knew Adjani was coming with us, and we just had to negotiate that. Her owner looked totally perplexed as he shrugged his shoulders and told us if we wanted her, we could have her, "but you won't be able to catch her," he said, "she's in a massive paddock, and she's not keen on people."

We left jubilant, undaunted by the size of the paddock and the mission we faced to bring Adjani to our camp, though I was very aware of that little voice within. *What the fuck are you doing? What if you get injured? And you don't even have somewhere to live, and you are taking on another animal and a dangerous one!* The voice of little me who always appears so deprived of power that she tries to bring the me that's living in a fuller way, aligned with my own knowing, trusting in what I feel, down. *Be gone, little me. There is no room left for you here. Gill and I have a mission!*

That night I could feel Adjani's presence so keenly. She knew we were coming and was waiting. We would find her easily. I knew this because, by this time, I had no doubt Adjani had called us to her. She wanted to leave. She felt very alone and wasn't happy, and Gill and I were most likely the only chance she had of leaving that paddock. What other crazy people would pass through and want to take on an apparently dangerous camel?

The following morning, we drove through the gate, and I was eager and excited to meet our new friend. I couldn't wait to see her. I had no idea what she looked like, what colour she would be. So I could scan the horizon and see her at the earliest opportunity, I hung out of the car window. Clinging tightly to the roof as Gill drove us down the rough and bumpy track. A few times, we stopped, and Gill checked the ground for tracks, there were many hard-edged hoof marks from the horses, but soft-footed Adjani had left none. This hard-sharp stony ground was not good terrain for her soft camel feet.

That little voice whispered to me again, *you won't find her*, and I felt a wave of sorrow at that thought. Then I dismissed it. I had to trust. Adjani had called us, and we *would* find her. It was in that very moment of rebuking my doubt that we drove into a clearing, and there she was. She was standing on a rocky rise in the vast splendour of that dry landscape, looking like a mythical beast with an appointment with destiny. Her destiny had not let her down.

Her face and legs were black and the rest of her a charcoal grey. I had not seen a camel that colour before. I was awed by her, but it wasn't just the exquisiteness of her colouring. It was everything about her. Her size, she was big like a mountain. She also emanated dignity and stood in such power. I felt a little nervous about how to approach such a noble creature, especially after being told she was dangerous.

Of course, it was Gill that gently walked towards her, speaking soft words of reassurance, and in some ways, looking back, I felt like a dumb human in the animal realms once again. She had called us in. She was expecting us. We didn't need to reassure her. She had been waiting expectantly for us. Even so, perhaps my own fragility in the presence of such a huge camel led to the soothing words that were ultimately reassuring me. "We are not here to hurt you. We have other camels, so you won't be alone anymore. We just need to put a rope around you. Then we will tie that to the back of our car and drive really slowly back to our camp." She stood still and ready as Gill gently put the rope around her neck and led her to our car. There was no resistance, no aggression. It all happened with an ease that was verging on miraculous after everything we'd heard about this girl.

It took us half an hour of driving slowly to reach the gate of the paddock. Waiting for us in his 4WD was Adjani's old owner. He looked astounded when he saw her with us and kinda stuttered, "Oh my god, you caught her." I pushed the boundaries just a little further, "She knew we were coming," I replied, "she was waiting for us."

And just as we had with Abdul and Banjo, we led our new camel home.

Even the word home had a new meaning for me. It had become wilder and freer. It had bloomed from a noun to a verb and was always moving and changing. That little patch of earth where our wagon was fleetingly parked and our chickens scratched around in the dirt. It was our fluttering, chomping, barking, stinky love-filled haven. It was my beating heart, and that's where we led this new girl too.

I wanted her to meet all our camels straight away, and while they were tethered further out around us so they could reach the best feed, we decided to bring them all close. After years of living with horses, we wanted Adjani to receive the best welcome.

Just beside our wagon was a circle of small trees with long swooping branches. They looked like little stout people with really long arms. They had survived on these parched planes and grown in their misshapen way by growing around a mined hollow in the earth that often-held water. Gill surmised it could have been created by sand being taken away for the roads. The hollow had long grown over, and a lot of vegetation grew around its banks, but the long arms of branches were perfect for tethering our camels too.

While I'd cared for injured and traumatised animals my entire life, I had never seen a previously abused animal give us their trust as fast as Adjani did. In the past, it had often taken weeks, months even. Lots of time sitting quietly with them, speaking in soft whispers, sometimes silence, but definitely never rushing them through their pain. I could tell Adjani had trauma. While her sighs of relief that she was finally home were palpable, I could also feel her deep wound. A trauma still embedded in her that stuck out from her heart like a spear. I didn't know what had happened to this beautiful camel, but she had come to the right place to heal.

Gill and I had a suspicion her old owner had not expected us to catch her *at all*. We even pondered if he'd said we could have her, thinking we would never succeed. Had this man given her to us, thinking she would still be his? Had he even seen us as a bit of a joke? After all, he was very well known for his camel handling skills. If he couldn't do anything with her, had he considered Gill and me presumptuous to think we could? He had certainly been struggling to find words and had looked utterly flabbergasted when he saw us leading Adjani out of his paddock.

I was incredulous, too, not because we'd caught her, but at how Adjani had overridden all her fears, resistance and defensive, protective behaviours to come and be part of our tribe. Even letting me put a head collar on her. Another event that had her old owner muttering, "Oh my god, you even got a head collar on her," when he called in the following morning to see how we were going with this recalcitrant camel.

His mouth had fallen open in incredulity when he saw Adjani, standing like a queen among all our camels. She was wearing her new bright red head collar with its sheepskin-lined noseband, looking so at home it felt like she had always been there. Had he anticipated us to be black and blue after being brutalised by Adjani, expecting us to plead with him to take her back? That thought crossed my mind. He had tried his best to handle Adjani, eventually giving up, and yet we were doing everything with such ease. He was witnessing a transformed camel, and she looked peaceful as she stood amongst her new tribe. Our camels were all standing so close together. It occurred to me that perhaps this arrangement of camels looked strange to a cameleer, so I explained that we'd had a welcome party, a sleepover so all our camels and Adjani could meet. This airy-fairy chatter was not outback camel handling talk. He shook his head, perplexed. No one in the outback had camel sleepovers but us.

I really liked her old owner, he was friendly and warm and full of interesting tales. He'd told us he'd been angry that Adjani had been hurt by someone he'd trusted enough to lend her to. Beyond all the surface stuff, I did feel he was relieved that a change was happening for Adjani. He'd had a good relationship with her for many years. Of course, he wanted the best for her. He was just utterly baffled at how we did everything. Nothing in his revenue of experience gave him insight into what was going on. Love is so underrated; its power happens unseen. Combining the power of love with the awareness that animals feel and know so much more than we do and being willing to learn from them creates a fantastic foundation for co-creation.

Working, connecting, and co-creating with them in a more conscious way may take a few more lifetimes to permeate the entrenched and often ruthless animal husbandry of the outback that often failed to recognise their own sentience, let alone that of an animal. Still, just like those Afghani cameleers, I did hope it would eventually happen because I loved being in the outback with its vast plains and big skies. It was the very limited awareness of animals that was my constant bane. I saw and heard things I didn't want to know happened, and there was nothing to do to change any of it except welcome this traumatised camel into our folds and keep being me. We plant seeds with our actions and deeds. In the times I would find myself choking back my tears or running to sit under a big tree and calm myself, I always saw this trail of light and all the seeds we had planted along the way that, when the rain came, would sprout.

Change is as inevitable as night becoming day. People may think they are experiencing the best that animals can offer with their bull musters and rodeos and camel races, but how captivating, jaw-dropping, and utterly phenomenal outback events could be if they began to showcase the horse and bull whisperers. Then people could witness the incredible flow of communion and syntropy that occurs from conscious communion with our noble creatures of this earth. This time will come! I know it.

We met many wonderful people in the outback who did love animals. Some shared their own heartache at some of the things they'd seen done to animals over the years. I won't go into details, but as hard as it was for me, I let these people speak. I could sense that what they had seen and experienced had become bottled up inside them because they'd not had anyone to share their grief with. I listened with my heart breaking. I felt so helpless, and later when that moment had passed, I would sit with the camels, my tears falling, and soak up all the beauty and kindness and love we shared. Our lives were made up of so many moments that were holy and kind. They joined together like a golden rope that stretched back through time. In my moments of sorrow, it was that rope and all those moments of love I held on to.

On the night of the Afghani reunion, we also met another animal lover. His name was Bobbie, and we'd laughed when he told us his last name. It was that of a famous musician, a name so memorable we would never forget this Bobbie. Not that this big middle-aged man needed a renowned name to be remembered. He was memorable in his own right. He wore a blue work shirt, faded jeans, and cowboy boots and had a very battered straw hat on his head. In the busy bluster and enthusiasm of so many people, I found his presence calming. He was like an anchor I kept going back to. It had been a long time since Gill and I had been with *any* people, let alone a huge mob of them. As much as I loved every morsel of that night, there were times it was overwhelming. All my senses were on high alert, so many people wanting to chat, so many offers of food and then repeated checks we'd had enough to eat and couldn't fit in a huge dollop more. I soaked up every moment of that gathering as if it was nectar. Still, periodically I found myself returning to this gentle giant of a man. He had a current flowing through him that felt ancient and still. Just being around him felt so restorative.

I was disappointed when I saw him get up to leave. We'd heard titbits of some of his stories, but it had been hard to converse with so many people talking excitedly. This was a reunion, and many cameleers had come from far-flung places and travelled many miles, even days, to be there. Many old friends were meeting for the first time in years, and there was a lot of excited chatter. As Bobbie pushed through the crowd, saying his farewells, and thanking all the women for the food, when he passed us, he pushed a piece of paper into my hand. It was his phone number. This was a man I definitely wanted to call, and we did the following day. He came and picked us up and took us for a visit to his home.

Bobbie lived on a hundred acres on the outskirts of the town. He was a horseman, and it was evident he loved animals and couldn't stand any type of cruelty. Some people just exude a presence that's so affable, gentle and kind you love them immediately. That was Bobbie. He even had a roguishness I liked. I just felt a connection with him. He had many interesting stories, but one really stood out. Many years previously, this man had reared and lived with a pack of dingoes. You have to be a bit outside of the box to do that, and I was fascinated.

"There were five of them," he told us, "and they saw me as the pack leader."

"How did you feed them?" I asked with an incredulous look on my face. Wondering if they went out killing stock.

Then he told us that every night he and his pack of dingoes would go out driving in his Ute down remote bush tracks. There were so many rabbits around, and they'd get blinded by the Ute's lights. The dingoes would jump out from the back of the Ute, catch and kill the rabbit, and jump back in with it until they saw the next rabbit in the headlights and they'd jump out and grab that. Sometimes Bobbie would drive for hours. He had to drive until there were enough dead rabbits in the back of the Ute to keep his pack well-fed for that night!

"If I kept them full-on rabbits, they had no interest in killing anything else."

Bobbie told us it had been one of the most fascinating experiences of his life. He had learnt so much about dingoes from living with this pack, but one day he made a mistake that almost cost a child his life.

The dingoes were used to Bobbie peeing outside. Any worthy pack leader would mark their territory. During the years, he'd had many visitors call in, and the dingoes had never been a problem. They were well behaved and used to people, until one day something unexpected happened. None of his previous guests had ever peed in his yard, so he had never faced the situation about to unfold.

On this particular day, a friend had come to visit, bringing his young son. They got out of the car, and the son, needing to pee, had gone to do so by a bush. Suddenly the dingoes raced over to the little boy and leapt on him. It had been terrifying. One even had the child's head in his mouth and may have killed him if Bobbie hadn't heard the screams and raced to the rescue. Never having faced this situation before, it had not occurred to Bobbie that someone other than him peeing in his yard was an open challenge to their territory and his place as pack leader. An innocent pee from a child had alerted the dingo's instincts to defend their home and, if need be, their pack leader.

Very clear signage went up in Bobbies yard after that, warning people that peeing in his yard was dangerous!

Later, down the track, Gill, on a trip out to a small town with Bobbie, would meet this victim. Now a grown man, he'd chuckled with Bobbie about the day the dingoes had almost killed him. There appeared to be no hard feelings between them. I excitedly asked if you could still see the bite marks on his head. Gill told me that there had been no external indication that this man's head had ever been inside the mouth of a dingo! He'd looked!

I loved our time in Maree. I wished I could find a little dark niche to settle into and hide out the summer from the heat, but nothing had happened to indicate that our time in this tiny little town with its kind people wasn't over. I knew we probably wouldn't find our permanent home for us and our animals in station country. There are just no small pockets of land, but we had to find somewhere to pull up over the summer. It was getting hotter, which made the daily jobs more arduous. Even though I knew each step was always unknown, and each day of our trip had been unknown, it had all felt easier when we'd been on the track, not needing to even think about the next stage.

It reminded me of when Gill and I had lived for a couple of years travelling around Australia in an old truck we had a home in. I would love the journeys to places. The long stretches of road we'd drive without a care. The way we would camp in wild places and feel so free, but it always changed when we arrived at our destination. Then we couldn't camp in many places, everything was ordered and organised. It became hard to find a place to pull up and let our dogs out, and so many bush areas around towns would have rangers patrolling, fining anyone they caught sleeping in their vans, cars and trucks, huge fines. Everything was so controlled that the only way to survive was to find a base, and then we could relax. While we didn't have to deal with rangers and being unable to walk our dogs, we were still moving through other people's land and were deeply respectful of that. The sooner we got a base, the sooner we'd be out of the heat, and I could relax. After all the hard work it had taken us to reach this point on the map, I was ready to let all the animals out in a paddock and sit back.

When I shared my concerns with Bobbie about how we needed to find a haven, he told us he would ask around. "There's got to be somewhere," he'd replied optimistically. "Leave it with me. If I find somewhere, I will catch you up further down the track." We only had a couple more properties to travel through before we met the tarmac. I hoped he would find a place for us all and soon.

The day we left, Maree, Gill and I felt that Adjani wanted to be in the team pulling the wagon. Usually, I was the sensitive one picking up on the subtler communications from our animals, but Adjani's focus and intention was so strong that we both felt her. After all these years of living in this tiny little town, she wanted to be leaving her way. Not being led, but leading, and it was her choice, not ours. Neither of us would have considered putting a camel we didn't know, had been warned could be dangerous, who we knew had experienced trauma, and, as if that wasn't enough, had never pulled a wagon before in her life into a position in our team. On the surface, it seemed foolish, but we had both learnt in the hard gruel of along the way, to trust, without sway in what we felt. Concussion, being run over and trampled flat like a pancake into the dirt, not to forget potential death, were just a few of the consequences we faced handling all these animals if we *didn't* listen to ourselves and trust in our own knowing, *even* when it appeared crazy. I had learnt that foolish can be wonderful. Foolish can bring the greatest gifts. Foolish can be wildly freeing. We had done many apparently foolish things, like leaving on this trip with so many animals, welcoming a stinky and dangerous billy goat and a camel that crushed the bonnets of people's cars and loved chasing people. Now we were trusting yet another wounded soul to guide our camel wagon as we headed out of town. Still, every fibre of my being, down to my blood and bones, told me that Adjani wanted to be in our team.

And this big girl didn't want to be in the middle. She wanted to be beside Zu, leading!

Whenever we harness the camels, we begin with the two camels closest to the wagon. When they are in place, the next two, then the next two and finally the two camels in the lead. The brakes are always on during this process for safety and because Lady Caroline was always keen to get moving and likely to create a few false starts before we were ready.

I couldn't believe Adjani. She stood tethered to a tree in the shade as we got all the camels ready, and finally, with only her to put in place, we led her up to Zu. With the same innate knowing that Zu had shown, she swung her bum around and stepped in beside our king. She was already wearing her sheep's wool harness, and Gill clipped her into place as he gave her lots of praise. When he gave the command to pull em up, she knew exactly what to do and pushed into her harness beside Zu.

The camels were all excited. The dogs were barking, the parrots were screeching, and the wagon rattled as it began to roll. Despite the ruckus, majestic and proud Adjani, with her head held high, the past already behind her, strode out on that desert road. She was one of our team, in heart and soul, for better or worse, and regardless of what we faced together.

And one of our team didn't mean the camels that pulled our wagon. It was every little creature that was our tribe. All our fellow travellers on our very own magical journey. It was The Colonel and his girls. It was Banjo and the Beebs. It was our crazy wagon launching happy howling dogs. It was Mr Bloss and Snowdrop, our doves and each and every camel with all their narks and nuances. It was all of our animals, big and small, each one a part of our beloved and beautiful hearts swooping with pride and love team, and there was no looking back for any of us.

Seventeen

Holy Pigeon

Over and over again, the same lessons cycled around in this *have you got it yet*, kinda loop. Be in the moment. Don't look too far ahead. Stay focused and a really big one, especially with the apparently dangerous animals we'd taken on, listen to ourselves and don't be swayed by the negativity of others.

It's easier to act with certainty when being cheered on and a little more daunting when people shake their heads in horror at our choices. Yet even when everyone was walking in the opposite direction, we had continuously done what felt right and true for us. We wouldn't have been on this trip if we hadn't.

Several times we had been warned by various people that the property owners whose station we were about to pass through were odd, unfriendly, rude or generally belligerent. Even though we had known not to listen to others, we had braced ourselves against whatever mayhem may be unleashed upon us as we entered these places. Yet, in every single case, we discovered the owners were lovely. What often made them strange to others was that profit was not the wind behind their sails, whereas a property that maintained balance and diversity and still had ground cover at the end of a drought, was. No wonder we got on so well with these odd people. It made us wonder what had been said about *us*.

Gill and I had soon learnt to take people as we found them and not as we were told they'd be, but we'd only ever experienced liking people we were told would be difficult or odd. We'd never had a difficult time with someone we'd been repeatedly told by many passing travellers was helpful and kind.

In fact, we'd heard such glowing praise about one such owner; Gill drove ahead to introduce himself and ask if he had anywhere we could pull up for a couple of days. We were happy to pay and knew he regularly had tourists camping on his vast property.

I waited at the wagon with the animals, sitting in my camp chair in the shade of the trees while Gill drove to see him. We were so close to the start of the tarmac. The prospect of a few days of stillness away from the constantly curious eyes of tourists so we could get in touch with our next move felt invaluable. I'd hoped we would have seen Bobbie with the good news that he'd found somewhere for us to stay, but the days had passed, and he'd not come.

Gill wasn't even gone long, but as soon as he got out of the car from visiting the station, it was clear something was wrong. He looked shaken. I couldn't imagine what had happened. He'd visited a man we'd been repeatedly told by tourists would make us welcome. Our little troupe of love had travelled so far on the kindness and love of strangers and not experienced one unfriendly person since that first station whose lost keys we'd returned. That was almost a thousand kilometres of kindness and welcome!

I felt shaky as I waited for Gill to explain what had happened. He was deeply stressed, which is rare for him. He walks this middle path through life, which keeps him pretty centred and stable through all the highs and lows. "Fuck, he was so nasty," he said before collapsing into a camp chair, needing a moment or two to gather himself. I listened in shock as Gill told me how accusatory and mean he'd been. "He said he didn't want us on his property because all our animals were diseased, and we were spreading disease."

"You gotta be kidding me," I replied. "We've not even met the guy, no-one in their right mind would say that if they'd seen our animals. How can he say that when he hasn't even come to look?"

I was astounded. All our animals beamed well-being. We both sat in shock. I felt sick in my guts and could feel myself trembling. I always want to be tougher than I am.

I would have loved to just say *Fuck him* and not take any of it on, but I felt so vulnerable like a hermit crab pulled out of its shell. We sat there for a long time and couldn't come up with any explanation as to why this person had been so vicious, especially after everything good we'd heard about him.

Sometimes you can't find answers to explain people's behaviour. It made no sense. But I did know that his attack and fear energy ended with us. Happy people don't do this to anyone. Instead, they communicate and discuss. They never accuse, and while knowing this helped me put this man's accusations in perspective, I'd be lying if I said we just switched from feeling confused, angry and upset to feeling fine. Changing the momentum in a new direction is a process. Gill had gone to this man wide open, in friendship, never for one minute anticipating the welcome he'd received. We both felt like we'd been doused in something dirty like a slop bucket and had to get clean. Nature and the animals were always our restoration unless it was our rotters of camels driving us mad.

I walked down to the dry creek bed, purposefully shaking my body as I went, freeing myself of this man's energy, letting all that tension I'd felt shake out through the ends of my fingers. The fears Gill had bought home with him were neither mine nor Gills, and we were not taking them on. I settled myself, bum in the dirt with my back up against a huge tree and closed my eyes, feeling beams of sunlight piercing the shady boughs, basking me in its golden glow. I sat there until I felt restored. Who knows what pain people are going through that causes them to act the way they do and who knows if it was just a hungry vampire wanting an energy feed? Some people intentionally stir negativity and then feed from the trauma they cause.

When I arrived back at camp, Gill was chopping up pumpkin and potatoes for dinner and paused from his food preparations; after checking, Banjo was nowhere to be seen. He came over and gave me a hug. I felt so deeply held by our love. The outside world could bluff and blunder around us, but it could not touch this love. I was so moved by the moment tears rolled down my face. Tenderness and pain intermingled, one soothing the other until all I could feel was gratitude.

In that moment of reclamation, we heard the sound of a noisy motorbike revving and spluttering towards our camp. Even with all the love I felt, I prayed it wasn't *him*, come to spew more of his fear and disease.

We were camped near the dirt road, on a station we'd been told the owner was difficult and obnoxious. That was why we'd been keen to find a refuge for a few days on the neighbouring property of a man we'd been told was lovely.

I held my breath in anticipation as the sound drew close. Then out from between the trees in a haze of smoke and splutter came a man riding an old motorbike. He looked like a villainous and cheeky musketeer with his handlebar moustache. I could imagine posters of his roguish jovial face plastered on all the trees. Wanted dead or alive. He greeted us with a hearty handshake, introduced himself and sat down around the campfire with us. He was the owner of the station we were on and so generous that he unwrapped all the food he had and offered it to us to share. He had the wildest, most mischievous twinkle in his eyes and was *really* funny. We laughed so much as we shared his food. "Rest up as long as you need," he told us before jumping back on his bike on a quest to locate some lost sheep. I didn't just like him. I loved him.

When home is the dirt under your feet, wherever you are, an owner's greeting can feel like a force of nature. It adds to the elements we already camped in. Thankfully it had seldom been the hot coals of an erupting volcano. I felt so grateful for the kindness we had been met with all along the track. Of course, it all comes down to us. We know that these little challenges, even if they feel volcanic, are simply experiences we can hone our own skills from. They force us to anchor more deeply into our peace. Gill and I had learnt to laugh on the edge of a volcano, but we were always aware it may erupt, and that, I felt, was wisdom.

Negative people can have such an impact until you meet a kind one. We laughed that once again, we had presumed an experience based on the views of others. The kind man had been a rotter, and the rotter had been kind, and we could relax. We were not on the rotter's land.

Since our beautiful night at the Afghani reunion, I'd felt totally flowing in trust. I knew everything would work out with finding a haven from the heat. It didn't matter that the dirt road was about to end. We were looked after. It didn't matter that we had totally unmoored from common sense and no longer even listened to the cautious advice of our intellect. It never spoke with any warmth and only offered sensible constriction anyway. That voice had warned us not to get Banjo. It had advised us that Abdul was not our concern, and it had tried its mighty best to scale down and diminish the boldness of our trip. Letting your intellect guide you is like trying to stay warm from a fire that's not lit. It has its purpose, but only a minimal one. Living aligned in each moment with what felt right, no matter what, and having the courage to act every time with what we intuitively knew we had to do, was the reason I knew we could trust. Trust doesn't happen outside of ourselves. It comes from within. It's not a cry for help but a knowing that our own choices have aligned us with a path where every experience, no matter how it looks, can serve us.

I felt like a warrioress, not with weapons of steel, but in the way, every aspect of me was being honed. My strength especially. I had been so weak and feeble when we left I had not even the arm muscle to pull myself into the wagon. Now I could jump in easily, even as it was rolling along. I could walk for miles and not get tired. I felt so strong. I had never lived so fully in my body, but I was also learning to soften and surrender as well. There is so much in life we can't control. We can only let go. I remember being given some excellent advice when I lived close to the ocean. "If you ever get caught swimming in a tidal rip, stop fighting. You won't win. You'll just exhaust yourself. Allow its currents to sweep you beyond its surge." Life is like that, too, and it's recognizing when to let go and when to push on.

The neighbouring farmer's hostility had been a tiny rip in the midst of all our abundant blessings. Still, I loved how we used it to strengthen our connection with love even more. To anchor down so deeply that almost in the next breath, a new current surged in and one that was supportive.

I felt overflowing with gratitude. The rose pink light of dusk was so beautiful. We had just finished tethering all our camels for the night and were walking back through the bush to our wagon. As we approached our camp with its fire burning and our dogs excitedly coming to greet us, I gasped in surprise. I could not believe my eyes. "Gill", I called, "come and look."

On top of our wagon roof was a domestic pigeon with a small leafy twig in its mouth. It must have been building a nest. Was it nesting in the wilderness, or had it come from one of the station owners? We had no idea, but the biblical symbology was not lost on me. This pigeon felt like our own personal messenger, and I felt ecstatic. While bible studies were not my forte, Gill had grown up dunked head first into Catholic indoctrination. Like all good altar boys, he knew his bible. He filled me in on the story of the dove that had landed on Noah's ark, letting him know that land was nearby. Yes, I know in our version of this biblical epic, our messenger was just a pigeon, but a pigeon would do. I wasn't about to knock this holy messenger who I had no doubt was telling us our home was near. I just knew it.

We did invite this pigeon to join our cavalcade of love, even throwing some food for it onto the roof of our wagon, but it flew off as if it knew exactly where it was going. Message delivered, mission accomplished, now back to building that nest.

Lo and behold, surprise, surprise, the following morning, on the heels of our heavenly messenger, Bobbie arrived. For a moment, he looked puzzled when I told him we'd been expecting him. He was, of course, unused to the heavenly messenger system we had that sent us Mother Mary's at moments of doubt, guided us to wedge-tailed eagles to remind us to let go and trust, and sent a pigeon carrying a bough to reassure us, home was indeed very near.

After his moment of confusion about how we'd known he was coming, Bobbie moved into the excitement of his mission. He had news. He had found us a haven for the summer. I danced and yapped around him like a happy dog. Our lovely new friend had scored us an old outstation on the edge of the Strzelecki ranges called Calcutta. He wanted to drive one of us out immediately to meet the owners and take a look, and he took Gill.

I paced with excitement the whole time he was away, and it was several hours before he returned. His first words were, "It is incredibly stark but really beautiful, and we can stay as long as we like. It's in a forty-five square kilometre paddock that the camels can roam freely in, and they are happy to let us have it for $150 a week." I was over the fucking moon. High-fiving Gill. What a waste of time every moment of stress had been. This trip was forcing me to expand beyond what even I had thought was possible. In a world where people often struggle to find a home because they have a couple of pets, we have manifested one *with* all our animals. Billy goat and all!

The following day we set off, keen to get to Calcutta before it got much hotter. We had another day travelling down the dirt road we'd followed since Alice. Then we veered west along another dirt road for ninety kilometres before arriving at our new home. Our haven from the heat, our temporary pause in a journey that would lead us to who knows where. I couldn't wait to rest and be still.

I'd felt a surge of anger inside me when I'd first heard that the land owner had accused us of spreading disease. But with a huge weight lifted and my trust in everything in life restored, as we travelled through his property, I could only feel peace. What space must someone exist in to see disease where there was love? What a bleak space to live in. Like a freezing cold winter without a warm fire. He didn't need our anger. He needed our compassion. Even so, on such a happy day, I had no desire to meet a fuming man in a hazmat suit unless he wanted a hug. Still, we passed through his property without seeing him. I was fine with that.

As we got closer to the end of the dirt track, several people that had heard months ago from the grey nomads and travellers on this route that we were coming came out to greet us. Ree, the lady we'd heard about who apparently spoke with aliens. This remarkable woman had been guided to open a beachside café in a tiny outback town a little further down the road. She'd even been told the inland sea would return. I was certainly intrigued by this tall, aristocratic woman who had no problem understanding our journey, including that we had no known destination. She even told us she had been expecting us. She'd been told some Arcturians would be arriving. I was intrigued that she had been told this, though also aware that while I knew many people who defined themselves by their galactic origin, it felt like a limiting label to me. I had asked myself who I was when I dropped beyond my labels many times, and I always came back to love. I was a being of love. Even so, I loved her passion and vitality and was keen to get to know her more, so we arranged to call in and see her after we had settled.

Another person we met was a wonderful man called Ron. We noticed him standing on the edge of the track, watching us from a distance. A lone figure, just a silhouette standing in the vast plain, looking as if he belonged there and was part of everything. As we got closer, I remember thinking he looked like a wizard. We called the camels to a halt and went over to meet him. He approached with his arms open, and we all hugged. I felt like I'd met a long-lost friend, and in that moment, with no words needed, I loved him. That feeling for this man never changed. He was also an animal person and had some camels and donkeys and the biggest heart. He lived in the same town as Ree. I felt even more curious about this tiny town. It was undoubtedly luring us like a magnet, and I had no idea then that we had our own journey there yet to unfold.

It took us several days to travel up the bleak rocky red dirt road called the Strzelecki track. Just a few kilometres into the journey, we called in to see the owners of this station and the outpost we were going to rent, ninety kilometres away, called Calcutta.

They had created an orderly oasis at their home. Sprinklers were watering the lush gardens and lawns, and all around the homestead, hundreds of young saplings had been planted.

The station owners, Jon and his wife Annie, were both friendly and welcoming, but there was one incident that left an ache in my heart. Jon had told us about an old shed we could see from Calcutta. Many years ago this shed had been used to dry baits. It hadn't been used for a long time, but some dried bait may have fallen through the floor laths. "Just watch your dogs," he'd said. Then he proceeded to name all the dogs he'd owned that had died from bait. He reeled off their names one after the other without giving any sense of remorse, sorrow or regret that these dogs had been killed in this hideous way. Once he'd left the freezer open, and his two dogs had eaten the bait and died. Then there was Sally. She must have picked it up in the paddock. Another one died when he drove his truck in after baiting out in the paddocks, and his dog ate some bait sitting in the back of his vehicle. The list went on and on. I listened, feeling sick, wanting to spew. I didn't know this man, but he appeared to be treating these deaths as if it was just a part of station life. When I asked how close to his homestead he baited, he replied, "two kilometres." No wonder so many dogs died. It was horrific listening to him.

We were heading to a home where our dogs could pick up a bait. There would be no relaxation. We had done everything we could to avoid baits. I needed fresh air. I had to get out. Gill sensed my trauma and made excuses, thanked them profusely for the offer of this house, and we left. Walking through a lovely garden where every plant was beautifully tended and mulched. I couldn't help feeling it all hid an attitude of such disregard and sloppiness for one's own dogs that over ten had died from the baits. Dogs that were their pets, little foxy terriers, dogs that worked for them, dogs that should have been kept safe from forgetting to shut the freezer door and all the various ways they'd imbibed this vile poison that should be banned. I was appalled and conflicted at my feelings. They had both been so welcoming, offering us food and willing to help in any way they could with anything we needed. What a fucking disparity, not just in their beautifully cared for gardens and home and their list of dead dogs, but in the way I felt. I want to think the best of people always. But I just felt so sick.

Back in the fresh air, with our animals, feeling the sun caress my tear, sodden face, Gill tried to soothe me. I felt despairing. We had no choice but to go to this house. We could not travel in this heat anymore. If we did, we risked the lives of our dear chickens, whose bodies wouldn't cope with the soaring temperatures. "I'll build a fence around the house so the dogs can't get out," Gill soothed. "We are only there through the summer. We can make this work. I saw the shed. I didn't know what it had been used for, but it's not close to the house. It will be ok, Kye." I still felt sick and worried, and a voice inside that I kept trying to erase kept saying, *you will lose one dog. No, no, no, that's not true. We will keep our dogs safe,* and even though I tried to reassure myself, I still felt ill. A cloud of foreboding had settled over me, and it wasn't about to leave. I would have times when it was in the background, times when I gave it no energy, convinced myself I was imagining it and got on with my life. Still, if I am honest, it followed me around like my shadow.

The trip to our new home, that I would come to see embodied shadows and light, birth and death, was undoubtedly expansive for our camels. While living at this outstation, we occasionally heard the faint rumble of trucks far away, like a soft mumbling on the horizon. Actually travelling this road was a constant negotiation with road trains.

The first time our camels saw a road train coming towards us, they veered completely off the road. Fortunately, there was a big wide-open space with a hard surface next to the road. Gill had been able to keep them moving as he'd guided them back onto the track. The second time our team kept going, travelling down that road as if they owned it. Even if they had looked a little nervous as the road train roared past in a bellow of dust, they'd stayed on the road. They trusted in their Gill, who was leading them.

Until the Strzelecki, they'd only seen a handful of trucks, and now they passed us in a constant spew of noise and dust. Most were polite and slowed down, but some didn't even bother. I felt mad they had such disregard for others, for our lives, but our camels handled these assaults like heroes. Heads down into the cloud of dust churned up by these massive monsters, pushing into their harnesses so we could swiftly reach the clear air on the other side of the spew. A truck could travel past a foot away from us all, and our camels wouldn't budge. Even Lady Caroline, known to like everything in her life 'just so', surpassed all her fears. I felt so proud of them, but it was a huge relief when we finally reached the turn-off to Calcutta. Just another five kilometres before we reached the driveway to our new home. From the road in, it was another two kilometres down the drive to the house. A long bumpy corrugated driveway across a stark and stony plain. Our own gibber flat! Yet it was high up on the edge of a vast plateau. As we walked down the driveway, I could just see the tops of giant gum trees down in a valley a short distance away that I would discover lined a dry creek that we *would* see run twice when we lived there. Even from our distance, we could hear the noisy chatter of corellas in the branches of the gums. Beyond the creek and the valley, it wound through, stretching across the horizon was the purple-hued vista of the ancient Strzelecki ranges. A range we would discover shifted its hues with the light, blushed with pink as the sun rose, blue or silver with the moon and purple in the stark light of day. Whatever colour, it was mesmerizing and spectacular. It was like living in the folds of an ancient beast. These ranges looked and felt as if they were alive!

But back to that day, as we came down the drive, heading to this lone house on its empty plains. The camels, who'd never the entire trip behaved in this way before, began to have a complete disregard for getting us all to the front door of this house. They started putting their heads down, so their harnesses slipped over their heads. They had to be unclipped from their harnesses before they could walk away. Still, they had disconnected so much from the job at hand that it made more sense to unclip them all and let them free and for us to tow the wagon up to the house with the car. They obviously knew it was holiday time, and our journey had temporarily come to an end.

We ran around unclipping our inpatient camels who were raring to go, and the moment they were free, they walked away. They didn't even look back.

Eighteen
Howling Winds of Calcutta

As I watched our camels walk away, I felt so achingly alone. After all our time of living and sharing together, I thought we were connected, heart and soul. Yet they had walked away from us without a backward glance. Had I got our relationship with these animals so wrong?

Then trying to fit ourselves into a house that felt full of sharp edges and had a musty smell from being empty for so long. There was no doubt the views were phenomenal, but I felt so teary as we began to try and make the worst-designed home I have ever lived in our temporary haven. After hearing about the baits, all my enthusiasm was gone. I felt like I'd been given an apple, but it was rotten inside. I knew I had to make the most of it. Travelling on in the heat was not an option, though I did have times I seriously wondered if we'd have been better camping out under a tree in our wagon. Each time I pondered this, I would hear my wise inner voice telling me to *let the camels wander freely and to make the most of this time. It will have its gifts!*

Gifts, there were many times it was hard to find them. Being on a gibber flat, our temporary home got the full wrath of the winds. They blew across that stark, unforgiving flat for miles and miles before they met us, and they always arrived hot and fucking mean.

There was a Telstra tower in the front garden that, on the best days, emitted a sound like ancient monks singing mantras. On the days when the winds rampaged and howled around us, the rabid squeal of demons fighting. Monks or demons it was a constant background noise as the winds blew almost all the time during the first few months we were there.

There were times I would come in the back door from the toilet, which was outside, and the wind would be blowing so strongly I'd have to fight to get in without being crushed. Then it took all my strength to shut the door. Using my legs as a brace, I would throw all my weight against that door as I struggled to lock it shut or, on bad days, scream above the howls of the wind for Gill to come urgently and help me.

In a straight line down a hallway, from the back door to the front one, was a total of four doors. If any were left open when the back door was opened, they would slam shut with such violence the wind felt like our abuser. I loathed the wind. I began to feel volatile and unhinged. Weeping at the slightest thing. I missed being outside with all our animals. I ached for campfires and our camels, but outside was so intolerable with the soaring heat and winds that all we could do was hide inside.

On rare days when the wind stopped, and I could sit in an armchair on the screened-in veranda overlooking the ranges, I felt like a prisoner out on day parole. I lapped up every moment of freedom with a sense of foreboding because I knew it wouldn't last long. Prowling in the background of any moment of fleeting calm were those predatory winds, and back inside, we would soon have to go.

Gill and I decided to get the few belongings we had left in storage sent down with the intention of setting up our industrial sewing machines in one of the bedrooms and making some clothes to sell. We needed to utilise this time of stillness, or should I say captivity, and make some funds. We still had some savings to buy a home, but we didn't want to keep dipping into that. I felt sewing and having a mission would help my mental state of mind.

I couldn't believe how weepy I had become and at the slightest little thing. It didn't make sense logically. I knew this space was only temporary, but I felt abandoned by all the goodness we'd had in our lives, and I so missed our camels. From the kitchen window with its epic views, I could see down into the camel's paddock. I would look out for them as they made their daily pilgrimage to the water troughs that were just down the hill from us. I could see them way off in the distance walking in single file through the bush. We had twenty minutes to get down to the troughs if we wanted to see them. An event that always left me feeling uplifted and yet still teary. They would stop for a brief cuddle and a scratch before ambling away, not looking back, off into their own realms where I would never belong. It was always so good to see them, they all looked so well and happy, but it was clear they didn't want to hang out with us.

I had thought our connection was so strong, and I felt like a needy child. Abandoned by the goodness in life, abandoned by the camels. Even as I write this, I can feel my misery. It engulfed me, but it wasn't just the loss of our life with all our animals and the current aloofness of our camels. It was the presence of a building that looked like a dark shadow every time I opened the back door. That fucking bait shed. It was down a steep rocky dip and up a hill, just five minutes away. I loathed its presence so much I would dream of it catching fire and being razed to the ground, but every morning as I fought the wind to get to the outside loo, I would see it, still there! Like the grim reaper, a constant reminder of its lure of death.

Gill had swung into action as soon as we'd arrived and built a fence around the house to keep our dogs safe. When we went out for walks, they were on leads, it was just how it had to be, and most of our dogs were content with that. With the heat and the winds, they were happy to shelter inside with us. We just had one dog, a Staffy cross called Jypy, who was constantly pushing the boundaries and trying to get out. Squeezing out of the door when we were struggling to close it, digging a hole under the fence. Sometimes I didn't even know she'd escaped until we heard her barking to come in.

It just added another layer of anguish to a place that already felt tormented. As much as we tried to barricade all of her escapes, Jypy would find another way out.

Then one day, she came back and, within a few minutes, began to really squeal. Something was wrong, and when she started to spasm, I knew she had taken a bait. The moment I had dreaded, fought against, and kept my dogs on leads to avoid, had finally collided with us, but there was a reprieve. It soon became evident that she had taken a strychnine bait, not a 1080. With strychnine, there is a possibility they will survive it with the proper treatment, but you have to keep them very still and warm and not touch them. Touching them triggers the seizures.

In moments like this, the gifts you do have become more evident, and I had never felt more grateful for an internet connection. To live so remote and still be able to access the internet via our phoneline and connect with the wider world was truly a blessing. We discovered we could neutralise the poison by giving her as much black tea as she would drink, which we syringed into her mouth every time she was thirsty. By the end of the day, though still very weak, she looked like she was over the worst. I had never felt more relieved, and nearly losing Jypy catalysed my focus. We were not here for long, and I needed to get busy sewing so that when we left, we would have enough funds to see us through the next leg of our journey.

There were many seams of both light and dark to our experience of living at Calcutta. Not only were we able to make money from this remote outstation, but we were also able to access fresh food for the first time in months. It was delivered twice a week by our postman, who'd picked up our order from the supermarket in Leigh Creek, over 150 kilometres away.

Getting to know our postman was one of Calcutta's blessings. He always arrived with a full load of parcels from the post office for us, as well as our food. We bought almost everything we needed online and were regularly getting huge cartoons of fabric and sewing supplies delivered. I always felt excited seeing his white 4WD coming down the long driveway. It was like Santa arriving on his sleigh, and with his long white beard, our postman looked a little like Santa too. His name was Talc Alf, and he was a big tourist attraction in the area. He was a philosopher and a sculptor and carved his art out of blocks of Talc that he picked up when he delivered the post to the local talc mine, another forty minutes down the road.

Being completely new to the workings of the outback postal system, it never even occurred to us that Talc Alf's extra services of delivering freight, our boxes of food from the supermarket and taking all our parcels of the clothing we had sold to the post office where it was processed on our account, was, in fact, a service we should have paid for. Talc Alf never mentioned money, and it was years later when I realised that this good man had gone beyond all his paid duties to offer us a service that would have generated some extra income for himself. For all the months we lived there, he didn't ask us for a penny. Yet he bought us mountains of freight and endless boxes of fresh food and was a major reason we could live so far away from everything and yet sell so many clothes. Everything we made sold fast, and feeling productive really helped my peace of mind. When I was sewing, I wasn't crying, and even if the wind was howling, I didn't care. I was totally absorbed by the beautiful clothing I created and my interactions with customers all around the world. They were my lifeline. The demons could be screaming from the Telstra tower while I filled myself up with the goodness and love of people I met online. Many were drawn to us because of our camel wagon journey, and many others because of our clothes.

If we wanted to do a big shop, the biggest town was over three hours away. While we did this trip a couple of times, it was so arduous driving so far in a day that it soon lost any appeal. An hour and a half away was the tiny town of Copley, where Ree and Ron lived. For a welcome respite, we would drive down for a cuppa in Ree's café and do our own shopping for a change. The supermarket was a couple of kilometres from Copley in Leigh Creek, a nearby mining town. On weeks we didn't drive down, they boxed up our orders and sent them up with Talc Alf.

The fresh food was always so fresh. Everything that arrived in our boxes was the best. I felt so grateful for all the services that enabled us to live in such a remote place and thrive. However, it was always good to get out. Have a cake and some coffee. Sit in a fancy beachside café, even if it was in the middle of a tiny outback town where the coal trains from the nearby mines still shuttled through. The first day we drove down to Copley, we pulled the car into a layby with a good vantage point to see all the coal mines. I had never seen one before, and I was horrified at the mountains of black coal that dominated the landscape, obliterating nature and its beauty. It looked like hell, and somewhere in the vast mountains of coal, a fire must have been burning. Thick black smoke so dense it looked like a demon, twisted and turned in the wind. It was all so ugly. We stood silently for a long time, shocked by what we could see and appalled that this view was a tourist attraction! And when we turned to each other to speak, we both uttered the same word. "Mordor."

I had been very curious about what Ree was doing in Copley. As we got to know her a little better, I can only say she had a vision that was undoubtedly magnetic. She was unapologetically herself and had complete disregard for unbelieving responses about how she'd been guided to this tiny town to set up a beachside café. There was also a lot more to her vision than the café.

During the time I was there, I witnessed many wonderful and creative projects she initiated to bring tourists into the town. A town that was the gateway to the Oodnadatta track, yet it had offered very little for passing tourists.

On one occasion, she bought all these kilns so they could be set up in the town to make pottery. The kilns were all being sold cheap in a bulk lot, and recognising a great opportunity, she grabbed them. The region was well known for all its ancient rocks, minerals, crystals and fossils. The idea was to create pottery that had images of fossils on them. A wonderful idea and a souvenir I am sure would appeal to many tourists. Ree also bought the old blacksmiths building that had been left intact with all its old tools to open as a tourist attraction. She described herself as a mover and a shaker. While she was certainly that, something made me feel uncomfortable. I couldn't put my finger on it. I was aware of this feeling even though I liked her. Everything she was doing looked so good, and she wasn't just working to bring in tourism. Ree saw a community of conscious people living in Copley that would be creating this together. There were already a group of people living there that appeared to be working for her.

Copley is an extraordinary place on the edge of the Flinders ranges. It is at a pivotal intersection of the earth's grid at a reference number of grid 44. It's a very powerful place energetically, and I have no doubts that it won't change, even with the demise of the old grid. The image I was shown of the new earth grid was that it overlayed the old grid. Even if it didn't overlay, the earth was so rich in minerals that it would always be a powerful place and continue to attract the numerous healers and travellers drawn to the area. On one visit to the café, Ree shared that her guidance had told her a woman who walked the earth healing would arrive.

In the same way, she'd told us she knew we'd come; this woman also arrived. She'd travelled through the Arab countries healing the earth and had finally made it to Ree's beachside to be outback bakery. It was hard not to be impressed by the extraordinary pulse of life that Ree lived on. Yet always underlying my respect for what she was achieving was that strange feeling. I couldn't understand it, and it didn't go away. Despite this, I felt drawn into her vision, as were many others. There was a group of people that appeared to be doing her bidding. If it was an ant colony, she was the Queen, which unsettled me more. I was much too independent, and besides, I had my own visions.

Her beachside bakery would have been equally at home in a trendy Sydney Suburb, except right next door lived a grubby old Irish man called Tommy. He was quite at home exactly where he was. His place took up two huge town lots and was covered in a sprawl of old rusty cars, bits of tin, broken machinery and old dongas. It was a Steptoe's dream. It was a vintage car enthusiast's dream, too. Some of the old models he had decaying on his block were highly sought after, but to Ree, it was just an eyesore. She had tried to buy him out so she could get the whole mess cleaned up, but Tommy was not going to budge.

To be honest, I loved Tommy's place. The chalk and cheese effect you got from walking from the bakery to his place seemed to create a perfect balance. There was no doubt this wild Irish man, who often forgot to put his teeth in so he was difficult to understand, would have most likely only been able to be himself in a tiny outback town. In the suburb's there would have been endless placard-wielding protesters urging the council to clean up the mess. Tommy was home right where he was.

On one of our visits he showed us around his rambling estate of rust and decay, and while it was hard to decipher what he was saying, we gleaned enough to understand, that some other person had come in and nicked lots of stuff. Everywhere we went, Tommy would spew. "The fuckers nicked it. There used to be a car here until the fucker nicked it." When the lights failed in a huge building that looked like it had many rooms, he spat and fumed for ages that he'd nicked all the lights as well. It seemed that everything that wasn't there or didn't work was due to this villain he'd let in. "The fucker had taken everything." We had no idea who the fucker was.

Despite all his fuming, I liked him. He was friendly and welcoming. There was no doubt he lived in squalor, the place was filthy, and he was a grimy toothless old man with his trousers held up with string and what looked like rust under his nails!

The final place he showed us was a donga, where a large pot of soup bubbled on the stove. A dog was lying on its back, filling up the small settee, balls exposed, in doggy bliss. The smell of the soup was noxious, and as I tentatively peered in the pot, I could almost see dead rats and cockroaches he'd thrown in for some extra taste. I don't know if those things were there, but the hygiene levels of Tommy's kitchen were so low that having a bowl of his soup was definitely *not* on my menu. We politely declined, telling him we'd just eaten, bid him farewell and went to the bakery for muffins. As we crossed from one neighbour to the next, I felt like I'd jumped timelines. From one man's rusty falling down ruin of palace to a hoity-toity beachside outback café, but it wasn't just the extremes of visage that created these opposing realities. It was the conversations we had too. From toothless Tommy spitting and hissing about the fucker to sitting drinking cappuccinos while chatting with a new age-ey healer who was all love and light. Like I'd once been before I had camels. I could imagine my camels looking at this woman as they had once looked at me. That haughty condescending look that immediately conveys you've got some growing up to do before you're worthy of their time. Oh, I knew that look so well!

When the conversation veered to gibber flats and howling winds and our life at Calcutta, she looked at me so patronisingly and said, "Oh, you must know you can talk with the winds and ask them not to blow." At least Tommy had been real! I gulped back my immediate response. Partly because we were in a bakery but primarily due to me not wanting to appear inadequate in my wind talking skills. "Oh yes," I replied truthfully, "I speak with the winds all the time." I didn't mention that I screamed and howled at them too.

While I do experience myself in a constant process of expansion and don't want to limit myself in any way, I can't even control a camel, let alone the blimin winds. I had to laugh because even as I pondered the possibility of being able to command the wind, I was immediately given a vision that wasn't very flattering.

There I was, bruised and broken, my dirty face streaked clean by tears. Laying in a foetal position in the dirt, shaking all over. Sobbing, howling, hurting. On the edge of passing out, dizzy and sick. My ego is not the voluminous thing it once was. It's had to run for its life, too, been thrown around on the ends of ropes and almost been trampled to death. It is looking pretty battered, let me tell you.

Do I think I can control the winds? Humbly, no! Not at this present time, anyway. But *if* I could command the wind as it rolled in across the gibber flats in its gritty red fury, surely it wouldn't be ethical to send it to someone else? As long as I don't get it, all is good! *Really!*

I'm just a part of nature, like a leaf on a tree, but I didn't say any of this. I just drank my coffee, smiled and thought *I couldn't be bothered.*

While Tommy's timeline may have won out for his realness, I did prefer the food on the bakery timeline. I loved it when Bobbie, who was friends with Ree, was in town, and we met him for a cuppa and cake at our beachside oasis.

One morning as we sat around a table in the early morning sun, enjoying our cappuccinos, Bobbie told us about a recent visit with Tommy. The old man had been moaning; he'd lost his teeth and hadn't been able to find them for months. During the visit, Bobbie glanced down at Tommy's dog and noticed he was chewing on some dentures, "Look, Tommy, there's your teeth," he exclaimed.

Tommy had wrestled his grubby dog chewed teeth from his dog and popped them straight into his mouth unwashed. Those gnashers had been lost for weeks, laid in the dirt, were chewed and covered in doggy saliva, but he didn't care.

I understood Tommy's lifestyle may have been considered bad for business. Still, something deeper than that niggled me, and it took me a while to realise what it was. I kept asking myself these questions, trying to understand what I felt. Was it possible to create a conscious community if we moved anyone on that didn't fit in? Surely it is more accepting of others to embrace our neighbours as they are?

Yes, he lived in a mess, but he had lived there for a very long time, much longer than Ree. This was his home, and he was as much a part of this town as anyone. Did wealth and vision give anyone the right to determine who was acceptable and who was not?

I often left my visits to Copley feeling an unease that I still couldn't place. Ree had come from a very high-profile working career in politics and had many contacts within the media. When a double-spread article came out in a Sunday paper about her, saying she had come to save an outback town, with a large photo of her standing in the street while a tumbleweed blew down it, it was evident that others within this small community that had lived there all their lives resented her. They didn't want someone coming to save them. It did feel a little Messiah-ish. Of course, the paper could have distorted her words, made her out to be saving an outback town when all she'd done was share the projects she'd initiated to bring more tourists. I don't know. She was friendly and welcoming. She even invited us to share Xmas dinner with her and a few friends, including Bobbie. After travelling for so long and rarely being able to be open about who we were, it was a relief to be with someone we didn't have to explain our trip to. She was on her own journey of trust and had taken a huge leap of faith to leave her home in the city to travel to this town and create a new life. In many ways, we shared the same language, and while there were little things that happened that bothered me, I ignored them for the vicarious pleasure of just one aspect of my life, being understood. Though even that premise for ignoring what didn't sit right, what I had yet to understand, was untrue. We were as different as an apple from a cherry. With Ree, I couldn't communicate the love we lived with our animals. Even our connection with nature and our own wild ways that had come from living outside for over a year in all of nature's whims and graces. But that wasn't clear to me then.

On two occasions, I had left a visit with her only to have to stop the car to puke. If it had only happened once, I would have dismissed it as an upset, but it happened twice on two very different occasions separated by a gulf of time.

On another occasion, we shared a meal with her, said goodbye and walked out to our car. As I got to the car, I realised I had left something behind and ran back. As she looked out her window to see who it was, I saw a look of such distaste. It was only fleeting, but I saw it. I felt sick that someone I was friends with was looking at me like that. Of course, she could have been dealing with her own dramas, and I had merely interrupted the moment. Still, that look stayed with me.

Call it loneliness or my raging desire to belong somewhere, but I kept pushing all these experiences away. I shoved them into the background of my knowing. Calcutta was a harsh and lonely place to live. I loved these excursions to town. There was a vibe and an energy happening that was enticing, and I wanted to be part of it. I was also very curious about the discrepancies between Ree's vision and the unease it triggered in me. Was this my stuff? Was I sick because of my own stuff? I was certainly willing to look. Ree would have most likely said it was because the energy was too much for me. I'd heard her say that about someone else.

In some ways, I had thrown our entire journey of over a thousand kilometres and everything I'd gained from living with our animals, out the window. Questioning myself and constantly asking *what is wrong with me that I struggle to fit in?* Instead of trusting myself enough to know that something didn't feel right. It wasn't even about Ree. What she was building and creating was epic and I had no doubt she was a woman of immense vision. My confusion was in feeling swept up in her vision while simultaneously feeling it was unaligned with me.

And yes, maybe the energy was too strong for me, perhaps because it wasn't love, I felt. Gill and I lived love. Throughout our trip, we connected with so many people we *had* shared love with. They may not have grasped the trust in how we lived, but they felt what we were doing, and it moved them deeply. Whether it was those beautiful people in their 4WDs that towed us out of our bog on our first day of travel and thanked *us* as if we'd done something for them. Saying goodbye with tears in their eyes as they shared how moved they were by what we were doing. Or the circle of love we felt when we shared Abdul's story and got to hear a heartfelt tale of love from a complete stranger. Whether it was a steaming tuna bake delivered under a bright blue sky by the bush postman, I knew what love felt like. So why didn't I feel it here? It was a question I would ask myself again and again as I struggled to make sense of an energy that felt attractive and compelling, yet at the same time repugnant.

And always when I listened, I would hear my wise inner voice say, *the energy of love is the most potent force, and that's the place you live from, Kye. Trust more in yourself.*

And I knew I should, but I kept going back for more,
caught up in the Copley dream.

Nineteen
Beautiful & Charlie

We occasionally saw the owners of the station we were on. Sometimes on our trips to town, we would call in and have a cuppa with them. There was always such grace and charm in their kitchen, cakes coming out of the oven and everything home cooked. Even with Jon's previous talk of baits, I liked them. They were jovial and fun and always welcoming.

When Gill got a phone call saying they had been let down by a worker and had all these sheep to shear, would he come in and help? He answered yes. "It's a paid job," Jon told him, "and we know it's a long way to come, so we'll give you fuel money as well." That was good to know. It was a ninety-kilometre trip just to get there!

I wasn't keen on Gill leaving. We were a team when it came to making clothes and had so many orders to finish. I wouldn't be able to finish them without him and that would put us behind, but he wanted to help Jon out, and I understood that. He is always a very giving man who looks out for others. If Jon was stuck for a worker even though it was far from his ideal work situation, he'd be there.

It felt like the middle of the night when I woke to find him dressing in the dark, trying to be as quiet as possible so as not to rouse me. "It's 4 am," he answered when I asked him what time it was, "I've got to go."

It was such a long day at Calcutta without him, and I felt really lonely. The heat and the winds rampaged the outstation like an angry invader all day. Even though I tried to keep busy, by the time the evening came, I would be listening keenly for the sound of Gill. I felt sheer relief when, late at night, I heard that familiar roar of our 4WD as it turned into our drive on its last leg home. I ran outside excitedly to greet him, but he was so shattered that all he wanted was a cold drink and to fall into bed. He had to be up at 4am again and needed his rest.

The weather could not have been worse for working outside. Every day was ricocheted by hot howling winds, and the temperature was insufferably hot. Most sane people stayed indoors. They certainly didn't do major sheep work. I felt for Gill working in such extreme conditions, and it soon became evident it wasn't only the workers being pushed. The sheep were not faring well either.

"It's a fucking nightmare down there, Kye," he groaned as he collapsed into a chair after his second day of gruelling labour. Even though he always wore a hat to protect himself from the sun, his face looked red. "They bought in all these sheep that hadn't had a drink for two days because they'd been held in yards that didn't have water. They were exhausted and dehydrated when they arrived. The water in the yards they were finally offered was so salty they were dropping like flies from it. Dead sheep were everywhere!"

I listened, horrified. Gill told me he'd done his best to make them comfortable and help get as many back on their feet as he could. "They just don't know what they are doing," he said, shaking his head sadly. The owners had moved to this property from a more serene and lush environment in a temperate zone. They were inexperienced with handling sheep in these dry and hot conditions.

For two more days, he continued to go and help. Would we have been kicked out of Calcutta if he'd said no? I don't know, but when I asked Gill why he was going again, perplexed that he would want to work in such awful circumstances, I was a little flawed by the selflessness of his response. "At least I can be there for the sheep Kye and hold a kind space for them."

When he returned from his last evening away working at a job where over a hundred sheep had died, our car was loaded with kindness. In the back were five baby goats, bleating pathetically for their mums, their little mouths blackened with thirst. There had been a muster on the station of wild goats. Their babies were left behind to fend for themselves or get taken by the eagles. Most of these little loves die of thirst. I felt sick knowing this but would come to see that in the wild goat industry, this lack of compassion was the sorrowful and devastating norm.

I felt heartache for all the little lives left behind, crying like these goats for their mammas. I couldn't help them all, but I could at least help these five. Wrap them up in the loving presence of two people that know the power of compassion and kindness and live by it. We refused to walk past suffering and would continually expand our lives to help those we met along the way that needed a helping hand.

There was one very tiny black goat, only a few days old, who willingly accepted a bottle of milk from us. The others were just old enough to be clear I was not mum and, despite trying, fought having bottles the entire way. We eventually gave up and provided bowls of milk that they lapped up. Bottle rearing would have made these wild goats quieter and connected them with us, but we were not going to fight them to achieve that.

Gill returned with not only the baby goats but a cheque for his work. Neither of us could believe it when he opened it up and saw it was for only $300. Gills still red face blanched white in shock. Four days of working from sun up to sun down in extreme temperatures, and they paid him less than $8 an hour and didn't pay for any of his fuel. Gill shrugged his shoulders. I could tell he was really disappointed in how they'd treated him, but I felt angry. Gill would have gone and worked for nothing if they had told him they were stuck or too broke to pay him, but they'd promised payment, fuel money, and told him not to worry about bringing lunch. If that had been me and I was stuck for a worker, I would have gone out of my way to look after Gill, not rip him off.

It was just another *what the fuck* are we doing here moment. After calming down, we began to think that perhaps the owners had charged us for the weekly rent. A payment that automatically came out of my bank account to theirs. Maybe we should check with them? Or have they charged for the goats? I asked Gill. "No way, they'd left them out in the yards to die. Absolutely no way."

We finally decided to send a polite email just querying the amount. They replied, telling Gill they had charged him $25 for every can of fuel he had taken and $5 for every sandwich he had eaten. They had charged him for driving $180 kilometres a day to work for them when they were short! We were staggered. We had improved Calcutta in the time we'd been there, put up a huge fence, painted the outside of the entire house white, covering up the graffiti on the back wall. It left a sour taste in our mouths. If it hadn't been so hot, we would have packed up and left right then.

As the months passed, the winds waned, and there were odd days when Calcutta truly was a magnificent place to be. One of Calcutta's infinitely enjoyable treasures was its massive vista of stars. We had been looking out for a tin bath we could light a fire underneath. I was keen to luxuriate in hot water while watching the sun going down over the ranges or enjoying the stars. Despite numerous enquiries, we couldn't find one. Only in retrospect did we realise that not getting what we wanted was a blessing. Gill, who is so creative, transformed two sheep troughs into the most amazing bath. It had the most beautiful curvaceous shape, and its rolling arms gave it the look of a comfortable armchair. It had fancy legs made out of old railway irons, welded together, and it would have been just as at home in an expensive gallery as it was in our bush garden. It was a work of art, and we could finally lay out under the stars, sharing a bath, up to our necks in hot water, with a glass of wine. Though I'd rarely drunk alcohol, a glass of wine was often my panacea for surviving Calcutta.

Even on its best days, when its beauty was laid out for all to see, there was something achingly, hauntingly lonely about being there. Even when the Telstra tower was playing its Buddhist chants, there were other voices that wept and wailed. Sometimes I thought it came from the millions of stones that covered the vast treeless plain that Calcutta was perched on the very edge of. Sometimes I felt it was in the air. Every breath I inhaled was an ancient wail resounding like an echo through time. Perhaps that's why I was always crying. Even when the sky was blue and the days were incredibly beautiful, my tears would fall at the slightest thing.

Then one morning, we woke up, and there was no sign of Banjo. None anywhere. We walked for miles calling and calling his name. Then drove even further, but our beloved pissy stinky loveable oaf, a billy goat, was gone.

At first, we couldn't understand what had happened. Banjo never left home. His mates were the Beebs. He got distressed when he couldn't see them. Where had he gone? We both realised what had happened at the same time.

The little tiny black goat that Gill had bought home had not been thriving. I had been beside myself with worry about what to do. Eventually, Gill had gone down to the station to see if they had any goats left from the muster. They had just a handful left in the yards that they hadn't been able to load on the trucks that would be shot. Gill was told he could take one.

We had hoped if we could find a mother goat with some milk, we may be able to bond the little black baby goat with her. Many mothers had lost their babies, and many babies, their mums. We didn't know if it would work, but for our little goat Majella who we adored, we were willing to try, though sadly, it didn't work. The poor mother goat was traumatised and terrified.

So many people don't realise that when we round up these animals from the wild, we only have to imagine how we would feel in the same circumstances to understand how *they* feel. This mother goat had lost her home, her kids, her mates and her friends. In the hell, she experienced what milk she may have had, had dried up. We decided the most compassionate thing we could do for this wild girl was let her go. It had not occurred to us she might be in season and would lure Banjo out into the wild with her. It was one of those things you do and berate yourself after for not thinking about the consequences. Not that we would have kept her, but we would have tethered Banjo for a few days until she got far away. We had given a wild mother goat back her life but lost Banjo. Majella, already weak when we found her, had also passed away. I was inconsolable that Majella had died but not ready to give up on Banjo.

We called every station in the area and told them to keep an eye out for a very distinct and friendly Billy goat. Then we drove down every station track in the region we could find, looking for our old mate. How would he manage without the Beebs, and how would he cope without his nightly campfire? We had to find him, we just *had* to, but as the weeks passed, I began to give up hope. Banjo had left a crater size hole that an entire town could fall into. I missed him so much. We still went out on forays searching, but when you have so many animals to care for, we had to focus on them. We had spent weeks driving down every bush track. Getting out and calling him. The loss of our beloved billy goat followed me everywhere. Then something really extraordinary and unexpectedly beautiful occurred with Beautiful and Charlie. Something I would never have thought possible.

Knowing we would be pulled up at Calcutta for several months, we had turned the framework of the big water tank outside into an aviary for Beautiful and Charlie. It was a huge high space, and I could tell Beautiful was content. However, Charlie, since the day he had flown all around the wagon, wanted more. How he felt was palpable. I wanted him to have his freedom but didn't know how to do this without Beautiful being left alone. I should have known we can never work these things out with our heads, though we can ask to be shown the perfect way. And that way was far more perfect than anything I could have imagined or thought up.

Down in the gully, giant gum trees lined the dry creek bed that only flowed in flood. With all their nooks and hollows, these trees provided the perfect environment for nesting parrots. Hundreds of corellas lived and nested in them. They were so noisy we could hear them from the house, and they had evidently heard the calls of Charlie and Beautiful. Every day they flew up to their aviary and hung out with them. We had corellas sitting in all the trees and on the fence posts around the house. This went on for weeks, and those birds didn't miss a day. Of course, I could feel Charlie's frustration building, but I could also sense that whatever unfolded would do so in its own time. Then one day, I came out, and the latch on the door of the aviary had come undone. Charlie had gone.

Beautiful was anxious and calling out for her mate. I tried to talk with her reassuringly, but she was very agitated, and I was so relieved when Charlie returned. He had all his new mates with him, and they all sat around the aviary. Charlie looked as if he was talking to Beautiful. She sat on a perch next to the wire. Her head was so close to Charlie's. It was easy to imagine what he was saying to Beautiful. *Come on, Beautiful, we can have the life we were meant to live now. We were never meant to be in cages. Imagine what you will feel as we soar through the sky in our flock. Come on, Beautiful, come with me.*

Each night Charlie would leave with his flock, a wild bird now. Beautiful, would pace and call out for him, and it would be like that until he returned in the morning. Since Charlie had got out, I had left the aviary door wide open. Both these parrots were free to do as they pleased. This was their life, not mine, and whatever they were working out, they just needed a safe haven and time.

Then one morning, I went out to feed Beautiful, and she was gone. I am such a worrisome mum. Would she cope, would she get anxious? She was such a nervous little bird, but I felt sure her nerves had come from being forced into a life that wasn't natural. Life in a cage had disconnected her from the purity of her own wild expression. I would soon see this was the truth.

It took a couple of days for them to return, and I wept with joy seeing Beautiful's excitement. They were both screeching with delight as they flew laps of the house before taking off again to their mates in the giant gum trees in the dry creek bed. I was happy and sad. Sad to see my dear friends go but so intrinsically delighted that I wept with joy that these two precious little beings had reclaimed the life that was theirs. It was an outcome I had never anticipated, and it was perfect.

They often visited during the next few months, but the space between visits slowly increased. I felt so grateful it had happened like that. Their visits had shown me they were both OK and that I didn't need to worry. The love we shared was real. They knew I loved them enough to let them go, and I felt their love and gratitude. They *wanted* me to know they were really well.

Then they stopped coming. I had no doubt the wild had swallowed them completely. I was sad that I would most likely never see my two precious little mates again. Our worlds would now no longer meet. But I was also fine with this. I knew we would not be living at this remote outstation for long. They would have kept me anchored to this place if they were still returning to see me and made it hard for me to leave. I was relieved they had become totally independent of us. They had taken their freedom and given me mine. This is one of the many blessings and heartaches of love. Being together, yet letting go to change, even to death. How much easier it would sometimes be to not love so deeply, and yet how bereft life would be without that holy flame that lights us up from deep within.

Calcutta would always remain a magnificent yet harsh and unforgiving place for me. Still, it had allowed Beautiful and Charlie to expand beyond a tiny wire cage. After twenty-two years of captivity, they could finally fly free and soar. Not just an unexpected gift, but a miracle, and maybe the stones and the air would weep and wail much less on this harsh arid plain because freedom and the gift of love had been anchored here so deeply. I didn't know, but I let out a massive sigh of relief for all that had been. For all the things that happen that we cannot control, only flow with. We were all expanding beyond our limitations on this trip. Perhaps Banjo was also experiencing bigger vistas than he could have shared with us. I had to trust in the flow of his life as much as I did in the wonderful liberation of my two little mates. I had to trust in it all.

With Beautiful, it was her circumstances that had led her to be anxious and afraid. This was not her natural state. It was a space she had fallen into because she wasn't living her wild self. We all need our connection with nature. On the times she had visited, swooping excitedly around our home with her mate Charlie and their rather loud flock of rowdy friends, I had seen her anxiety had become exuberance, and her fear had become excitement for the life she now lived. Finally, back where she belonged, she was a noble Queen.

But life at Calcutta gave, and it also took away. As much as we had done everything we could to keep our escape artist of a dog Jypy within our yard, she had gone to extreme lengths to dig her way out. She always seemed focused on that shed. That loathsome building and true to that day when a voice had whispered in my head, you will lose one dog, we did. Our dear Jypy.

And I am not going to talk about it. Nothing is served by dragging others through the agony of that experience. It was heart-achingly tragic, but it was also tinged with a sense of relief and please don't mistake me. If I could have changed that outcome, I would have done anything. I loved all our animals dearly. It was only because I had carried the burden of knowing one of my dogs would die. I had pushed the thought away a million times and tried to convince myself this inner knowing was wrong. The deed had finally happened, the worst was over, and I felt I could relax more. Our other dogs didn't try and get out. It was easier keeping them all safe. The tension had gone about our dog's safety, and even though the winds had waned, I still found life in this house gruelling and hard. Living on such an exposed plain bought everything I needed to let go of to the surface. I could not from hide from anything. There was no pretence, and all I could do was face whatever emotions came up. Everyday!

But on one of those days when the wind was so still I could almost hear dead leaves fluttering to the ground from the gum trees in the valley below, our phone rang.

It was the most unexpectedly magnificent news. Banjo had been spotted by a farmer, who gave us precise directions to where he'd been seen.

We jumped in the car so fast. Our route took us a few miles away, up rough and rocky dirt tracks, down into steep gullies, past falling down stone shepherd's huts built by the early settlers. Looking, looking, looking. My whole body was tense with the anticipation of finding him and the dread we wouldn't. The rough rocky track we followed wove between some giant boulders, and all of a sudden, there he was. Sitting on a grassy knoll was our stinky love of a friend, Banjo. I wept with joy, I was so happy, and it was blatantly evident the feelings were mutual. He gave a huge happy bawl when he saw us and ran over to the car. I opened up the back door, and he dived in. Settled himself happily along the seat and fell into a deep sleep that lasted the entire way home. He was exhausted. He was also missing a horn. When we'd spoken to the farmer who'd initially seen him, he thought he may have been trying to follow some wild donkeys. He'd seen a herd nearby, and Banjo appeared to be calling them. That could explain the broken horn. Our little lost love had been following donkeys, looking for a familiar face, his old friend Bella, and a wild one had booted him. We could only surmise, but going by the look of him, he hadn't had an easy time. Not only was he without a horn, but he'd also lost a lot of weight. This must have been from stress as there was plenty of wild food around. When we got him home and gave his broken horn a closer examination, we discovered the root of it was badly fly blown. Another week or two, and Banjo wouldn't have made it.

It was late afternoon when we arrived back from our rescue mission. Bella and Blossom were still out grazing, which gave us time to treat his head wound before reuniting Banjo with his mates. We led him into our yard and got organised to clean his maggot-infested wound. Its times like this, I am so grateful for Gill. He is the one that can get in there and do what needs to be done without flinching, cringing or spewing. Just looking at it made me feel ill, but I have another job. I am the soother, reassuring our patients that everything is ok, they are safe, and we are only helping them. Banjo didn't need any reassurance, though. He just stood quietly and let

Gill clean up and flush out his wound before dressing it and finally, to keep it safe from any more fly invasions, wrapping Banjo's head up in a bandage. By the time he was ready to meet up with his mates, he had looked like a returning war hero. I thought he would rush out calling them, but he settled himself in the shade of a tree and waited for them to come home. When they finally did, in the last rays of the sun, Banjo bawled with excitement to see them, and they looked just as happy to see him.

I had prayed and pleaded for Banjo to come home. As the weeks had turned into months, I had given up hope, yet here he was. Home again. Our wayward traveller had returned, and even though the following day bought us a dust storm that we saw approaching from the horizon in a big red tsunami-like wave, that spurred the winds into a hot fury and had the Telstra tower devils screeching and wailing, I smiled all the way through. There was nothing I couldn't cope with.

My beloved beautiful Banjo was home! I could not have been happier.

Twenty

Freedom

One of my favourite people in Copley was Ron. The beautiful middle-aged man who'd stood looking like a wizard on the edge of the track waiting for our cavalcade of love, just so he could greet us. He beamed kindness and had an elegance and grace that always felt soothing. Seeing his bright, cheery face when we went to Copley was always a lifesaver for me. A moment of recognition that however much some things felt strange in this outback town, here at least was a friend.

He'd worked with the local aboriginal people for many years and organised many exciting and inspirational workshops in town. I was delighted when he asked us if we would be interested in running a couple of sewing and fabric dyeing workshops with the local community. It was an excellent opportunity to get to know people and be a part of the vibrancy and empowerment happening in this little outback town.

Our first workshop was held at the local school and was like walking into a headwind. While it was primarily white kids who really couldn't be bothered to make any effort, the whole day was redeemed by one Aboriginal girl. She was very shut down and communicated very little, just in nods and grunts. Yet she sat at a sewing machine, sewing up a top we had cut out together. Despite numerous setbacks, when she sewed the wrong bit, the machine broke, the cotton snapped, she kept going. She didn't give up until her creation was finished. I was delighted to hear she would be coming to the next workshop. It was an opportunity to help her build her confidence in her creativity.

The following day our workshop was in the village hall. It was supposed to begin at 9 am, but by 9.30, no one had come. At 9.45 am, a car pulled up, almost tossing two young kids towards us before driving off. They had green drinks in their hands, snotty noses and one had a dirty nappy. Gill and I just grimaced at each other. *This ain't what we had in mind!*

By 10 am, a few more stragglers had arrived, and after that they kept coming and coming and coming! By elevenish, we had a village hall full of people, and it looked like the whole community had turned up. Mostly aboriginal people with a handful of white fellas thrown in.

With Ron's help, we found a few extra overlockers. I helped the girls cut out and sew up their creations, keeping the designs very simple so it was, more or less, straight up and down the seam, sewing.

There were a lot of young girls in their pre-teens, and I asked them what they would like to create. As we went around the group, they answered, "something for my sister or auntie." None of them chose to create for themselves. "What would you make if it was just for you?" I asked them. Their faces looked puzzled as if doing something for themselves was a new concept. "For me?" They queried. "Yes," I replied. "Just for you?"

There was a visible shift in the expressions on their faces. They began to lighten up with excitement. The thought that they could create something for themselves had not occurred to them. As they started to offer suggestions for what they could make, I noticed an interesting dynamic occurring. Several of the younger girls wanted to make miniskirts, and the older girls told them, "You can't make that. It's too sexy. You know gran won't let you wear that." It was evident that these little girls were already becoming aware of the image they were projecting. At an age when they hadn't even developed breasts, they were toning down their expression in case they appeared 'sexual'.

There were two other girls, sisters, who I'd been advised may create problems. They were known to be very disruptive. They were both big girls in their mid-teens, and everything they wore was big and baggy and hid their bodies. While the others were rethinking their choices after realising a mini skirt wasn't a good idea, the sisters were antagonistic toward everyone and mocked their new choices.

I felt a yearning in one of the sisters that was so strong I focused my attention on her and asked her what she would love to create. She looked bored by me as if I was merely an irritating mosquito. Still, with a little more coaxing, I could tell that a desire inside her may get an opportunity to be born. I began to be silly, suggesting outrageous things to make. A space outfit, a ballroom dress, a magician's coat? Then I heard her speak so softy, it was almost a whisper, "A poncho." This tough little cookie with all her armour wanted to make a poncho. The most unique and creative suggestion any of them had given and so doable, I was excited.

I managed to get these girls to cut out their visions and sew them up. One was making a poncho, and the other had finally let go of resisting and decided to create a top. When the sister making the poncho finished, she began collecting all the scraps of fabric left over, and she sewed herself up a matching bag. I felt so overwhelmed watching her. I almost felt like crying. She was completely focused on what she was making and spent a long time arranging all the bits of fabric she had gathered for her bag. Then she worked out what seams she had to sew and what could be used for a handle until she had a design she loved. She did it all herself!

Outside in the hall's yard, Gill was coping with the dying. Lots of kids pepped up on green fizzy drinks was not helping, but everyone was having a lot of fun, even if it was flicking cords of fabric dipped in dyes at each other!

Running this workshop was like trying to bottle up and contain a willy-willy, one of those swirling eddies of wind that sucks everything up into itself as it spirals across the land, gaining momentum. We did our best and were delighted when Ron turned up to help. We had bought heaps of cotton t-shirts to dye, and between colouring those, the girls were outside dyeing the clothing they had created. Some of them had even made dresses.

It was an astoundingly successful event. We were told two families had been fighting, and many were surprised to see them in the same place at the same time.

It was a day that was exhausting. I felt like a deflated balloon by the time everyone finally left. But standing at that doorway saying goodbye to young girls that were leaving all fluffed up with pride, their own creations being carried out across their arms that were stretched out in front of them as if they'd just picked up their dry cleaning and didn't want to crease anything, I felt overwhelmed with joy and a sense of community I'd not felt before.

I told the girls before they left, "Now, any time you doubt yourself and think you can't do something, I want you to look at what you created today and remember how amazing you are." Honestly, they were beaming from ear to ear. Even the young woman who had created the beautiful poncho and bag and hand-dyed them in beautiful blues and purples had a faint grin. Difficult to see, but visible to me. I had seen her opening up throughout the day, and she left carrying her creations as if they were treasures.

So many people were calling for another workshop. Someone even yelled, "Let's have a curtain dyeing workshop next. We could dye everyone's curtains, so the whole town has bright colours hanging in their windows." This idea was met with overwhelming enthusiasm, and we promised to consider it.

Was it possible that we could fit into this tiny town and find a place we could call home? Right then, we both wanted to. We had certainly received so much encouragement to stay not only from Ree and Ron but many other locals. When we were offered a falling-down stone cottage on four houses blocks on the edge of town a few days later, we went to look, determined to fit in somehow.

We knew another couple hadn't followed through on the purchase, so Ree made it available again. There was a bit of angst in the town about the unnatural inflation of house prices as Ree bought up every property available. Of course, people were selling for as much as they could get, but if Ree hadn't bought them, there was a solid chance they would have remained on the market as some of them had been for years. This was a town where you could buy a basic house on a town block for a few thousand dollars. An affordable town for anyone to live in.

I was aware the price we were offered the stone cottage for was a few thousand more than was asked of the previous buyers, who'd not followed through. Yes, for sure, they were friends of hers, but it was clear it wasn't *just* beneficence that had Ree purchasing all the real estate. She was making a profit too. Once again, I felt uncomfortable, but I ignored it, and we agreed to buy this property. I was even excited, though I had this unease. *How would we fit in here with all our animals? Could we find a paddock nearby for the camels? Would people in town complain that we had a stinky old billy goat?* While this was an outback town and certainly more relaxed than most eastern states towns, it was also made up of a mixture of people who could complain.

We bulldozed over all our doubts, wheeling out that word trust again and again. We even spent a couple of days down at the house site cleaning out all the rocks from the collapsed walls of the cottage, planning where we would rebuild and what would go where.

And then we signed the contract, and that's when the unease settled in. A nag inside like a dull toothache. Sleepless nights tossing and turning because I felt like we'd given up on our dream and settled for a home we would have to contract to fit into. How fitting that the awareness of contraction came from signing the contract!

Finally, after a few days of both feeling sick in the guts, we went and saw Ree and told her we couldn't go through with it. She was gracious and happy for us to back out and accepted our offer to pay any costs incurred, which we did.

The sense of freedom we both felt when we left Copley that day was immense. I felt as if I had the wing span of a wedge-tailed eagle and could soar from the top of a mountain, riding the thermals higher and higher. In that moment of rapturous release, we could not even comprehend how we had become meshed in a vision that didn't feel like it had love as its foundation. What was happening in Copley was fantastic from a business perspective. It was brilliant and dynamic. There was no doubt Ree was implementing so many wonderful projects in that town. Creating opportunities for more tourism and jobs for locals was admirable if that was the direction the town wanted to go in. I just couldn't feel the love.

I couldn't get past how old Tommy's place was judged as an eye sore, and a speedier outcome for getting him out of there and the area cleaned up was welcomed. I also recalled a time when we had called into the bakery and sat outside at a table. We had our little dog Chia on a lead, and she was sitting quietly at our feet. I have mentioned before what an odd little creature she was. Her tail had no hair, while between her toes and out from her ear's hair tufted with the density of a tropical forest. She looked like she was part hyena and was one of the wildest-looking dogs I have ever seen. Those who knew her absolutely adored her as we did, but I had noticed Ree looking at her with such distaste. At the same time as we were sitting there, another woman, one of Ree's disciples for want of a better word, was further in the café with her sweet little dog. A pretty little bandana around its neck, a pretty coloured Indian Bindi on its third eye. There is no doubt it was a beautiful little dog, but love loves the unloveable as well as the easy to love, and that for us included Tommy and our little wild Chia, who lived life so fully, with such passion and zest. She was often a wise guide for me.

This wasn't our place, it wasn't our dream and our life aligned again when we finally woke up and got it. We made some lovely friends in the area. I was disappointed that our time with them would be short-lived, but we lapped up every moment with our friends and made several long excursions to visit them at their farm.

Life at Calcutta felt less lonely. We had both realised that even being with people can be lonely. I would have loved to do more workshops, but it wasn't to be in that town, though hopefully, we had inspired a few young women to realise they were more powerful than they'd previously thought.

On the home front, Banjo's wound had healed up entirely though I would never get used to seeing him with only one horn. He had such wild curly horns, and it was sad to see one go, but he was back, and for that, I was eternally grateful. Our little goats were thriving. While they had maintained their wildness and didn't like to be touched, they always came running home if they felt afraid.

One day they ran back so fast and dived into a small shed. We had never seen them do this before and went into the shed to look, but just before we did, a huge wedge-tailed eagle swooped so low above our heads that we realised it had been chasing our young goats. When we finally got the goats to come out, one of them had some wounds on his back, and we realised the eagle must have caught it with its talons and tried to pick it up. It was a little black goat, and he was an odd little thing. We called him Taffy toes, and he always walked with one shoulder to the front as if he was walking into a headwind. I often would sit and watch him and puzzle over what made him really different from all our other goats. There was a quality that I found undefinable. It felt bizarre that he was the goat to be grabbed by a wedge-tailed eagle. As if there was a quality about Taffy toes that had lured this eagle in. Thankfully the talon wounds were not deep. Though our little goat had struggled and fought us as we cleaned his wounds and put antiseptic on them. If he'd fought the eagle with the same force, he had fought us with, no wonder he'd escaped.

We were certain that our journey would continue soon, and all our focus went towards that goal. Once again, we had so much stuff to sort out and organise, especially since we had taken all our belongings out of storage. We didn't want that cost again and decided to buy ourselves an old horse truck. We could store all our stuff in that and park it at our friend Gina's farm until we had a base.

After making a few enquiries, our friend Bobbie who we had come to know and love, told us about a truck he knew was for sale a few hours away. He reckoned it had been really looked after and was a great buy. We got it. Problems all solved. When we were ready to leave, we just had to pack it up.

I felt so relieved knowing we only had a short time left at Calcutta, perhaps one of the most beautiful yet gruelling places I had ever lived. We had really tried to make it better. I had even planted numerous pots of flowers out on the veranda. They had looked so beautiful for about a week before all the flowers began to wilt and die. I had not thought about the salt content of the bore water that killed them all.

We had planned to give ourselves one final month, so we had time to prepare everything for our imminent escape when Gill got a phone call from one of his sisters. He was on the phone for hours, and I didn't give it much thought. He often chatted for a long time with this particular sister. I also knew she was having a few challenges on the home front. I was, however, completely unprepared for what Gill would ask me when he finally put the phone down.

His sister was absolutely worn out. Her fifteen-year-old daughter had attempted to kill herself, and not only that, she was cutting herself as well. Gill's sister had been hiding all the knives in the house and watching her daughter's every move, terrified she would attempt to retake her life. "Can she come to you," she'd asked Gill, and that's what he was asking me. I must have looked stunned. *Holy Fuck! I couldn't speak. My thoughts were on a rampage. A suicidal teenager landing in our midst! My god, what were we to do? Would we have to hide all our knives? Does she know we live in a bleak old outstation with only a tiny generator for power? Is she mad? She wants a teenage girl from Melbourne to come out here. Does she know we are only here for a few more weeks?* I was gob-smacked and horrified. We lived so far away from normal reality. It was a suggestion that verged on insane.

"She is so worn out," Gill said, speaking about his sister. "She doesn't know what to do. I don't feel she can cope with much more. It will only be for a few weeks to give Lisa a break."

I just sat there in stunned silence. This was a shocking contemplation. It wasn't like we even had a lovely house to welcome her to, and we were leaving. "Have you clarified that we are going in a few weeks?" I asked Gill. "Yup, she knows that. If we are willing to have her, she will talk with Teghan first and see how she feels about it. Honestly, Kye, it will only be for a week or two."

I sat there a little longer, still in a stunned silence, before spluttering, "Well fuck, she is going to have to come then, isn't she." It wasn't that I didn't want to help, but the thought of dealing with a suicidal teenager on top of everything else we had to do was almost insane. I had no doubts we'd take her if she was a camel or a stinky billy goat. We wouldn't even pause to think. We would embrace them immediately. *Surely that same trust in the flow that brings all things to us could embrace a wounded teenager as well?*

"Fuck," I said, "well tell her she can come. I really can't believe we are doing this." Gill smiled, he felt the same consternation but wanted to help his sister and his niece, and I did too.

I wasn't quite prepared when after another phone call, he came and told me they would be arriving tomorrow.

"Tomorrow," I screamed.

"Fuuuuuck!"

Twenty-One
Two Becomes Three

I spent the following day knotted with anxiety, pacing up and down, unable to focus on anything other than the impending arrival of Teghan. We had spent a lot of time with Teghan and her three brothers over the years, and Gill was very close to Lisa, one of his four sisters. It was a family we loved, and we wanted to help, but I knew how hard it was being at Calcutta when you began in a great frame of mind. I was usually cheerful and optimistic, yet I had times living at Calcutta where I felt so bleak. I had no idea how a suicidal teenager would cope. Would it send her totally over the edge? My concern had been for the environment she was entering, not because I didn't want to help. However, if I am honest, give me a dangerous camel or a vicious billy goat any day over a wounded teenager.

But she was coming. Lisa had left early in the morning, driving from Melbourne so she could deliver her daughter into our safe hands and finally get some respite.

It was late afternoon when we heard her car coming down our track. A tiny and old sedan car that was so low to the ground that it must have travelled the ninety kilometres down the rough surface of the Strzelecki track on its belly. Somehow it had survived.

The only saving grace I could see was that the weather had at least begun to get cooler. As we stood outside, ready to welcome our new guest, there was a slight nip in the wind that still swept and blustered around us. I had hoped for some sunshine and stillness, but Calcutta wanted to introduce itself and was determined to be authentic. No pretty veneers here. This is who I am. Get used to it.

And all too soon, there we were. Standing on the edge of a moment that would rock and sway the harmony of our days. At least for a while. Teghan arrived all pretty in pink. Despite her sweet little pink hairband, her long hair was lashing around her face in the wind. She wore a sweet powder pink puffy jacket that Gill and I both thought, *oh dear, that's not going to stay pink for very long*! We had laughed that night in bed when we shared our initial feeling and fears about our new guest.

We had anticipated after such a long drive, Lisa and her son, who'd come with her for company, would at least stay the night. But no, after a quick cuppa, they returned to their car to drive home. Lisa was working in the morning. A part of me wanted to plead with her to stay. Not just have a struggling teenager dropped off with not a clue what we should do. Did she come with instructions?

Should we have hidden all the knives? We hadn't. At that moment, the responsibility for this young and troubled woman felt more burdensome than keeping our dogs safe from that grim reaper of a shed. Despite visualising it every day burning down, it continued to mock me with its presence every time I came out the back door. It had been a challenge living with such menace on my doorstep, and now we had a troubled young woman to protect from the perils and pitfalls of this lone outstation as well.

The days that followed Teghan's arrival were challenging. There was no doubt about that. She was very shut down and uncommunicative. During the day, she often sat outside with her headphones on, hunched up, hat down over her face as if she wanted to shut us all out. She gave the most basic grunts of answers to any question and didn't do anything to help. That was fine, though. I was happy to give her time to settle in. Coming to stay at such a remote location was a huge adjustment and even more so for a Melbourne teenager, used to shopping malls and lots of girly friends.

In the morning's Gill and I would be in the kitchen making breakfast, often laughing and being silly when she would come in all hunched up, unspeaking and almost hostile. I realised later that it wasn't hostility I'd felt. She was used to having so many blockades and barriers around her a swat team couldn't have penetrated her resistance. *Just trust, I told myself. This will work out. You know it will.*

While deep down, I knew that having Teghan stay with us would get better, dealing with her every day was exhausting. It's hard to be jovial in a field ploughed by depression. It felt like a black hole that, if I didn't watch myself, would suck me in too. This was harder than dealing with Banjo or Adjani. We couldn't just tether her outside, and she was with us almost every minute of the day. There was little to do, nothing to see, and nowhere to go. We *were* her life now.

We had turned our wagon into her bedroom, and I made a considerable effort to make sure she was OK. Every night we found a movie to watch, and I was always asking her if she was warm enough at night. Did she need more blankets? Had she had enough to eat? I was concerned about her. I knew she was experiencing a massive adjustment. I wanted to help her in this enormous transition. Still, with such little communication, it was gruelling trying to determine if she was OK. We were really busy. We had lots to organise to get ready for the road. We were also making the most of the last few weeks before we left and still making lots of clothes so we wouldn't have to think about money for at least the next six months.

Teghan would sit through our entire busy day, completely unphased that we were doing everything. Cooking every meal, working every day, preparing stuff for the next leg of our big camel trek. She wouldn't even get up to make a cup of tea. After two weeks of doing everything for her, I was exhausted and worn down. I knew I couldn't keep doing this without being real or putting myself first.

One day I asked her, "Just out of curiosity, Teghan, how do you show others that you care because you have been here for two weeks now, and I haven't seen you care for us once. How do you show it? I just want to make sure I am not missing it."

She looked at me astounded as if to say *how could you not notice me caring. Of course, I care!*

It had taken me two weeks to finally front up and be honest. After everything I'd gone through, I couldn't believe it had taken me so long. I knew how much strength and flow I accessed when I came from my truth.

If the camels had been there, they would have given me those superior looks. I would have perhaps heard them tut as they shook their heads in astonishment that I was again showing behavioural issues they'd assumed I'd worked through a long time ago. *A little bit of time out of our company, and look what happens, she resorts back to her old pleasing ways.* Well, I had, but for two weeks only. I hadn't known how to deal with or cope with someone suicidal. I didn't want to be the one to send her over the edge. Of course, I was extra caring, but all that was happening from this one-way flow of energy was that I was the one being pushed over the edge, not her! Well, no more.

After asking her this really sincere question that had come in complete spontaneity, our relationship began to slowly change. Later that day, I came in and found her washing up. She began to help more and make some of the meals. I could feel her starting to open up, which was a relief. We had no room for passengers. The burden was just too great. If she wanted to stay with us, she had to be part of the team and not expect us to do everything.

On one of our trips out to Copley, a trip Teghan enjoyed as much as we did, we picked up a tiny little baby goat that was the most adorable kid I had ever seen. Mottled tans and white and tiny yet so chunky, it looked like a little teddy bear. Teghan cuddled him the whole way back in the car. She loved animals, and I was delighted we had a baby goat for her to help care for. I know how healing animals can be. We had laughed on the way home because the person with the baby goat hadn't initially asked us if we could give the goat a home because they knew we were leaving on a trek. It's clear they didn't know us very well. Welcoming animals and leaving on a trip was perfectly compatible in our world.

We had a loose arrangement with Lisa about Teghan staying when she'd first come. It had been said, it was only for a week or two, yet picking her up again was never mentioned in any of the numerous phone calls. I understood. I knew Lisa had been worn down and needed some recovery time. Having Teghan with us was actually starting to feel OK. It was still a strain at times, especially not having any personal space. Still, we were all generally in a much better flow together. Gill had also done something so outrageous that it had shocked me at the time. Yet unexpectedly, it had really broken the ice.

I had tiptoed around the subject of knives, not really sure whether to mention them or the cutting or not. In the end, I decided to leave it to timing. It would happen when Teghan was ready, if she ever was. She may not even want to share so deeply with us. We hadn't removed our knives. That just felt ridiculous. What were we supposed to do every time we wanted to chop vegetables for dinner? Would we have to creep out to a secret location? All the while looking around us furtively, making sure she wasn't peeping as we discreetly reclaimed a knife from our hidden stash? Then dole out dinner knives each time we were ready to eat, ever watchful as Teghan washed up after dinner, that she didn't secrete one away? I had zero enthusiasm for that much stress. Even if we hid all the knives, if she wanted to hurt herself, she would surely find another way. There are many sharp objects you can use if you are intent on cutting yourself.

Gill and I had spoken to each other about asking Teghan if she wanted to come with us on the next leg of the trip. We both knew how transformational living out in nature was, especially with all the animals and felt it would be a fantastic adventure for her. But we also needed to be really clear we had no room for passengers. She would probably fall into bed every night knackered and have to push herself beyond all her limits every day, but travelling with all our animals was a once-in-a-lifetime experience and worth every bit of hard work.

I hadn't wanted to put her off, but I knew we needed to be clear. Teghan had to know what she was going into. When we asked her, she thought about it for a little while and unexpectedly said yes. I was kinda surprised but felt glad she was seizing the opportunity. While my relationship with her was improving, she was still hard to work out. She kept everything close to herself. Still, if Teghan was looking for her own transformation, she'd definitely come to the right place.

The moment Gill obliterated the ice happened one morning as we waited for our porridge to cook. The old agar we used to cook on was so big it took up almost the entire kitchen wall. In the pause before breakfast, Gill handed Teghan a knife. "It's really sharp," he told her, "If you're going to handle camels, you must have it with you. It's vital when dealing with ropes. If you're going to use it to cut yourself, though, remember it is sharp and do it outside where you won't make a mess."

He said it in such a matter-of-fact way, and when I heard what he'd said, I was momentarily horrified. I am sure Teghan was as well. People had been shuffling around the subject of cutting and knives with her way before we'd begun. Gill's words were like a giant sledgehammer smashing the pretence we had all been living in. It was now out in the open for us all to see. There was a moment of shocked silence before we all cracked up laughing, and Teghan was laughing most of all. The pressure release valve had finally been opened. I hadn't realised until then how much tension I'd felt since Teghan had arrived in our life. It was truly such a relief.

Yet another lesson in honesty and facing what's uncomfortable rather than pretending it didn't exist. The door between Teghan and us creaked open a little more.

One subject that really intrigued me was her description of life at school. It was a culture so far away from the one I'd experienced decades previously where no one I knew in my all-girl school cut themselves. Whereas most girls in Teghans class had some dysfunctional body image behaviour. They were either cutters, bulimic, or anorexic and appeared to wear these labels like a badge. Though I'd certainly had my own body image issues at school, problems like this had not existed.

I was also surprised when she talked about the popular girls at school because, in my day, these girls would not have been held in high esteem. They would have been wagging school or fagging it down at the bike racks, just out of sight from our classrooms. In Teghans school, these girls appeared to be popular because they had sex with multiple boys. In contrast, when I was at school in the seventies, the girls we looked up to were generally good-looking and cool in their clothes. They always wore the latest fashions and the latest design of cool shoes. They were the trendsetters for the rest of the class. Within days we'd all be wearing the same style. Whether they were having sex or not didn't come into it. I was shocked to hear girls became popular by having sex. No wonder many of her classmates had body image issues and a distaste for their unique beauty. It appeared that 'popular' was determined by what the boys thought and no longer the girls. As the days passed and I got to know Teghan more, so many aspects of the life she shared with us stuck with me in an unpalatable way. She described so many psychiatrists she'd been to see. Some were so depressed themselves she had felt like hugging them. Others had told her that her own depression and suicidal thoughts were genetic. After all, her father had committed suicide. This suggestion really pissed me off. That a young woman struggling in life could be given an even greater burden maddened me. It was an ignorance that should be held accountable.

When I listened to her describe her days, I would have felt suicidal. She lived on a five-lane highway at traffic lights on a busy Melbourne road. The fumes were so nasty that they never opened the windows in the front of the house. She had a mum who did the best she could and gave everything to her five kids, who she'd bought up single-handedly. I remember visiting one Easter when the kids were all young. They woke up to the most magical treasure trails of Easter eggs going all around the garden. I felt quite teary at how mum had gotten up way before the kids and created an enchanted world for them to discover and explore when they woke up. But mums can't do everything. When teenagers try to commit suicide, they get sucked into a system where they have to attend counselling, however unwise or foolish that council may be.

"It doesn't mean that because your father killed himself, you will too." I told her. "What is very likely is that your father did not have the tools or the support he needed to deal with his own trauma, and anyway, I would feel depressed if I was living your life. It all sounds so grey."

Not once had Teghan been asked by any of the therapists what she was doing in her life to ignite passion. When did she spend time with people that inspired her? How much time did she spend in nature, or was she doing anything she loved? The answer was nothing, no, very little and no. No wonder this girl was depressed! Who wouldn't be depressed? And yet their only cure was medication so toxic it made her migraines even worse, so she came off it and was driven to us.

In the short time, she'd been with us, I could already see some colour in her once grey cheeks. She laughed a lot more. She often snuggled our little goat, who had been anointed with the nickname Weebly because he weed everywhere and his silly name had stood. I'd realised pretty soon that Teghan, like so many people, had learnt to get energy from people through either illness or suicide attempts. She had come to us with a long history of suffering from migraines. I had been really sensitive to that, yet there was one occasion that made me rethink my own attentiveness to her during her illness. And for sure, this is a dicey subject to navigate because if someone is really sick, I want to be there for them, but I wasn't sure this was the case.

She woke up one morning and came into the house complaining of a migraine. I'd done the usual. I told her to go to bed and searched for a pain killer, some lavender oil, or anything I could think of that would help. When I came outside ten minutes later to go and check on her as she rested in the wagon, she was climbing up the side of our water tower and was pretty high up. I've had migraines. They are debilitating. How could she go from a migraine to doing something extraordinarily energetic so soon? It just made me rethink.

From that point on, when she complained of migraines, I simply told her to go and rest. That was it. I just shifted the focus of my energy. When she did something empowering for herself and achieved something for the first time, and there were plenty of opportunities for that, I really praised her and gave her so much encouragement.

In so many ways, I really admired her. What fifteen-year-old depressed city girl arriving at a bleak remote outstation on a wind-swept plain with no power would willingly choose to stay on. This girl had guts, and the more we got to know her, the more obvious that became. She was willing to face her fears, even if that made her radically uncomfortable, and I loved that about her.

We all started to move in a much better flow together as we got organised to leave Calcutta. Leaving was an event that surprisingly had me shed a tear. So many different chapters of our lives had come and gone. Each one had left us more empowered than we had been before. Calcutta had been a cruel queen as she had stripped me of my bullshit and realigned me with what felt true to me. To think we had almost bought a house in Copley was unimaginable. Back in the total flow of our own lives, back into the love and compassion that guided us, there was no doubt we would never have fitted into someone else's dream. We couldn't even grasp how we ever had thought we could.

Give us our big expansive life any day. A life that was OK with imperfection and mess. One that could stretch beyond the bounds of easy and love the unloveable too.

Let us always embody the reality we want to see birthed on our earth. If we would love more kindness, we have to be kinder. If we ache for more compassion, our choices have to be compassionate. We are the change we want to see. Messy Tommy and his dog-eaten teeth, Banjo with his pissy yellowed beard, Abdul with his penchant for crushing people's cars and now a teenager who was still pretty spiky, well, they could all gather around our fire. We had hearts big enough for them all.

Twenty-Two

Farewell my Friends

I was surprised at how much my feelings for the harsh and barren windswept plains that our lonely whitewashed homestead of Calcutta was perched on had changed. She was still an uncomfortable place to be, but when she unveiled her treasures, they were jewels, and one of these was the sky.

I had never lived under a more immense sky, and on the nights that were still and clear, Gill and I often carried our swags outside, built a fire and lay gazing up at the stars. They were so bright at Calcutta. Once, as we lay in our silent reverie, we had both exclaimed in wonder at the same time. Shooting across the sky was a vivid magenta-coloured blaze of light, much bigger than any shooting star we'd ever seen. We had no idea what it was, but we often saw inexplicable things in the sky, strange lights moving in erratic ways, which we would watch for hours.

Looking up at those stars, I always felt so infinitesimal. In the vast oceans of stars, I was only a tiny particle of light. How could I ever be on a quest that had an end? A journey with a destination. Surely in this infinite universe, journeys only morph into new experiences. How can anything ever end?

Sometimes I would stare up at the sky for so long that I lost all sense of myself. I felt lifted up from the mortal realms as the sky came down to me, wrapping me in its cloak, melting the boundaries between sky, stars, moon and earth and little me, just as we did with the animals. All I felt was the love within us all. A beautiful merging beyond all illusions of self. I was a star, and the moon was a river, and the stars were the stones. Star me, bone white water, earth light, golden dusk, rocky plains of brilliant lights and jewelled splendour. When Calcutta unveiled herself, she was an absolute Queen, and I felt so grateful to her for these rare yet precious nights.

But the stars also showed me truths about my own life. They only shone brightly in wild places and brightest of all in total darkness. Not only could I see that a disconnection from nature is bound to dim our light, I saw my own path. As someone who's often guided into the heart of darkness, I'd experienced few people I could honestly and openly share with. Yet what I had gained from these experiences was profound. I'd been given the awareness to be in my light, even in the darkness.

Over the years, I have often experienced a discomfort in new age and spiritual circles to even speak of darkness, as if by mentioning it, we'll be sucked into its power. On a planet in such turmoil and transition, being able to hold our light, no matter what has always made more sense to me. No one would buy a torch that only shines in the day, so why embrace such a weakened ideology. I want to be the star shining in the darkness, not the ones we can't see because they are dimmed by false lights!

Though we would still see the stars when we left Calcutta, I was confident I would never live on a gibber flat again. There was no doubt I would miss its vast, beautiful skies, the pulsing beauty of the purple ranges, its wild and reckless beauty, but not its bleak and barren windy ways. I was ready to leave them in the past and felt excited by the unknown road that beckoned.

While being tangled up in Copley had been an awakening experience and certainly reiterated the necessity of trusting in what we felt, it had delayed our departure. We needed to make the most of the cooler months. Half of the winter had already gone, and we could not delay leaving any longer. The last week at Calcutta was busy. The truck with all our belongings was packed up and driven to our dear friends. We were back sleeping in our wagon while Teghan got used to sleeping in a little dome tent she could pop up in minutes. Once again, our life was being lived outside around the campfire as we organised and decided where everything would go. Fixing hobble straps that needed new sheepskin, stitching harnesses that had come undone, and packing our food containers. It was hard to remember where everything went. We were no longer the sleek, well-oiled team we'd once been and would have to fine-tune as we went.

Our five young goats and Banjo would travel on the back veranda of the wagon, and Weeby, inside with his mama's where we could give him his bottles. We needed extra flasks of hot water, so each time he needed a drink, we had it on hand and didn't need to stop the wagon, light a fire and boil the billy just so we had warm water to make his milk.

We had no parrots boarding for this leg of the trip. Just before Teghan had come, Yumyum had unexpectedly died. We woke up and found him lying in his open cage. Our last remaining parrot had flown the coup on his wings of light. I felt so sad when I found him and walked down the long track to the dry river bed and sat on the roots of a giant gum tree and cried. I hadn't been there long when all these raucous chattering galahs landed in the branches of my tree and peered down at me. I couldn't help smiling. A flock of galahs had come to remind me that my little love, Yumyum, was already flying free. As they chortled and chattered in the trees above my head, I was filled was a feeling of pure joy. Yet, at the same time, aware of how often in the death of those we love, our response focuses on the empty vessel of a body instead of the expansion of that being into pure love. Yumyums death was a cause of celebration. Our wild and wicked galah had completed his life in expansion and love. He had miraculously outflown a hungry hawk and known what it was to be loved. We had accepted him for better and worse, and let me tell you, the number of bites he gave us, we were absolutely true to our word. Rotter or not, we loved him and, in that love and expansion, he had transcended the mortal realms and completed his earthly cycle. We should all be singing with joy because of that.

As I walked back along the dry bed of the sandy creek, I could hear corellas in the trees too. *Could it be that Beautiful and Charlie were here too? Could they even be nesting in one of the many trees, hollows?* It was certainly a possibility. I called their names, "Beautiful, Charlie, I love you. I love you, my dearest friends." I felt teary again. Goodbyes can be so hard. Two corellas screeched as they flew overhead, but I didn't know if it was them. It had been months since they'd returned. I'd have worried if the wild hadn't reclaimed them so gradually, with their visits becoming less and less frequent until they hadn't come at all. They'd chosen their path, and with my heartfelt blessing. It was an outcome that was miraculous, but I felt like I'd said goodbye to dear friends I may never see again. I was heartbroken and happy for them all at the same time.

Finally, in the last few days before departure, there was one big job left to do. Bring all the camels in. They were roaming in a paddock so big that it could take us days to find them. With the cold weather and lots of green vegetation, they came in a lot less for a drink.

Sometimes, they wouldn't come in for a week, so we couldn't wait for that.

I had no idea how our camels would respond to being taken out of their paddock. They lived in a camel's paradise with a massive space to roam. Soft sand's for their padded feet that were so gentle on the earth if I walked behind them, I often saw little seedlings they'd stepped on spring back up as soon as they passed. They were really happy in their paddock. Calcutta had certainly been good to them. When we'd last seen them at their troughs, Gill and I had both commented on their rather bountiful girths. They had plenty of bush feed to eat.

I wasn't looking forward to bringing them all in. It was likely to be a very long day. We would have to drive really slowly over bumpy terrain with the car and the trailer, the camel's ropes tied to the back of the trailer so they could walk in a few strings behind. We planned to get up really early, at first light, two days before we left. That gave us two days more to ensure everything was ready for us to go before we got the camels in.

We arose the following day, and I was in the kitchen making breakfast when I heard Gill yell out, "Fuck, looooook." His voice was so loud and insistent that he momentarily startled me, and I went running out, anticipating some calamity. When I saw what he was calling me out for, I was staggered. It was unbelievable, and I couldn't help asking myself, why had I ever doubted that our camels had chosen to come on this trip with us.

Walking up to the homestead in single file, winding up the track that rose from the gully below, where the giant gums lined the dry creek bed, up past the old wrecks of vintage cars dumped by early settlers, proud and majestic came our camels and in the lead our magnificent white king of a bull camel, Zu.

In the eight months, we'd lived at Calcutta, our camels had *never* visited the homestead. I would have loved them too, but since the day we'd arrived, when they'd dumped their harnesses and stopped pulling our wagon up the long drive, they'd been gone. Even when we walked down to the troughs to say hello, while they were friendly, it was apparent we were no longer a big part of their world. This had upset me. How could I claim to have an amazing connection with them when the minute they were free, they walked away without looking back. Had I imagined the love we shared? I'd asked myself this question many times during our break from them and was always left feeling confused. Now they were back and had come because they'd chosen to. I was giddy with relief and joy and could not have been happier.

As I watched our noble dromedaries walking proudly towards us, I got it. I'd behaved like a little kid, not getting attention, doubting our relationship when I knew the truth. I had lived it. The camels had known this was their time of replenishment, and they'd taken it. I should never have let that undermine the extraordinary connection we all shared. That was real and unwavering. I danced around in pure joy to know this. Despite experiencing a much more beneficent and nurturing time at Calcutta, our camels were as ready to leave as we were.

I was so excited that Teghan had witnessed our camels coming in by themselves. We shared many stories about the incredible bond we had and how we communicated with them. Yet, each time we took her to meet our herd at the trough, it felt like we'd invaded their secret camel business. They'd have their drink, and with little more than a fleeting glance, off they'd go, back out into their arid wilderness. Wild and free, without us. How ridiculous I'd been for ever doubting.

Gill and I went out to greet them all as they arrived at the homestead, walking right up to our garden fence. Our long-lost tribe had returned, and they were even back to being their usual friendly selves. After eight months of cold-shouldering, Lady Caroline came down to give me a sweet little nuzzle with her big soft lips. A puckered trembling of velvet softness on the side of my grateful face. I was adored again. I felt whole, complete, and in sync. I was on the right track, and I had a herd of camels to prove it. I stood as tall as the moon and as happy as the heavens.

A big silver moon came up over the icy blue ranges of the Strzelecki for our last night. I felt as full as the moon of gratitude. What an incredible journey we'd had since leaving Alice. Lifetimes had passed since we'd sat in the hulk of our unfinished wagon, looking at maps and imagining the freedom of the unknown road and all the magical places we would camp. None of those imaginings had come anywhere close to the reality of our experience. Sitting by an open fire, on the edge of a vast gibber flat, where every stone looked silver in the moonlight, with our camels all chomping and chewing around us, I felt like I'd been given the holy grail.

Over and over again, I had underestimated our camels and had no doubts they would have even more to unveil on the road ahead. The more we expanded in our own awareness, the more we saw who they were. I felt so elated that my life would once again be lived in the midst of a herd of camels and the animals we loved.

I felt as if we were riding a phenomenal wave when we shut the door of our homestead for the last time. It was a cold and cloudy day of Buddhist monks and their mantras. I couldn't help wondering how many more years she would sit empty and alone with nothing but the winds and the voices in the tower to chant and ricochet around her.

As we gave the team the command to "Pullem up," Zu pushed into his harness, and the rest of our camel team supported from behind. They were all keen to go and pulled with such vigour that our big wagon lurched forward in a powerful surge that gained us the momentum to begin the next leg of our journey.

Calcutta, on the wild Strzelecki track to the city of Silver, a town called Broken Hill, approximately eight hundred kilometres away. It was a place I had never been and never had a desire to visit, and yet it was calling us and the feeling to go there was intense.

I felt a pang of loss when the dogs began to screech and howl, and there were no accompanying parrots. The wind section of our orchestra was all gone. Their screeches had been so shrill and deafening they'd almost pierced our eardrums, yet that noise had meant our friends were with us, and I missed them.

The rough dirt track we followed joined up with the Strezlecki track a few kilometres further on. It had begun at the back of Calcutta. It led down a hill into a small valley before rising up past the old grim reaper shed. Then the track climbed higher, so high that when we turned around in a wave of nostalgia to get the last glimpse of our once was home, we could see further than we'd ever seen before. For a moment, she looked tiny and lost in the vast ruthless landscape of shale and stones and stubby little shrubs that grew beaten and twisted from all the winds. It was not a landscape for thriving, yet I was surprised from my distance to see a softness I'd not recognised before. In the soft wintry morning sunshine, as the Strzelecki ranges pulsed and beat their purple hues, they no longer appeared to dominate the gibber flats with their presence. They cradled them softly instead.

"Farewell Beautiful and Charlie." I called, "Be happy. We love you, Jypy and Yumyum," I called to the graves we'd left behind. Our little friends we'd buried in waterfalls of tears. In that moment of farewell, a ray of sunshine broke through the dull cloudy day and lit Calcutta up in a dazzle of white render and red dirt. I smiled.

We may have left their bones, but the spirits of all the animals we loved travelled with us.

Thank You

I am a self published author and all profits from this book help us to continue to care for not only ourselves, but an already large family of previously rescued animals.

The more books we sell, the more we can do to help even more animals and build our vision of kindness.

If you have enjoyed this book please let your friends know.

Share it on social media. Gift it to your friends. Leave feedback if you buy it on Amazon. Even if you didn't buy it on Amazon you can still leave a review there and this will help me build sales.

And if you know anyone I can send this book to that can help me get this epic and beautiful journey of trust out there into the world in a much bigger way, beyond the realms of little me, let me know. I am often so busy caring for animals, or trying to write my next book while bottle feeding an orphaned lamb, mucking out the horse poop, or welcoming the latest animal that's arrived worn down from abuse with their trust in people broken.

Finding time to focus on building sales, attracting media, getting interviews, all of which would be an enormous help gets lost in the midst of all these animals. If you can help, be part of our beautiful network - even if it's just by letting others know about my books.

We thank you.

We appreciate you.

So much LOVE

Kye & Gill & all the animals.

Ps . If you would like to join our mailing list for periodic love letters

www.kyecrow.love

Wild Holy Love - A true mystical adventure

Love We Live – My Leap of Faith with fifty rescued animals {book one}

Tracks of Love - A heartfelt Journey of Love {Book two}

Sacred Journey into the Animal Realms

Sacred Journey into the Animal Realms Wisdom Cards – 55 gold edged cards - available only from our website

www.kyecrow.love

www.ingramcontent.com/pod-product-compliance
Lightning Source LLC
Chambersburg PA
CBHW011147290426
44109CB00023B/2519